LC   30449100018319
5800   Peters, Otto.
.P48   Otto Peters on d[
        education

Otto Peters on distance education

Otto Peters is generally recognized as one of the world's leading authorities on distance education. His theory of distance education as the most industrialized form of education is the most original and far-reaching analysis of distance education yet produced.

This book brings together the best of Peters' work, most of which has not been previously available in English. Drawing on German sociologists and philosophers of education, Peters builds up an impressive analysis of the advantages and defects of the industrialization of education. His essays cover the historical development of teaching and learning at a distance, from the correspondence schools of the 1950s through to distance education in the post-industrial societies of today, including a fascinating account of his central role in the foundation of the Fernuniversität. Desmond Keegan has provided an introduction to each chapter and a concluding chapter which situates Peters' thought for English-speaking readers and gives frameworks for the evaluation of Peters' position.

Otto Peters on Distance Education will be essential reading for researchers and practitioners of distance education, open learning and the sociology of education.

Otto Peters is Professor Emeritus of the Methodology of Distance Education at the Fernuniversität, Hagen, Germany. **Desmond Keegan** is manager of the European Virtual Classroom for Vocational Training project at the Audio Visual Centre, University College, Dublin and the editor of the Routledge Studies in Distance Education series.

Routledge studies in distance education
Series editor: Desmond Keegan

Theoretical Principles of Distance Education
Edited by Desmond Keegan

Distance Education: New Perspectives
Edited by Keith Harry, Magnus John and Desmond Keegan

Collaboration in Distance Education
Edited by Louise Moran and Ian Mugridge

Otto Peters on distance education
The industrialization of teaching and learning

Edited by Desmond Keegan

London and New York

First published 1994
by Routledge
11 New Fetter Lane London EC4P 4EE

Simultaneously published in the USA and Canada
by Routledge
29 West 35th Street, New York NY 10001

© 1994 Otto Peters and Desmond Keegan

Typeset in Times by Intype, London
Printed and bound in Great Britain by
Biddles Ltd, Guildford and King's Lynn

All rights reserved. No part of this book may be reprinted or reproduced or utilized in any form or by any electronic, mechanical, or other means, now known or hereafter invented, including photocopying and recording, or in any information storage or retrieval system, without permission in writing from the publishers.

British Library Cataloguing in Publication Data
A catalogue record for this book is available from the British Library.

Library of Congress Cataloging in Publication Data
Otto Peters on distance education: the industrialization of teaching and learning/edited by Desmond Keegan.
p. cm.
   Includes bibliographical references and index.
1. Distance education. 2. Educational technology. 3. University extension. 4. Peters, Otto. I. Keegan, Desmond.
   LC5800.088 1994
   371.3–dc20
                                                                93–28823
                                                                    CIP

ISBN 0-415-10384-3

Contents

Preface	vii
Acknowledgements	ix
Introduction	1

Part I Data collection

1 Distance education by correspondence schools (1965)	27
2 University-level distance education (1968)	36
3 Models of university-level distance education (1971)	46

Part II Analysis

4 Didactic analysis (1972)	57
5 Distance education and industrial production: a comparative interpretation in outline (1967)	107
6 Distance education: a historical, sociological and anthropological interpretation (1973)	128

Part III Distance education in practice

7 The concept of the Fernuniversität (1981)	173
8 The Fernuniversität after ten years (1985)	179

Part IV Contemporary analyses

9 The iceberg has not yet melted: further reflections on the concept of industrialization and distance teaching (1989)	195

10 Understanding distance education (1990) 210

11 Distance education in a post-industrial society (1993) 220

Conclusion
Desmond Keegan 241

Appendix: Major publications on distance education by
Otto Peters 253

Author index 255
Subject index 258

Preface

For over 20 years Professor Otto Peters' research on distance education has been extensively cited and referred to by writers in English. His work sets out fundamental landmarks in this field of study that require consideration in any scholarly treatment of the subject or in any course on distance education.

To date most of the citation and comment on his work was from paraphrase, as nearly all the major texts were published only in German. The publication of this book enables all who work in the field of distance education to access a considerable amount of Professor Peters' work in English.

The concept of the industrialization of education is important for sociologists and educationists beyond the field of distance education and it is one of the aims of this book to bring the concept to the wider audience it deserves.

Professor Peters and I worked together on the selection of the chapters for this book in 1992. Professor Peters translated Chapters 1 to 3 and 6 to 8. We are grateful for permission to use existing translations of Chapters 4 and 5. Chapters 9 to 11 were originally drafted in both German and English and the English versions are used here.

Professor Peters wrote the introduction in April 1993. I have supplied a short abstract to give the reader the context of each chapter and the conclusion.

Desmond Keegan
Dublin, May 1993

Acknowledgements

The essays and articles included in this book were previously printed by the following publishers:

Chapter 1: Distance education by correspondence schools. In O. Peters: *Der Fernunterricht. Materialien zur Diskussion einer neuen Unterrichtsform*. Weinheim: Beltz, 1965, pp. 7–22.

Chapter 2: University-level distance education. In O. Peters: *Das Hochschulfernstudium. Materialien zur Diskussion einer neuen Studienform*. Weinheim: Beltz, 1968, pp. 17–30.

Chapter 3: Models of university-level distance education. In O. Peters (ed.) *Texte zum Hochschulfernstudium*. Weinheim: Beltz, pp. 2–25.

Chapter 4: Didactic analysis. In O. Peters: *Die didaktische Struktur des Fernunterrichts. Untersuchungen zu einer industrialisierten Form des Lehrens und Lernens*. Weinheim: Beltz, 1973, pp. 51–107.

Chapter 5: Distance education and industrial production, a comparative interpretation in outline. In O. Peters, *Die didaktische Struktur des Fernunterrichts. Untersuchungen zu einer industrialisierten Form des Lehrens and Lernens*. Weinheim: Beltz, 1973, pp. 162–212. Reprinted in P. Clever, W. Heßhaus, M. Lücke & G. Mus (eds) *Ökonomische Theorie und wirtschaftliche Praxis*. Herne/Berlin: Neue Wirtschaftsbriefe, 1981, pp. 47–64.

Chapter 6: Distance education: a historical, sociological and anthropological interpretation. In O. Peters: *Die didaktische Struktur des Fernunterrichts. Untersuchungen zu einer industrialisierten Form des Lehrens and Lernens*. Weinheim: Beltz, 1973, pp. 253–307.

Chapter 7: The concept of the Fernuniversität. In O. Peters: *Die*

Fernuniversität im fünften Jahr. Köln: Verlagsgesellschaft Fernsehen, 1981, pp. 11–16.

Chapter 8: The Fernuniversität after ten years. In O. Peters: *Die Gründung der Fernuniversität. Wagnis und Gelingen*. In *Gesellschaft der Freunde der Fernuniversität. Jahrbuch 1984*. Hagen: Schröder, 1984, pp. 9–30.

Chapter 9: The iceberg has not yet melted. Further reflections on the concept of industrialization and distance teaching. In *Open Learning*, November 1989, pp. 3–8.

Chapter 10: Understanding distance education. In B. Holmberg and G. E. Ortner (eds) *Research into Distance Education*, under the title 'Towards a better understanding of distance education: analysing designations and catchwords'. Frankfurt am Main: Peter Lang, 1991, pp. 48–57. Reprinted in K. Harry, M. John and D. Keegan (eds) *Distance Education: New Perspectives*. London: Routledge, 1993, pp. 10–18, under the title 'Understanding distance education'.

Chapter 11: Distance education in a post-industrial society. In D. Keegan (ed.): *Theoretical Principles of Distance Education*. London: Routledge, 1993, pp. 39–58.

The author and editor are grateful for the authorization to reprint these articles and essays which has been granted by the publishers indicated.

Introduction

The essays and articles brought together in this book were written during the last thirty years. Most of them mirror the time in which they were prepared and worked out. This does not, however, mean that they are outdated or obsolete. They remain relevant in the current situation as they deal with fundamental problems of distance education which have not changed at all in the intervening years. If they remind us also of the dynamic development of distance education in this period, so much the better.

In this introductory section I should like to characterize the eleven chapters of the book by referring to and considering its main findings. This will be done under three aspects: the chapters will be seen in a historical context; the inception and the genesis of the concept of industrialization of teaching and learning will be made clear and many of its more important points of reference will be commented upon; some personal experiences connected to the themes and events described will also be included.

The first three chapters can be appreciated fully only if one realizes that until 1965 distance education had very seldom been an object of scientific research or scholarly work – this holds true equally for German-speaking and English-speaking countries. It was, as it were, unexplored ground. Even specialists in the methods of teaching and learning had never taken notice of it, although distance education was by no means a new phenomenon – even though it was admittedly far away from the mainstream of education. If anything had been written about it at all, it came from people who were engaged in the correspondence school business. This means that scholars who wished to deal with this subject were at a loss: they lacked reliable, impartial information about the practice of distance education, let alone theoretical explanations of its extraordinary methods and approaches with relevant empirical data. They could, in addition, learn practically nothing about the significant role distance education had already played in educational systems abroad. In other words, they were unable to work in this field, which was so alien to the thinking of traditional experts in teaching methods.

In this situation the then Minister of Education of West Berlin, Carl-Heinz Evers, asked me to write a report about distance education. The German Congress of Municipal Authorities intended to deal with this subject. They were concerned about the fact that the educational systems of their communities were not nearly able to produce the rapidly rising number of highly qualified persons required by industry and they had just learnt that there was a close relation between the educational standards of a society and its economic growth. Therefore, they were ready to consider even unorthodox methods of teaching and learning, including programmed instruction and distance education. The report was to provide background material for their discussions.

Why did the Minister of Education ask me? At that time I was helping to establish the Berlin Educational Centre and specialized in the methodology of teaching and learning – in schools, of course. Being a product of my professional socialization I thought little of distance education. I even felt that supporting it was the last thing to do if the Minister intended to increase the efficiency of the educational system. My report was begun with the intention of revealing the obvious pedagogic deficits of distance education and of deploring its commercial misuse. However, the more information I acquired from many countries all over the world, the more I learned about its techniques, its merits in educational emergency situations, its significance in the field of continuing and adult education, the more I was attracted by the new theme. This feeling was reinforced by the conviction that I had the rare chance of breaking new ground. I felt challenged by having entered a new field of educational research.

AN INDISPENSABLE TASK: COLLECTING INFORMATION

Chapters 1 to 3 indicate that at that time first things had to be done first. They represent specimens of three books (Peters 1965, 1968, 1971) which were mainly of a documentary nature. They describe distance education in Germany and in twenty-nine other countries mainly at the secondary and tertiary levels in order to enable members of the academic community to be well informed when dealing

with the new subject. Taken together, they represent the first comprehensive international documentation on distance education.
   The impact of these books was considerable. For the first time educationists in the Federal Republic of Germany became aware that in this country the number of persons learning at a distance was greater by far than assumed, and that distance education supplements and even replaces important elements of the public educational systems in quite a number of other countries. This was certainly a surprise for those who had the vague idea that distance education was essentially a communist invention developed in Russia and in its satellite states, and for those who thought that persons advocating it should be suspected of doing this for ideological reasons. Even more: a discussion about university-level distance education began and lasted for about ten years. It was stimulated mainly by the German National Union of Students, the German National Association of Students, the Federal Conference of Non-Professorial Teaching Staff, the Volkswagen Foundation, some broadcasting corporations, and the Scientific Council of the Federal Republic of Germany. Never before and never thereafter was the desirability of distance education and its function in the tertiary sector dealt with in such a lively manner, so intensively and so continuously.
   Chapters 1 to 3 are sections of the introductory chapters of these three books providing the reader with informative overviews.
   Chapter 1 deals with correspondence schools. Its function in the book is to remind readers of the traditional basis of distance education. Indeed, private correspondence schools had been pioneers in establishing this unusual way of teaching and learning. They had handed down unique methods of dealing with great numbers of students scattered widely across the country. And they had accumulated a number of practical experiences which turned out to be useful for the amazing and unpredictable developments in the last three decades.
   The chapter describes correspondence schools under the perspective of the teaching and learning process. A first definition is given in order to characterize distance education as offered by correspondence schools. Then, the students are described, stressing a feature which is characteristic of many distant students. Very often they are, for several reasons, denied the opportunity to attend regular schools to acquire the desired qualification. The main reasons are that they are poor and socially disadvantaged. This reminds us of the fact that it was the very process of industrialization which created many new

situations in which individuals could be disadvantaged. It was the function of correspondence schools to help to compensate for these limitations of opportunity. We have to admit that the correspondence schools catered to many groups of students, including those who were in poor health or institutionalized, who were neglected and even ignored by the public school system. Finally, the teachers and their typical activities are characterized as well as the special qualities they should possess as authors of course material and as correctors of assignments.

It might be appropriate to mention that there is already an allusion to the industrialization of education in this early publication. When describing the particular role of the teacher in distance education offered by correspondence schools, the intensified application of the principle of the division of labour is reflected upon. This, indeed, was the starting point of trying to understand distance education as a way of teaching and learning which differs structurally in many ways from face-to-face instruction, as it adopted the ways and means of industrialization.

Furthermore, it should be noted that these correspondence schools were related to the process of industrialization in two further ways. First, it is certainly significant that they were founded in industrialized countries. It was industrialization that created the demand for many new qualifications for many new jobs and caused the geographical, vocational and social mobility unknown in an agrarian society. And even more, it also provided the means of transportation necessary for the delivery of distance education. Second, the production and distribution of printed teaching material is an industrialized process itself. Thus, instruction has become a commodity and an object of trade. It is true that private schools are also paid for their services. But they only raise 'fees', and this is basically a pre-industrial mode of rewarding someone. The correspondence schools, however, profit from the mass production of the printed material, which is to be 'bought' by as many students as possible in order to make the highest profit. This is a convincing proof of how far functions of the teaching–learning process and of the industrialized production process have intermingled and even merged.

Chapter 2 makes the reader aware that another development of distance education concentrated on higher education. This feature in particular was at that time virtually unknown in the Federal Republic of Germany, as until then no university or other institute

Introduction 5

of higher education had ever considered making use of this method of teaching and learning.

When the book on university-level distance education was published, German readers were amazed to learn that there were sixty-two universities in the United States which regularly ran courses in distance education, that the University of South Africa, of good repute, catered exclusively for distant students, that the USSR had established seventeen all-union universities for applied sciences teaching mainly at a distance, that about 25 per cent of the students in East Germany were distant students, and that rough estimates of the number of distant students all over the world amounted to 2.3 millions. The descriptions of the achievements of well-known universities in distance education helped to dispel some of the deep-rooted doubts about distance education caused by commercial misuse of correspondence schools. In those years the image of distance education seemed to be improving so much that the idea of establishing some form of university-level distance education in the Federal Republic of Germany could be advocated without any opposition worth mentioning.

The perspective of teaching theory that this chapter represents is a description of three types of distance students and their different motivational situations as well as of five types of distance teachers with their different tasks. The affinity to the industrial production process is suggested again by the functional specialization of teaching activities described, and by pointing to the necessity of managing the complex organizations of large institutions of university-level distance education which must be established in order to be able to teach great numbers of students at a distance. Not only was the term taken over, but also the very procedures and techniques it denotes.

Chapter 3 is a short section of the introduction to the book *Texte zum Hochschulfernstudium* (Essays on university-level distance education) which stresses the international perspective of distance education by presenting descriptions of models of university-level distance education in nine countries. The authors of these contributions were well-known specialists in their countries, among them Gail B. Childs, Charles Wedemeyer, Börje Holmberg, F. E. Rädel, Howard C. Sheath, David Hawkridge, as well as Horst Möhle, Ludwik Bandura, Frantisek Singule, A. S. Zav'jalov, and Mitoji Nishimoto. At that time these names were entirely unknown in the Federal Republic of Germany.

In the introduction I tried to categorize the models of distance education described and found distinct differences between a typical western and a typical eastern model. In consideration of the fact that even today very little is known about the eastern model of distance education and its variations, one can say that its description should still be of interest – even if we can assume that the eastern model will undergo considerable changes if a market economy is introduced in these countries. Maybe this model will then be only of historical interest. For theoretical reasons, however, it will remain important as an example of university-level distance education which is heavily subsidized by the companies employing the students.

A second theme highlighted in this introduction is the importance that educational technology might have in the further development of distance education. Reading this part of the chapter today is a little embarrassing as it is inspired by the *Zeitgeist* of those years. Educational technology had a wide appeal and was seen as a kind of panacea with the help of which many difficulties could be overcome and many new tasks could be solved. Flechsig proclaimed the 'technological turn' of didactics. And I expected much of this new way of dealing with problems of education as well. Today, I am certainly less enthusiastic about this approach as I see it more critically and distantly.

Nevertheless, the impact of educational technology in those years was just another indication of the fact that the industrialization of education was on its way. Methods were applied which had proved to be successful in projects of industrial research and development. Instruction was to be constructed, perfected and optimized in the same way as industrial products, and it was no longer to remain the creation of the teacher as an artist or artisan. The seductive assumption behind this thinking was, of course, that the success of such technologically constructed instruction would be also as extraordinary as that of industrial production processes.

The increased use of modern technical media such as, for instance, television, radio and computers in distance education, which were already noticed at that time – the Open University of the United Kingdom had just been founded – is another feature of educational technology and reminds us strongly of the extensive and more sophisticated mechanization of working processes in industry. This could be considered another decisive step towards the industrialization of teaching and learning. It was precisely this feature which induced me to foresee the advent of the third model of distance education, the technological model, which would supplement both the western and the eastern model in the years to come. According to this model, the institutions of distance education would use technical mass media and begin the era of mass education – just as industry developed techniques of mass production. Such a development was discernible in 1970. Time has shown that I was, as it were, a prophet of an unbelievable development. It is true, such a technological model of distance education was already vaguely discernible in 1970, but who could foresee that about thirty open universities and distance teaching universities patterned after this model would be founded all over the world in subsequent years? And who could imagine the wide range of technical media which would become available for them, among them the information carriers – audio cassettes, video cassettes, discettes, compact discs – as well as the information channels – telephone (conference call), telefax, viewdata, teletex, telex, datex, video conference and the already rather conventional radio and television (Wurster 1989: 9)? Indeed, the technological model of distance education assumed an overriding importance. It changed the whole field and the outlook of distance education. Garrison (1989: 8) is right when he considers the emergence and adoption of new communication technology as 'the most important and visible change of distance education'. And I am with him when he thinks that this change is so important that it is justifiable to take it as the main feature of a new period in the development of distance education which he calls 'the modern era'.

TRYING TO EXPLAIN THE REAL NATURE OF DISTANCE EDUCATION – TWO FAILURES

Having finished the documentation of distance education I proceeded from description to explanation. I felt that this task was important as there were quite a number of questions I could not answer in spite of having described distance education at great length and in great detail. What is its characteristic feature? Is it distance? correspondence? the socially disadvantaged students? the student studying on his or her own? Why was distance education ignored, disdained and neglected for about 100 years although it managed to provide instruction in many cases in which face-to-face teaching was unable to help? How far does it differ from other mediated forms of imparting knowledge? Today one might add: what are the reasons for the wide appeal distance education has had during the last two decades?

The circumstances in which this kind of work was done had

improved immensely after I joined the German Institute for Distance Education at the University of Tübingen in 1969, where I was charged with comparative distance education research. Here, I analysed the university-level distance education systems in many countries, starting with the Open University of the United Kingdom which was founded in the same year and had a spectacular impact on educationists over the whole world. In this way, the theoretical interpretations of distance education worked out in those years were not just lofty speculations, but were based on the study of practical experiences. Furthermore, it was certainly pleasant to work in an institute devoted entirely to the research and development of university-level distance education and which was funded amply by the Volkswagen Foundation.

In a first approach to explaining distance education, presented in Chapter 4, I analysed distance education by trying to relate it to other forms of imparting knowledge which are all accepted and of good repute and have proved successful both in education's past and at the present time. I found no less than ten forms of distance education: teaching using writing, teaching using printed material, teaching by means of periodicals, teaching using learning and work aids, audiovisual lessons, communication of knowledge by radio and television, programmed instruction, computer-aided instruction, individual tuition and independent work. Even more: twenty-seven didactic forms were identified which have been taken over from indirect teaching and incorporated into distance education. Consequently, distance education could be explained as being composed of some or more, or even all, of these elements. Seen from this angle, distance education is shown to be clearly rooted in a long tradition of indirect teaching, and profits from the experiences of modern ways of imparting knowledge as well. It is by no means the extraordinary, queer form of instruction that many people think. One could even be astonished and ask why a form of instruction which is composed of these well-known, widely used and well-reputed elements has been ignored and criticized for such a long time.

This structural analysis is certainly an interesting one and, so to speak, reassuring, as it integrates this rather singular and isolated method of instruction into a wide range of practices of imparting knowledge. It helps to discern important elements of teaching which could and should be investigated further. On the other hand, the question arises whether such a composite picture, such a mosaic of methods, helps to identify the specific structure of distance education. Does it answer the questions raised? I have to admit that this is not the case.

Therefore, I made a second approach (Peters 1973: 110), which is not included in this book, but is mentioned here in order to refer to yet another effort to understand distance education. This time I proceeded from a more pragmatic level to a level of theoretic reflection and described distance education with the help of categories taken from Heimann's structural concept of instruction which claimed to be applicable to all forms of learning at all levels and for all age groups. He postulated that all instruction consists of six structural elements: aims, contents, methods, media, the human beings involved, and the socio-economic conditions. From this statement it can be concluded that if one or more of these elements is lacking one cannot possibly speak of instruction in a proper way. I intended to find out whether distance education would comply with these prerequisites. If not, it could not be considered as instruction at all. This question suggested itself in view of the disparaging disdain of its critics.

The findings were that according to this concept distance education could be principally considered a complete method of teaching and learning, that it was, indeed, instruction in its own right. A few restrictions, however, had to be noted: not all intentions can be achieved, not all contents can be dealt with, not all methods and media can be employed, not all human factors in the teacher and the student can influence the instructional process. If one, in addition to that, considers the spontaneous dialogue between teacher and taught as an indispensable element of instruction, one cannot but define distance education as a reduced and denaturalized form of face-to-face instruction.

Such a concept of distance education was unsatisfactory as it did not answer the questions, did not lay open the true nature of distance education and could not explain the enormous teaching potential which at that time had already been proved by the Quadriga-Radio-College in the Federal Republic of Germany and the Open University in the United Kingdom. I became aware that it might be futile and misleading to try to analyse distance education with categories of traditional teaching theory. Therefore, I looked for categories which are inherent in distance education, categories which maybe are lacking in face-to-face teaching entirely and which may answer some of the unanswered questions and the enormous impact of distance education all over the world. In doing so I arrived at categories which so far had not been seen, let alone reflected upon, by experts in teaching theory.

GETTING A DIFFERENT PERSPECTIVE ON DISTANCE EDUCATION

Chapter 5 reveals that distance education has quite a number of structural features in common with the industrialized production process. The findings were, indeed, amazing: both processes are decisively determined by the principles of rationalization, the most important ones being the division and subdivision of labour, specialization, mechanization and automation. Both processes have to rely on careful planning, intensive preparatory work, adequate organization (bureaucracy, management approach), regular evaluation (quality control) and permanent optimizing. Both processes profit from the increased emphasis on research and increased cost-effectiveness, and both of them suffer from increased depersonalization.

In evaluating these findings, the questions raised can be answered as follows. First, *What is the characteristic feature of distance education?* After having read Chapter 5 it should be apparent that it is its high degree of industrialization. Hence, distance education can be defined as the most industrial form of teaching and learning. This definition points to a general characteristic of the new form of teaching and learning, it illuminates its structural peculiarity, and separates it sharply from all conventional forms of face-to-face instruction. It applies to all forms of distance education as it can be more or less industrialized – just like the production process. It is useful as it conveys a sense of direction and proportion and clarifies the typical approach of distance education to politicians responsible for education, planners of education, managers of distance teaching systems and their staffs as well as to teachers and students. This is an important task as nothing can be more counter-productive than not acting according to the principles of the system one is working in. Two examples are given as illustration:

- A Minister of Education accepted the idea of establishing an open university, but suggested that one should begin with a small unit which might grow, if successful, in subsequent years.
- A professor of a distance teaching university rushed to the nearest study centre as often as he could in order to tutor the students personally after he had learnt that most of his students had failed their tests. Both of them had certainly not understood the

structural peculiarity of distance education. As it is an industrialized process based on division of labour, a high degree of mechanization and on the economy of scale, it is absurd to plan a small beginning. And the professor fell back to an artisan mode of teaching and met a small number of students instead of improving the teaching material in such a way that all students could profit from it.

In view of the difficulties I had to face when trying to define distance education in more pragmatic and more theoretical educational terms – as just mentioned – and in view of Garrison and Shale's remark that 'a definition of distance education has long been something of a Jason's Fleece for those working at the enterprise – tantalizing, much sought after, but ever elusive' (1987: 7), such a definitory characterization of distance education is already a step forward. But there is more to this definition as it provides us also with essential principles which help us to explain also the peculiar structural pattern of distance education. I refer to only five of them: rationalization, division and subdivision of labour, mechanization, automation and depersonalization. There is no doubt that they are at work in distance education in a very developed way. Everyone working in and for systems of distance education should be aware of them.

It can be easily seen that such a definition is a real definition which characterizes a structure common to all objects to which this term should be applied, and that it is not merely a nominal definition which – like most designations – takes into account such distinguishing marks as, for instance, the correspondence between teacher and student, the distance which is to be overcome, the relative independence of the learner, or the fact that this kind of instruction usually takes place in the home of the student. Such definitions simply explicate a meaning that the term happens to have according to existing verbal usage, which is quite often not logical.

Similar objections can be made with regard to the definitions of writers who select and highlight other characteristic features of distance education, as, for instance, 'independent study' (Wedemeyer 1971: 36), 'apartness and autonomy' of the self-directed learner (Moore 1977, 1983), the support model 'continuity of concern' (Sewart 1981: 8), the 'helping organization' (Delling 1991: 61) and the 'guided didactic conversation' (Holmberg 1981: 30). In my view these definitions are not as precise as they should be as there are also forms of independent learning, of apartness and autonomy and support models at our schools and universities, and face-to-face instruction is even the model of the 'guided didactic conversation'. I also feel that all these definitions do not reflect the everyday practice of distance education, but try to improve it by underlining its desirable features. In this way they reveal a rather optimistic view of distance education.

The second question to be answered is this. *How much does distance differ from other forms of mediated teaching and learning?* The definition of distance education as the most industrial form of education helps to relate it to other forms of indirect or mediated forms of imparting knowledge, as they can be distinguished by their relative degree of being industrialized. Obviously, instruction by writing lacks most of the specific marks of industrialization – with the important exception that the teaching is objectified in the form of a letter which can be read again and again and by many persons. Teaching by printed material requires careful preparation, mechanical reproduction and some sort of organization for the distribution of the material to a great number of readers. Here, the process of industrialization of teaching and learning is far more advanced. In teaching by television the complexity of this process can hardly be surpassed, and the mass education effects are evident. But it is surpassed by distance education. In this case industrial production processes with regard to printed course material and radio and television broadcasts merge with developmental procedures and the systems approach of educational technology in a unique way in order to reach as many students as possible. It is clearly unbelievable how complicated the technical processes are which have been designed just to substitute the simple dialogue between teacher and student.

The third question is this. *What is the reason for the almost universal lack of esteem for distance education?* The comparative interpretation might lead us to assume that distance education was suspected and rejected for such a long time just because of its industrialized structure. It is true that this was not seen clearly and understood in the beginning, but it was certainly sensed. There was a vague but strong feeling about its being different. People did not accept the breakup of personal links between teacher and taught, they disliked the obvious depersonalization which took place as a result of mechanization, and they queried the artificial way in which the gap between the teacher and student was to be bridged. Above all, they rejected the idea of producing and marketing education just like a commodity. These may also be the reasons why this particular method of teaching and learning was normally not adopted by traditional schools and universities, and, hence, did not belong to the mainstream of education for a long time.

The fourth question is, *What are the reasons for the world-wide appeal distance education has had during the last two decades?* The attractiveness of distance education for educational reformers and politicians responsible for education as well as for millions of students all over the world can be also explained by its industrialization. It is the principle of mass production the application of which enables distance teaching institutions to supply high-quality instruction at comparatively low cost for great numbers of students. The teaching of only a small group of excellent teachers can be duplicated *ad libitum*. It is the industrialized mode of education which makes it, above all, possible 'that an increase in the number of educated people in a nation can be achieved *faster* than in any other way' (Perry 1986: 17).

One might want to test whether the other definitions quoted could contribute to the answering of questions like these. Obviously not. This shows the interpretative power of the definition of distance education as the most industrialized mode of teaching and learning.

Chapter 6 deals with some of the theoretic underpinnings of distance education in order to prove that there is more to it than just a new label or a more or less attractive catchword.

The findings of the first approach – a historical interpretation – are that the process of industrialization is not such an alien element in education as many people think. Rather, it is the result of a long historical development and perfectly in line with six dimensions of change. Thus, it is in harmony with historical tendencies to become more egalitarian, more profane, more determined by the students, more mechanized, more accessible for larger groups of students, and less tied to special persons, places and times. The decisive difference between industrialized education and traditional instruction is not due to unusual exterior influences, but originates basically from the slower development of the latter along the same lines. Judged in terms of this historical model, distance education is more advanced in the categories given, and traditional instruction is lagging behind.

A second approach deals with socio-cultural and intellectual preconditions of distance education. Here, the findings indicate clearly that distance education is a genuine product of the era of industrialization, as it requires motivations, attitudes, social experiences and dimensions of consciousness which could have developed in this period only and never in former periods in the development of mankind. In other words: people in the industrialized society are prepared in very special ways for this particular mode of teaching and learning. This, by the way, explains also the tremendous difficulties of developing countries which hope to profit from industrialized learning and, therefore, have established institutions of distance education.

The third approach – a sociological interpretation – contributes to the further clarification of the concept of industrialized education. With the help of categories developed in order to describe relevant structural changes of institutional subsystems which were caused by industrialization it is possible to characterize distance education as such a subsystem. It can be conceived as a subsystem of action determined by rational means–ends thinking, whereas traditional face-to-face teaching appears to remain a subsystem of communicative action. It could be shown that they, indeed, differ with regard to seven pairs of categories. Whereas in face-to-face teaching as a subsystem of communicative action the students' and the teachers' actions are predominantly determined by social norms, the intersubjectively shared everyday language, reciprocal behaviour expectations, the internalization of roles, the aim of preserving the institution, the punishment of the students by conventional sanctions and the goals of emancipation, individuation and the extension of dominance-free communication, it appears that distance teaching as a system of educational action determined by rational means–ends thinking is predominantly determined by technical rules, a context-free language, conditional prognoses and imperatives, the learning of skills and qualifications, the attainment of objectives by applying means-to-an-end principles, the students' failing because of their inability to cope with the reality of learning at a distance, and the goals to increase and to extend the teaching system. It may be deduced that face-to-face instruction and industrialized instruction are, therefore, two structurally distinct and separated forms of education.

The fourth approach tries to interpret industrialized education in anthropological terms. It reveals that technology and being human have the same origin and that technical activity belongs essentially to the distinguishing marks of man. Seen from this angle, it appears only natural that this technical activity is developed in education too and that man uses industrialized education if no other way of providing instruction is possible for all the students asking for it.

These four ways of looking at distance education as industrialized education underline the relevance of the new concept. They make clear that it is theoretically substantiated and that it helps us to see important structural patterns and elements which remain invisible if treated in terms of conventional theories of teaching and education.

This does not, of course, mean that the current theories of teaching and learning are to be replaced by this concept. Here, I have to oppose a misconception caused by speakers and writers who, in a somewhat careless use of the word 'theory' continue to refer to 'the theory of distance education as industrialized teaching and learning'. This phrase suggests or even implies that the concept of industrialized teaching and learning could become instrumental when goals, contents, methods and media of instruction are to be discussed and decided upon. Nothing could be more absurd. Quite the contrary: all theoretical approaches which reflect critically, for instance, the pedagogical value of given teaching and learning goals or relevant content, and justify and legitimate it, naturally apply to distance education in the same way as to all other forms of instruction in spite of its being highly industrialized. Obviously, too little is done in this respect. And the classical teaching–learning models can also be very helpful in analysing and constructing distance education. The practice of distance education has shown that some versions of educational technology are widely used – probably because of its definite affinities to distance education and to industrialization as well. It is telling and symptomatic that most distance teaching universities have established centres of educational technology which help to design, construct, and operate instructional systems. Together with a pragmatically orientated curriculum theory they provide the theoretical background and framework for the analysis and construction of distance education. They can be used according to the philosophical outlook and theoretical approach preferred by those in charge of and responsible for this kind of instruction.

It must be stressed that the concept of distance education as an industrialized mode of teaching and learning surely cannot perform these functions. On the other hand, this concept is relevant to other factors. It can draw educationists' attention to the fact that industrialization, which has thoroughly changed our lives in most areas, has done so in the realm of education as well. It can convince those who up to now preferred not to see this process or even indulged in denying it. It can make them see clearly what is different in distance education and induce them to act accordingly. Whatever the readers' attitudes to this process may be – amazement, optimistic confidence, sceptical interest, profound contempt or even sharp rejection – the industrialization of teaching and learning has taken place in spite of them. And chances are that it will develop further if the industrialization of society continues to grow so rapidly and irresistibly. Is such an extension of distance education to be desired? My personal views on this issue are ambivalent.

On the one hand I would certainly advocate it if the industrialization of teaching and learning continues to enable us to offer education to deprived adults who were previously denied opportunities. This is basically a moral question. One cannot keep distance education from the disadvantaged on the grounds that the further spreading of industrialized forms of teaching might be a menace to humanity. We have to realize that this can also be a matter of social justice.

Furthermore, I envisage that industrialized forms of imparting knowledge will, by and by, also permeate and finally partly substitute for face-to-face instruction on all levels. In other words, the importance of industrialized forms of teaching and learning will increase in the industrialized world civilization of the future. Will this be harmful to men and women? I do not think so as I believe optimistically that people – anthropologically speaking – will continue to change and adapt to the new structures of industrialized education of the future. They may then differ from us as we differ from agrarian peoples. They may change to such a degree – also with regard to their values – that they will not understand our present fears and doubts.

On the other hand I am pessimistic and join those critics who are convinced that the continued process of industrialization will finally destroy the foundations of life on this planet. As distance education is a part of this powerful process it is more than likely that it will contribute to the disintegration of society as it isolates people from one another, reduces the forms of shared learning, and keep learners away from personal interactions and critical intercourse. This may remain true even if post-industrialism will try to mitigate these more obvious weaknesses of the industrialized mode of teaching and learning – as is described in Chapter 11. Seemingly, such a sense of uncertainty, such a splitting of consciousness, is typical of times of transition.

Finally, in order to defend myself against the reproach that I have developed a theory which is not related to pedagogical theories, I should like to mention that I never claimed to have developed a theory of distance education at all. Rather, I, very modestly, interpreted distance education only with the help of the metaphor of the industrialized production process and found similarities. Later I understood that distance education is not only similar to an industrialized production process, but is itself thoroughly industrialized. This is a special way of conceiving distance education – and nothing more. Therefore, I prefer to speak of the concept of industrialized teaching and learning. It helps us to see a number of criteria which distinguish distance education from all forms of face-to-face instruction. It is not an approach of general teaching theory, but rather a sociological analysis. Will the findings ever be integrated into general teaching theories? I am doubtful about this as didactic theories, indeed, lack the categories for grasping this strange phenomenon.

PUTTING DISTANCE EDUCATION TO THE TEST

The establishment of the Fernuniversität by the *Land* North Rhine-Westphalia in 1974 was not the first initiative towards introducing distance education in the Federal Republic of Germany. The preceding ten years had seen the foundation of the *Telekolleg* of the Bavarian Broadcasting Corporation, the *Funkkolleg* of the Hessian Broadcasting Corporation, and of the *Deutsches Institut für Fernstudien an der Universität Tübingen* (German Institute of Distance Education at the University of Tübingen), which was to conduct research into distance education and to develop distance teaching material. But the establishment of the Fernuniversität was a major thrust forward in the development of distance education in the Federal Republic as, and this was new, a whole university was founded in order to provide new opportunities for acquiring degrees and for university-level continuing education. I was involved in it as I served first as a member of its Founding Committee and then as its Founding Rector (vice-chancellor).

Why did I accept the new job which called for such a great effort and so much time mainly spent on administrative affairs and which would keep me away from my scholarly work? There were, among others, mainly three reasons. First, I was challenged by the sheer importance of the new university. I had the idea that after the implementation of universal *primary* education and universal *secondary* education the general trend in highly industrialized countries would eventually lead to universal *tertiary* education, to which distance education would have to contribute a great deal. With regard to the future I considered the adult student studying at a distance no longer as exceptional, but rather as normal and even typical. In other words, I could not imagine universal tertiary education without a distance teaching university. Secondly, I had another reason which originated from my personal history. Since I myself, in the fifties, had to work as a teacher and to study at the university at the same time, I was strongly motivated to help establish a university uniquely for those in a similar position in order to alleviate their double burden. And thirdly, I was challenged by the newness, the unusualness and the extreme difficulty of the task.

I need not describe the Fernuniversität here as there are two accounts of it available in English (Keegan 1982: 88; Bartels and Peters 1986: 97). Therefore, I limit myself to just a few remarks in order to indicate more recent developments.

In spite of extraordinary financial problems which have lasted now for thirteen years, the Fernuniversität has been able to consolidate. It caters now for 52,500 students who are provided with tuition by sixty-one full professors, fifteen assistant professors, 278 academic staff and 686 administrative staff. In 1993 the parliament of North Rhine-Westphalia allotted a budget of 102 million German marks for the Fernuniversität.

The Fernuniversität has been able to extend and to develop further its system of educational technology. Since 1983 the West German Broadcasting Corporation has provided 45 minutes' television broadcasting time fortnightly on Saturdays. Since 1989 the Fernuniversität has been able to broadcast its instructional television programmes for 45 minutes each week also via the satellite EURO-STEP, a project of the European Community. Surprisingly, there is a special demand for their programmes in the East European countries. The development of educational software has already become routine in several departments. Finally, it may also be worth mentioning that the university has been experimenting for many years with computer data, computer conferencing and video conferencing.

After the reunification of Germany and the dramatic political changes in Eastern Europe, the Fernuniversität had to reconsider its target groups. Many new students from East Germany and even from East European countries enrolled in addition to the previous students. It became necessary to establish study centres for the new students, including also a study centre in Budapest (as part of the TEMPUS project of the European Community). Further study centres will be organized in the Czech Republic and – together with the Polish authorities – at the newly founded Europe University in Frankfurt-on-Oder. These developments indicate the European dimension of distance study. The distance teaching institutions surely contribute to the growth of a united Europe.

In order to give additional information and to convey deeper insights into some of the problems of the new distance teaching university as well as into its first accomplishments and failures, two articles have been selected.

A key problem was, of course, to cope with the problems of the industrialized way of teaching and learning which was to be developed for the new university. The Founding Committee had already realized that there was a dichotomy in its instructional system. Scientific knowledge was to be taught according to the same regulations for examinations and according to the same standards as at other universities in the Federal Republic, but was to be developed and delivered in a highly mechanized way. Academic teaching, in spite of some effort at reform in the last decades, had remained basically traditional. In a very effective process of academic qualification the professors learn to know exactly – subconsciously and consciously – what and how to teach. Now, in the new university the professors were expected to adapt their traditional teaching to an entirely new situation. In order to increase the availability and accessibility of academic teaching they were expected to accept new – industrialized – systems of planning, organizing and communicating which ran counter to established practices. This means that they had to get acquainted and actually learn to deal with important aspects of instructional technology. The structural antagonism inherent in such a plan is obvious, as most professors disregard and even reject activities such as, for instance, the definition of instructional goals, curriculum construction, the use of technical media, tests and systematic evaluation techniques. The real accomplishment of the Fernuniversität was that this antagonism was overcome to a large degree. The two main elements of its instruction system, a traditional way of producing knowledge and an industrialized way of its dissemination – usually fitting together like fire and water – have been absorbed and integrated in daily working routines.

Chapter 7 deals with the functions that a distance teaching university should perform in view of its unique opportunities to reach out and to provide tuition for students all over the country, and abroad, and with the difficulties it necessarily has to face when these functions are carried out. This is just another aspect of putting distance education to the test.

These difficulties are the reason for a long discussion of the concept of the Fernuniversität. I exaggerate the opposing positions for the sake of clarity. There were those who wanted to do everything in their power to address a special clientele – namely, the disadvantaged, the deprived and the handicapped – and, therefore, wanted to open the university for them and to develop, mainly, continuing education. And there were those who wanted to do everything in their power to develop the Fernuniversität, at least as far as possible, like a traditional university and who preferred to cater for 'normal' students and, therefore, insisted on proper entrance qualifications and on a priority of undergraduate and graduate studies. This was by no means merely a theoretical discussion with political overtones, as vested interests were at stake. Quite to the contrary: its acuteness was caused by a clash between the legislative power of Parliament and the right of self-government of the Fernuniversität as an autonomous institution. This chapter describes the various factors influencing the quest for the right concept of the Fernuniversität.

Chapter 8 is an account of what the Fernuniversität achieved in its first ten years and a description of necessary measures to be taken to develop it further. It informs the reader about its structural features and specific problems and indicates that the Fernuniversität is a good example of putting the ideas of distance education into practice, which, clearly, have been able to stand the test of time.

CONTEMPORARY ANALYSES

Chapter 9 may very well function as a recapitulation and additional justification of the main thesis submitted here as it deals with the correction of its misinterpretations. Very much to my surprise, the concept of distance education as the most industrialized form of teaching and learning had attracted unusual attention which was to continue for thirty years. Not only was this aspect of distance education often referred to in discussions of the subject, but it was also quoted and referred to in the literature more than fifty times after Börje Holmberg's and Desmond Keegan's first reports of it in the late seventies and early eighties. As might be expected with such a controversial issue, the discussion suffered from quite a number of misunderstandings. In this chapter I respond to them and analyse them critically. One of the more important findings is that the concept of industrialized education is not just an expression of the optimistic trust in technology and empirical research and development so typical of the sixties and seventies. It is not tied to a particular decade of our century, but is rather an aspect of the most powerful process of industrialization which lasted much longer and which will continue to permeate most areas of our world.

Chapter 10 is an attempt to deal with lay theories on distance education by analysing quite a number of designations for it. This is done because it can be assumed that different designations mean different understandings of distance education. The same applies to catchwords coined in order to characterize distance education. If their implicit meanings are described and seen together, one becomes aware of a composite picture of distance education, which, of course, differs from the composite picture conveyed in Chapter 4. It has the advantage that it consists of features which actually influence the actions of people when they deal with distance education.

Chapter 11 deals with the question what will happen to distance education as the most industrialized way of teaching and learning when the era of industrialization comes to an end and a very sharp change of values takes place in a post-industrial era. It is relevant to deal with the problems which proponents of distance education will probably have to face in the future. It is high time to do this now, as the forerunners of post-industrialism can be already encountered in some areas. As post-industrialism is obviously a definite reaction to the damages the process of industrialization has done, it seems likely that post-industrial distance education will try to correct harmful exaggerations and destructive side effects of the industrialized mode of teaching and learning – as, for instance, isolating teachers from students and students from students by neglecting tutorial and group work. Therefore, it may well be that post-industrialism will strengthen personal ties as far as possible and highlight social interaction. This means that considerable changes of distance education are to be envisaged.

Seen together in retrospect, the eleven chapters of this book, covering thirty years, make the reader conscious of a unique development in the world of education: the unprecedented rise of distance education as a new method of teaching and learning; its world-wide acceptance; the unparalleled emergence of new big institutions applying it; the phenomenal growth of the number of teachers and students profiting from it; and the increasing importance of research activities dealing with this remarkable and unforeseen innovation. The reader becomes aware of how the previously neglected and often questionable practice of correspondence education in the back yard of education turned into an accepted, professionalized branch of public education – the importance of which is steadily increasing.

The theory and practice of some teaching methods have their up-turns and down-turns. For a while they are much sought after and actively discussed, and then they go out of fashion. Who, for instance, is still interested in programmed instruction, so much in vogue during the sixties and seventies? And who would still like to bother with set theory which was to revolutionize mathematics instruction at our schools in the seventies? The attractiveness of distance education, however, seems to have steadily increased during the last thirty, and especially during the last twenty, years. This form of teaching and learning has profited from its unusual flexibility and adaptability as well as from the ever-growing demand for education and continuing education, especially in industrialized countries. I was lucky to have been involved in distance education just at this time, as it has been not only extremely rewarding but also very exciting to feel oneself, so to speak, always on the way up. I am confident that distance education will continue this way.

REFERENCES

Bartels, J. and Peters, O. (1986) 'The German distance university: its main features and functions', in G. van Enckevort, K. Harry, P. Morin and H-G. Schütze (eds) *Distance Higher Education and the Adult Learner*, Heerlen: Dutch Open University, pp. 97–109.

Delling, R. M. (1991) 'Distance education as a multi-dimensional system of communication and production', in B. Holmberg and G. E. Ortner (eds) *Research into Distance Education*, Frankfurt am Main: Lang.

Garrison, D. R. (1989) *Understanding Distance Education: a Framework for the Future*, London: Routledge.

Garrison, D. R. and Shale, D. (1987) 'Mapping the boundaries of distance education: problems in defining the field', in *The American Journal of Distance Education*, 1, 1:7–13.

Holmberg, B. (1981) *Status and Trends of Distance Education*, London: Kogan Page.

Keegan, D. (1982) 'The Fernuniversität (Fernuniversität-Gesamthochschule in Hagen), Federal Republic of Germany', in G. Rumble and K. Harry (eds) *The Distance Teaching Universities*, London: Croom Helm, pp. 88–106.

Moore, M. (1977) 'On a theory of independent study', ZIFF-Papiere 16, Hagen: Fernuniversität.

Moore, M. (1983) 'Self-directed learning and distance education', ZIFF-Papiere 48, Hagen: Fernuniversität.

Perry, W. (Lord Perry of Walton) (1986) 'Distance education: trends worldwide', in G. van Enckevort, K. Harry, P. Morin and H-G. Schütze (eds) *Distance Higher Education and the Adult Learner*, Heerlen: Open Universiteit, pp. 15–21.

—— (1992) 'The birth of the Open University: an unwanted infant and its children', in G. E. Ortner, K. Graff and H. Wilmersdoerfer (eds) *Distance Education as Two-way Communication*, Frankfurt-on-Main: Lang, pp. 226–8.

Peters, O. (1965) *Der Fernunterricht*, Weinheim: Beltz.
—— (1968) *Das Hochschulfernstudium*, Weinheim: Beltz.
—— (1971) *Texte zum Hochschulfernstudium*, Weinheim: Beltz.
—— (1973) *Die didaktische Struktur des Fernunterrichts*, Weinheim: Beltz.
Sewart, D. (1981) 'Distance teaching: a contradiction in terms?' in *Teaching at a Distance*, 19:8–18.
Wedemeyer, C. (1971) 'Independent study', in *The Encyclopedia of Education*, pp. 548–57.
Wurster, J. (1989) *The Future of Media at the Fernuniversität, Hagen: Fernuniversität, Zentrum für Fernstudienentwicklung.*

Part I
Data collection

1 Distance education by correspondence schools (1965)

> Peters completed *Der Fernunterricht: Materialien zur Diskussion einer neuen Unterrichtsform* (Distance training: materials for the analysis of a new form of teaching) in 1964, and it was published by Beltz in 1965. The book has 537 pages. It treats government distance training, the provision of distance education for children and the achievements of private correspondence schools throughout the world in the 1950s and early 1960s. Detailed analyses are given of France, Denmark, the Netherlands, Norway, Sweden, Japan, South Africa, Australia, Canada, the USSR, the German Democratic Republic and the Federal Republic of Germany. The book opens with a 66-page overview from which this extract is taken, and concludes with 162 pages of tables, statistical analysis, eferences and research documentation.

DEFINITIONS

The term 'distance education' is predominantly used in its narrower meaning. It then refers to instruction by the exchange of letters between teacher and student, a process in which the contributions of both are usually based on specially prepared and methodically developed printed course material. This form of distance education is practised in most of the correspondence schools.

The wider meaning of the term is derived from the word 'distance'. It indicates more generally any form of instruction in which it is necessary to bridge a distance between teacher and student, which can be achieved not only with the help of letters and printed course material, but also by other technical media such as telephone, radio, television, audio and video cassettes, as well as by newer electronic media.

In both definitions – and this is of great importance, as it separates distance education from other forms of influencing people by giving information – *instruction* means a methodical process of imparting knowledge with the following characteristics.

- The contents of the instruction are chosen taking into account didactical and methodical considerations.
- The indirect contact between teacher and students is continued until the end of the instruction.
- There are possibilities for the teacher to influence the learning behaviour of the students.
- The learning of the students is measured and graded.

Self-instruction and *self-study*, which have been often used as synonyms for distance education, have none of these characteristics. There is, however, an intermediate stage between distance education and self-instruction, if, for instance, a student reads a series of methodically developed study materials. Such a form of instruction corresponds to face-to-face teaching in which only the teacher speaks – limiting himself or herself exclusively to the presentation of teaching material.

Supervised distance education has been used by schools which lacked teachers of certain subjects. In this case a student sits in the classroom at regular hours, studies course units and communicates with his teacher in the correspondence school somewhere else. The student – and others who might be studying different courses – is supervised by a teacher who, as a rule, does not interfere with the teaching–learning processes which are taking place under his eyes.

STUDENTS

As distance education is practised in many subject areas and in many countries it is difficult to describe features which are common to all students. However, if one tries to find out why they decide to enrol in distance study courses it is easy to see that most of them do so because they are prevented from attending regular day schools. If we categorize the respective impediments, the distance students can be assigned to the following groups:

Group 1: Students who have to work for a living in order to support themselves and often also their family: workers who want to complete their primary or secondary school education; workers, skilled workers, and technicians who want to improve their vocational qualification; agricultural labourers who intend to move into a town and therefore wish to prepare themselves for a new occupation; workers in occupations which come to an end and who, therefore, need retraining; immigrants who wish to obtain the citizenship of their new country and have to acquire specific knowledge about it.

Group 2: Students who live in sparsely settled areas: children of farmers in isolated areas, for instance in Canada and Australia.

Group 3: Students who live too far away from the nearest day school of their own nationality: children of diplomats, missionaries, military personnel abroad, children of experts employed in developing countries, children of persons in itinerant trades, sailors, boatmen, children of immigrants who are to be instructed in their mother tongues.

Group 4: Persons who are unable to attend regular schools for health reasons: sick persons who are bedridden, handicapped persons, children who have to stay in hospital for some time.

Group 5: Persons who are hindered from attending regular schools by the state: prisoners, children and juveniles in reformatories.

Apart from these five groups, there are distance students who do not come into this category. They might well be able to attend regular schools but prefer to enrol in distance education courses. Some do it in order to supplement the instruction of their regular school or to raise their level of general education; gifted students do it in order to reach an advanced level and still other students do it in order to find out whether they fit into a specific vocational pattern so as to clarify vocational options. Finally, there are also teachers who study courses at a distance in order to inspire and prepare themselves for teaching.

Usually there are fewer students who wish to complete their secondary education in order to obtain entrance qualification for institutes of higher learning. Many more students intend to improve their vocational qualifications. Generally speaking, both groups belong to the higher ranks of workers and the middle ranks of salaried staff – those wide, intermediate sections of the population in industrialized countries which wish to improve their conditions of life and to climb socially. They are interested in information and eager for knowledge. Many of them can be characterized by the fact that *The Reader's Digest* recruits its readers among them. It is not coincidental that many correspondence schools like to place their advertisements in this magazine, where they have proved to be most successful.

Students who enrol in distance education do not live predominantly in rural areas – although this is widely assumed as there is usually a lack of specialized schools in country areas. On the contrary, they typically dwell in big cities and overcrowded industrial regions. It is only there that many differentiated possibilities for employment and promotion prospects inspire the students to learn, that the competitiveness of industrialized production urges them to take the initiative, and that the urban environment and atmosphere provides for additional incentives.

Most students are between twenty and thirty-five years old, which means that they are adults. Their educational standard is, as a rule, above the average of the respective age group – and not lower, as again is often assumed by those who consider distance students as disadvantaged persons.

What are the motivations of distant students? The strongest one is certainly the ambition to climb socially, to change from a blue-collar job to a white-collar job. They seek economic security. This motivation is activated when the students have clear ideas of the job they want to have and when the competences they have developed so far will help them to reach it. Furthermore, this motivation is supported by the fact that these students are adults who are able to judge their life chances more realistically than, say, students in secondary schools. They are conscious of the importance of their educational goals and of the consequences of reaching them.

There might be more hidden motivations. Some students decide to engage in distance education in order to protest against their parents who insisted on certain vocational training for their children. Through distance education they want to remedy early wrong decisions. The 'ambitious wife' can also be a powerful source of motivation. Sometimes, there is a revolt against discrimination in their daily work which distant students hope to escape by striving for better jobs. The great number of distant students in developing countries can perhaps be explained by similar motives.

The advertising departments of correspondence schools systematically exploit such motivations and reinforce them by creating an image of distant students which is certainly far beyond reality but nevertheless appeals to them. According to them, distant students belong to the 'intellectual elite' of the work force, have 'better chances' when applying for a new job, obtain a 'higher income', enjoy 'more prestige' and look forward to a 'happy future'. Sometimes the advertisements contain pictures under the headline: 'Formerly an employee with a low income – now a leading personality', showing all those present at a meeting of directors listening attentively to the former distant student. Another picture visualizes the success of the distant student who himself, travelling with an attractive young wife in a large sports car in a holiday paradise, is obviously able 'to afford anything'. The distant students will, of course, lower their sights depending on their maturity and life experience. But more or less subconsciously such advertisements may encourage them in their striving for success.

The motivations of distant students are also influenced by the way in which they are looked upon by society. This differs considerably from country to country, and depends on the achievements of the correspondence schools and the social structures and traditions of a given country – whether they are, for instance, capitalist or socialist. The scale of possible attitudes reaches from condescending pity and derision for the poor guys who turn themselves into drudges in order to climb the social ladder, to the firm conviction that the economic future of society depends on the qualification of numerous distant students who work and study at the same time. In the first case, distant students appear to be strange characters and outsiders, showing all the disadvantages of the self-educated; in the second case, they are considered the blue-eyed boys of the nation.

An attitude has also emerged which is located midway between these two extremes. Thus distant students are persons who take the initiative in the planning and pursuit of their careers, who have considerable will-power and perseverance in mastering a difficult task, and who are often praised for their stamina.

TEACHERS

In distance education, courses are usually written for an arbitrary number of students. This shows the importance of the qualification of the teachers. A bad course written by one teacher which will be studied by 10,000 students will do more harm that the oral instruction of the same teacher in a classroom. Therefore, correspondence schools try to employ teachers whose competence is higher than average. Large correspondence schools with highly differentiated course programmes employ teachers who have not only studied their subjects at a university but who also teach at institutes of higher learning: graduate engineers, businessmen, and teachers. On the other hand, they also employ experienced practitioners, leading experts and managers coming directly from the world of work.

Little is known about the educational qualifications of these teachers. Generally speaking, their competencies are mainly subject-orientated. Often they are experts in a limited field only. Educational and didactical knowledge are, as a rule, missing. Some correspondence schools like to employ experts with a special reputation or persons who have become popular – mainly for advertising purposes. A correspondence school in Paris, for instance, took pride in employing a general as well as an opera singer, and in the United States 'famous artists' founded a correspondence school in order to offer tuition in painting and writing.

On the other hand, there are correspondence schools in which teachers have not passed the examinations for which they prepare their students. As there are often no public regulations about the educational training of teachers at correspondence schools, these institutes may become places in which ambitious outsiders can stand the test as well as in which arrogant know-nothings can do a lot of harm.

As a rule, a correspondence school has a small staff of full-time and a great number of part-time employees. Many of the part-time employees are teachers in the state school system. They work as authors of course material and as correctors of assignments. Correspondence schools are happy with this arrangement as they can tell their students that they are taught by 'real' teachers. And the state schools profit from it as well, as their teachers gain new insights in the methodology of teaching when writing course material and communicating with the distant students after having corrected the assignments. Experienced teachers can often also be found in the permanent staff of correspondence schools. Usually they are unable to work in state schools because they are retired, ill or have had to leave their schools for other reasons. Among them is also a number of younger, well-trained teachers who found that they could not cope with a normal class situation as they cannot get along with larger groups of students. They find teaching at a distance much easier and more rewarding.

The work of the teacher in distance education differs from face-to-face teaching in a classroom through the increased division of labour. This principle is fundamental in industrialized production processes. Its application to the process of instruction has therefore caused considerable resistance and, mainly emotional, opposition. Division of labour, however, is not alien to our schools and universities, although they postulate a special pedagogical relationship between teacher and student and deduce from this a holistic concept of instruction. Usually the long- and medium-term plans for instruction are developed by special teams of experts, special subjects are taught by special teachers and the final evaluation of the learning outcomes of the students is often decided upon by meetings of all teachers in a given school. Nobody objects to a professor who conducts a seminar himself but asks his assistants to read and mark the papers of the students.

Although the principle of division of labour has already influenced the teaching and learning of our day schools, the job of the teacher remains extremely complex, as it consists of a number of different activities. At large correspondence schools, however, this complexity is reduced by splitting the job into several functions which are assigned to several departments:

- *Preparation of the instruction 1*: selection of the contents of instruction by the author in cooperation with the directorate of the school.
- *Preparation of the instruction 2*: development of manuscripts by an editorial staff according to the special requirements of distance teaching.
- *Presentation*: typographical design of the teaching material by layout specialists and designers.
- *Assessment and marking*: correction of the assignments by specialized correctors.
- *Interaction*: exchange of letters between the student and various persons in the correspondence school.
- *Administration and supervision*: control of the whole process of instruction, registering of the corrected assignments, card filings by specialists in the office.
- *Counselling*: Passing on information about courses and examinations and writing of letters reminding the students to send in the assignments by the information section and the respective distant teachers.
- *Evaluation:* Examination of the learning results of all course students, recommendations of changes to the instructions and further development of courses, taking into consideration new findings by educational experts of the research unit.

The most important functions are the writing of course material and the correction of papers sent in by the students. This is what most of the teachers do. The division of labour frees them from the more bothersome extra functions which can be carried out by specialists in the various departments of the school. It stands to reason that these specialists can do their job more thoroughly, reliably and effectively.

Generally, the qualities of the persons teaching at a distance must be the same as in face-to-face instruction. As their functions are, however, reduced to course writing as well as to correcting and marking assignments, and as they have to specialize in these fields, they need additional qualifications. The *course writer* must have the ability to envisage the teaching–learning situation they want to create and to foresee possible difficulties of comprehending and learning, and must be able to circumvent them in advance as a precaution. And above all, the course writer must be able to write instead of instructing orally or lecturing – which is quite a different thing. Even more, the course writer must be able to write short, concise and succinct sentences which are understandable – a gift which is certainly not found very often.

The *corrector* must be able to react as if he or she were in a virtual instructional situation with a single student. Some correspondence schools help correctors to do so by supplying them with the student's file and photograph when sending the assignments. Their task is difficult, indeed. While they correct, mark, explain and comment they must endeavour to individualize the course material, which is, necessarily, the same for thousands of students. This can be attained by inspiring, encouraging and advising the student in such a way as is necessary in this particular teaching–learning situation. Correctors are able to devote more of their time to performing these important functions as the schools free them from written routine work. Often they use computers which print out long and very individualized letters according to the key numbers which the corrector has indicated. This very often enables them to comment upon a mistake comprehensively and to give just those hints which are required by the particular teaching–learning situation.

Some correspondence schools work with 'travelling teachers' who visit groups of distant students more or less regularly. They need special teaching skills, as they must not waste the short time available by lecturing on the topics exhibited in the course units, but must use it for identifying the most important learning difficulties and showing ways of overcoming them. This means again that the instruction is to be individualized. Furthermore, it suggests that the precious time of face-to-face instruction is also used for motivational purposes.

If the importance of correspondence schools and their possible advantages are more and more recognized their teachers will attract more public attention. It is certainly imaginable that special training courses for this group of persons will be established at teacher training colleges and at universities. For the time being, correspondence schools have to train their teachers themselves. The bigger the schools are, the easier it might be to cease improvising and to develop elaborated training procedures. The American giant correspondence school ICS, for instance, has set up a special training department which is connected to fifteen schools. Applicants are selected by tests and interviews. Then their educational and vocational backgrounds are considered. The training is strictly practice-orientated and has similarities to an apprenticeship. Trainees are assigned to a teacher who acquaints them with a course unit and demands that they study it in the same way as a student is expected to. This also means that the trainees have to pass the prescribed examinations. Their assignments are discussed and evaluated with the teacher, who will dwell upon typical mistakes and the best ways of dealing with them. Then the future teachers start practising themselves. They are asked to correct further assignments of the same course unit, but still under supervision of their trainer, and this usually lasts for eighteen months. By and by, the trainees increase the number of course units they are able to correct.

Part-time teachers and often full-time teachers work at home. A correspondence school may, therefore, employ hundreds of teachers without providing offices. The teachers need not live near the correspondence school, as contacts between them and their school can be secured by mail. At a correspondence school in Paris the teachers are obliged to be present once a week to deliver the corrected asssignments and to obtain new ones. This gives the teachers an opportunity to meet their colleagues and to discuss their experiences.

Objections are often raised against the depersonalizing of the teacher–student relationship in distance education. Teachers of correspondence schools, however, like to stress that they devote much more time to each individual student than could possibly be the case in the classroom. Quite often this leads, they say, to sustained personal relationships which result in distant students sending postcards from their vacations or announcements of engagements, weddings and births. When Hamburg was deluged by a big flood, a correspondence school there received many letters expressing concern for the well-being of their teachers.

2 University-level distance education (1968)

Das Hochschulfernstudium: Materialien zur Diskussion einer neuen Studienform (University-level distance education: materials for the analysis of a new form of education) was published by Beltz in 1968. It has 620 pages. It deals with university education at a distance throughout the world in the 1960s. The book opens with a 60-page overview from which this extract is taken. Detailed analysis follows of university distance education in England, France, the Netherlands, Norway, Sweden, Israel, Spain, South Vietnam, Australia, New Zealand, South Africa, Canada, the United States, the USSR, Poland, Czechoslovakia, Hungary, Romania, Bulgaria, Cuba, Jamaica, Mexico, Colombia, Costa Rica, Lebanon, India, the German Democratic Republic and the Federal Republic of Germany. A further twenty-three countries are listed as having no distance education at university level, and twenty-seven more from which it was impossible to get data. The book concludes with 300 pages of references, bibliography, statistical data and source materials for all the countries studied.

INTRODUCTORY REMARKS

'Distance education' is a form of education in which the students of universities and institutes of higher learning do not attend regular classes or lectures, but instead study teaching material especially prepared for this purpose by professors and their staffs together with experts in distance education – and interact indirectly with members of the teaching staff by means of technical media for the guidance and control of their learning.

This means that the distance between the living space of the student and their Alma Mater is not the decisive characteristic. It is true that this understanding of distance is applicable to most distant students – but not to the great number of regular students living on the campus who attend classes and study 'at a distance' as well, for instance, at many US-American universities. The term 'distance', therefore must be qualified in the sense that it means in the first place 'not face-to-face'. This means that the students are not pinned down to fixed times, places and persons, but are free to decide themselves when, where, what and how they wish to study.

Another important distinctive attribute of distance study is the *indirect* interaction between the university teachers and their students. This must be stressed, as many people believe that there is no communication between them at all. It is accomplished by means of letters, printed material, telephone calls, video and audio tapes and other electronic media. This separates distance education from lectures and classes at a university where this interaction usually takes place *directly*, that is, face-to-face.

There are four fundamental types of distance education in higher learning:

- *Type 1*: Distance education is accomplished by studying the printed material sent to the students by their university teachers, as well as by means of an exchange of letters between them, whereby the university teachers and their assistants correct the assignments and guide the further work of the students. This type was developed out of the traditional correspondence instruction and can be found especially in countries with long experiences in this field; for instance, England, France, the United States, Canada, Australia and South Africa.

- *Type 2*: Here, distance education type 1 is supplemented by regular and obligatory teaching–learning activities which take place face-to-face (consultation periods, weekend seminars and classes). It was developed in the Soviet Union and later introduced in eastern European countries. It has been organized especially well in eastern Germany. Variations of this type can be found in Japan, India, Sweden, Cuba, Mexico and Costa Rica. In extreme cases the face-to-face periods become so important that it becomes doubtful whether one can still speak of distance education.

- *Type 3*: Distance education types 1 and 2 are supplemented by lectures and demonstrations on radio and television. This multimedia approach has been tested in the United States and England.

- *Type 4*: Distance education is organized in such a way that a programed computer performs important teaching functions. This type has been tested by the US Air Force.

There are two special developments of distance education: *Combined distance education*: Here two or three forms of study, each of which could lead separately to graduation, are incorporated in such a way that they form a new teaching–learning structure. In East Germany, for instance, it is possible to combine traditional tuition on the campus with evening study and distance education.

Group distance education: A number of students enrol in the same course of distance education and meet regularly in order to recapitulate, check and discuss what they have learnt by reading the teaching material. They are often called 'self-help groups'.

DISTANT STUDENTS

No accurate information is available about the numbers of distant students. The statistical data which have been found are partially incomplete, and refer to different years and to courses of different lengths. They will be specified here only in order to give at least some indication as to how large the groups of persons are which will be dealt with.

The table below shows the numbers of distant students in selected countries in the 1960s.

The total number of distant students would probably be only slightly higher if the numbers of distant students of those countries

Table. Distance students of university level in the 1960s

England	8,000
France	7,000
The Netherlands	10,599
Sweden	8,283
South Africa	16,326
Australia	10,500
Canada	6,807
USA	642,789
USSR	1,438,600
Czechoslovakia	50,452
Poland	67,926
Mexico	1,500
India	35,000
German Democratic Republic	29,548
Federal Republic of Germany	1,300
Total	2,334,630

which are not in this list were added. It can, however, be supposed that the numbers of Chinese students would change it considerably.

As distance study differs from country to country in the same way as other forms of higher learning, it is difficult to describe the distant students in unified, general terms. However, it is possible to distinguish three types of them according to the goals and the duration of their studies. There are undergraduate, part-time and postgraduate distant students.

Undergraduate distant students take courses in order to prepare themselves for graduation. We find them, for instance, in England, South Africa, the Soviet Union, Poland, Czechoslovakia, Hungary, Romania, Bulgaria and East Germany. As they usually have also to work for a living they must extend their study time considerably. Often they have to carry this double burden for five to seven years, and in many cases even longer.

Part-time distant students are to be found among the regular students of a university. They enrol for courses the contents of which are normally delivered by professors or lecturers in one semester. This type of student emerged especially in the United States, but also in Sweden, Norway and the Netherlands. It includes regular students who had to discontinue their studies for health, family or financial reasons or had to go into the armed forces but wish to use their free time for studying single courses at a distance until they are able to resume their regular studies.

Post-graduate distant students are graduate students employed in the professions who wish to enrol in distance education courses in order to continue their education. They can be met both in eastern and western countries. Up to now this group has been comparatively small. But there are signs that it will grow considerably in the years to come.

Distance education will mean different things for the distant students of these three groups, and this will affect their motivation and commitment. For undergraduate students, studying at a distance is a central life task which determines their way of living for a long time in a specific way. If they drop out, their plans for a professional future have failed and they have to dispense with the vocational promotion they had in mind. For the regular students who enrol in only one or in several single courses, the new learning experience might merely be an interesting episode. And for the professional employees who are continuing their education, distance study will be considered as an additional task which will not bind them very much, especially if they volunteered to study at a distance and think that they can postpone it for any length of time.

A surprisingly large portion of the distant students are teachers or future teachers. In East Germany, for instance, there were more than 10,000 teachers enrolled in distance education in 1965. In the USSR, there were more than 261,000 distant students enrolled in teacher training colleges in 1961. Large groups of teachers can also be found among distant students in the Netherlands, in France, in the United States and Australia, in South Africa and India. In Cuba, Costa Rica, Mexico and in the Lebanon all distant students are teachers – as distance education was introduced in these countries just for them. The teachers studying at a distance can also be allotted to the three types described. In East Germany and eastern European countries they study mainly in order to pass the prescribed state examinations. In the United States younger teachers enrol in supplementary single courses. Postgraduate courses for senior teachers have been developed in Sweden, England and Australia. The number of distant students studying technical subjects is even larger. In East Germany, it is true, there are only 5,736, but in the USSR there are half a million. A third large group which has become more important in recent years consists of those persons who are studying economics at a distance.

Distant students are generally older than day students. In South Africa their average age is twenty-seven years, which means that on average they are seven years older. In the United States the average age is between 26.3 and 29.4 years. In the USSR distant students are also generally older than evening students, who also work for a living. Most distant students belong to the age group up to thirty-five years, but many of them are considerably older. In eastern countries there is an age limit (about forty years). In western countries, however, it is possible to become a distant student if you are considerably older even than that. At the University of Wisconsin, for instance, they have enrolled a seventy-year-old man and at the University of South Africa the oldest student was seventy-two years old.

As distance students are generally older than day students a greater portion of them are married and responsible for children. Experience has shown that married distant students are 'better' students. However, the years before and after their marriage are reported to be rather unfavourable for their studies. Female students often have to discontinue their studies for longer periods because they have had children.

The disadvantages of higher age, however, are compensated for by higher motivation. As distant students are more experienced in the world of work and in life, it is easier for them to judge the importance of graduation and continuing education for their professional development. Tutors, in particular, confirm that their maturity is obviously a favourable condition for the learning process and the general progress of their studies. If their study programme is related to their vocational work, their motivation can be supported in a unique way.

For universities and colleges the higher age of their distant students means that they are in the process of slowly becoming institutes of adult education as well, which will make considerable adjustments necessary.

As there are only a few distant students in the Federal Republic of Germany, misunderstandings are likely regarding their image. In this country it could happen that the traditional concept of the working student will be transferred to the distant student. This would, however, be wrong, as this concept refers to the exceptional case and to a low social prestige, neither of which applies to distant students in most cases. In east European countries, the percentage of distance students is so high that they are no longer the exceptions. In the USSR they are nearly on a par with the day students, who, by the way, have also to do practical work in the production process. And in the United States, the second large group, this concept would be wrong, as many distant students do not work at all whereas many of the day students are compelled to work for a living.

People often think that distance education is preferred mainly by outsiders. This cannot be said about distant students in the USSR because of the high proportion of distant students in the total number of students. There cannot possibly be so many outsiders. In western countries, however, one can often observe that distant students do indeed take a special course, and differ from the majority of students. However, in the United States nobody has any objection whatsoever to distant students, as this form of teaching and learning has a long tradition in that country. Distant students are even more likely to be respected than scorned, although group life is highly regarded on the campus. The students and the university teachers hold that distance education is 'more difficult' and compels the distant students to deal with the subject matter longer and more intensely than is the case with day students. If they have successfully finished their courses, their achievements are duly acknowledged – in spite of their special way of studying.

The status of distant students is also different in East and West, as the respective societies judge the importance of vocational work quite differently – mainly for ideological reasons. Whereas the necessity of working for a living is considered to be rather an impediment to university studies in western countries, it is appreciated as a necessary precondition for successful university study in eastern countries. Typical of the western attitude is the remark of a Canadian professor who said, 'Every encouragement should be given to all persons who desire to become better educated and more highly trained, particularly those who have sufficient zeal and ambition to learn while they earn.' Apart from the view that vocational work is such a great, but unavoidable, burden that it could be carried only by distant students with special qualities, these words convey an attitude towards distance students which still suggests a philanthropic benevolence. It would be worth examining whether this attitude is disappearing in western industrialized countries.

In eastern European countries distant students are systematically made conscious of the fact that they have an obligation to society which they are expected to live up to, and in government and communist party reports they are called the 'pioneers of a new socialist intelligentsia'. In addition, they enjoy considerable financial privileges, and this is the reason why the image of the distant student is much more clear-cut and positive in these countries.

TEACHERS

Whereas commercial correspondence schools are sometimes criticized because of the doubtful qualifications of their teachers, university distance education can rely on the high academic standards of their teachers as they usually have to have the same credentials as the teachers on the campus.

Because distance education can take place only when special teaching functions are performed and because it is organized at regular universities as well as at special institutes, it is possible to subdivide teachers in distance education into five groups, each representing a special type.

- *Type 1*: University teachers who are responsible for their day students as well as for distant students. Their traditional field of activities, which is already very complex, is extended by the additional functions of being an author of teaching material and a tutor of distant students. Many of them like these new functions and endeavour to become excellent in performing them. Writing teaching material for distant students is new for them as it differs decisively from writing down their lectures. They no longer write for the day student in the class or the auditorium, but for the student who sits at home and tries to reach his goals by reading the texts. As it is necessary to use their limited time economically, such teachers will have to calculate their approach very carefully and thereby realize the importance of new didactical perspectives which induce them to separate the two groups of students and deal with them in different ways. The function of a tutor of distant students is also new to such a teacher. It will call for developing further those guiding and counselling functions which are used when talking with the day students about their tests and seminar papers – a considerable educational task.

- *Type 2*: Teachers at distance teaching colleges and at departments for distance education in universities. They deal with distant students only, which changes the profile of their work. It consists mainly of writing teaching material and tutoring. As they can specialize in these activities, they are more likely to develop new concepts of distance teaching of their own.

   In the Federal Republic of Germany, professors and lecturers who deal exclusively with distant students are still unknown and do not correspond with the current idea of university teachers. In other countries, however, there are university teachers who even prefer this new form of teaching, as it certainly does not exclude research activities. This remains true, although an American professor for distance teaching, when asked about the difference between teaching day students and distant students, said frankly: 'I have to write more, to telephone more, to deal with more visitors and have less time for research.'

- *Type 3*: University teachers who conduct seminars for distant students regularly. A typical representative of this type is the *Konsulent* in East Germany, where a considerable amount of distance education consists of obligatory face-to-face teaching. Generally, they are lecturers and readers working under the supervision of a professor. They perform a very demanding job as they have to combine and adjust principles of face-to-face teaching with those of distance teaching, which is difficult as there are no traditional patterns for this special teaching approach.

- *Type 4*: The academic mentor, who can be found in the education of university teachers in the USSR. He is a professor who typically does not write any teaching material and does not correct assignments at all, but exchanges letters with a number of advanced students in order to guide and conduct their doctoral studies. These students usually live far away from the university and are working in the production process. At this level of university education the work of a student is already so specialized and individualized that regular courses will no longer do. Furthermore, these students are already so self-reliant and have become able to master the techniques of acquiring knowledge by methodical reading that they need professional advice which is given to them by their academic mentor. An experiment at the National Extension College in the United Kingdom shows that this type of distance education can also be tried out and be successful at a lower level.

- *Type 5*: University teachers who assume responsibility for the management of distance teaching departments of institutions. They are confronted with tasks differing decisively from the corresponding tasks at conventional universities. Vice-chancellors and presidents, for instance, do not normally deal with teaching problems, as this task is dealt with by the individual professors or lecturers. The heads of distance teaching universities or departments, however, have to see to it that the contributions of all departments and sections can be guided and adapted in such a way that they fit together and elicit the intended learning effects. Furthermore, they have to keep complex technical systems going as the success of distance teaching relies on them entirely.

The programmes of study of distance teaching departments and universities show that university teachers of all academic ranks contribute to it. Often the proportion of full professors is higher than at traditional universities, as they are responsible for the courses and often like to write them themselves. In addition professors from other universities are invited to participate in writing the courses. This indicates that distance education is by no means something which is accomplished merely at the level of lecturers and readers. In East Germany and in the USSR there are even Pro-deans and Pro-rectors for distance education in order to have this teaching–learning system represented fully in the hierarchy of the university.

Often the question is discussed whether teachers in distance education should have qualities different from teachers on the campus.

Ossian Mackenzie of the University of Pennsylvania thinks that they should combine scientific knowledge and intellectual capabilities with the rare gift to motivate and to guide. Charles Wedemeyer of the University of Wisconsin said that the distance teacher must be able to write efficiently, have a good sense of humour and, above all, be a good teacher. One might wish to attribute these qualities to every university teacher. It is, however, striking that opinions like these can be met very often. Presumably, particularly good teaching is expected from the teacher in distance education as a compensation for not having the students in the classroom. People might think that this 'handicap' can be overcome by special personal and methodical qualities. Perhaps teachers in distance education are also expected to be particularly good as they have to deal with adults calling for new and therefore unusual approaches to teaching.

3 Models of university-level distance education (1971)

A comparative study of open universities and departments of conventional university teaching at a distance in the late 1960s was edited by Peters in 1971 as *Texte zum Hochschulfernstudium* (University-level distance education texts). The first half of this book deals with western models of university distance education with chapters by Wedemeyer, Bern and Child (USA), Rädel (South Africa), Sheath (Australia), Nashimoto (Japan), Holmberg (Sweden) and Hawkridge (UK). The second half of the book presents the socialist models of university distance education by Möhle (GDR), Bandura (Poland), Singule and Kamiač (Czechoslovakia), Zav'jalov (USSR) and Chou Li-fang (China). Peters himself provided the introductory chapter from which the following two extracts are taken.

If we examine university-level distance education in various countries of the world we can see that the special educational traditions and socio-economic conditions of these countries have led to individual models of distance education in each case. This applies even to east European countries, although educational policy there is generally influenced by the standardization of ideological goals and the overriding prototype in the Soviet Union. In spite of this, it is possible to identify two distinct, supra-national models of distance education if we disregard some particular developments and minor exceptions: a western and an eastern one. They differ with regard to their rank in national educational policy, the competent and responsible persons for it in the hierarchy of the university, the degree of their organizational integration into the university, and the methods of teaching and learning employed.

RANK IN NATIONAL EDUCATIONAL POLICY

The rank of the two models in the national educational policy can be easily identified when we consider the reasons for establishing distance education. In western countries the universities originally intended to help certain fringe groups to take part in university studies. Here, they were very much in the tradition of private correspondence schools or colleges. They were aimed at the individual person who was prevented from attending university by adverse circumstances. The number of distant students was, therefore, usually relatively small. Hence, distance education was not an important issue with educational politicians. As a rule it was neglected in the same way as correspondence education.

In eastern European countries the situation was entirely different. Here, distance education was introduced and developed systematically by the respective ministries of higher education in order to increase the number of qualified specialists in many branches of the economic and political system. At the same time, the governments intended to provide for additional access to the professions for wider sections of the working people. Finally, the governments believed that distance education was a good example for reaffirming the ideological concept of the close connection of theory and practice. Such a high degree of political motivation and, above all, the enormous demand of highly qualified specialists meant that the number of distant students increased so dramatically in the fifties and sixties that they made up a considerable percentage of the students in the universities – that is, 20 to 50 per cent, and in some disciplines even more. Only recently have these high numbers of students been somewhat reduced. This does not, however, detract from the great political importance of distance education at universities in eastern European countries. Experts assure us that this form of university study has become a permanent part of higher education. Legally, it is entirely on a par with that of traditional university study.

AREAS OF RESPONSIBILITY

The different goals of distance education have also led to different areas of responsibility. In the western model the establishment of distance education rests usually with the departments of university extension or adult education. These departments decide the contents and procedures of their distance education themselves. The result can be highly differentiated programmes, as, for instance, at the

University of Wisconsin and the University of Nebraska. On the other hand, one can also find meagre programmes with a small number of accidental and unrelated correspondence courses often administered by only one secretary.

The relative autonomy of these departments has a special negative effect, in that they do not coordinate their programmes with those of other universities. For instance, American universities have developed fifty-eight different courses for distance education under the title *Survey of the History of the USA*. Clearly, this goes against important principles of distance education, especially against those of rationalization and centralization.

The eastern European model of distance study, however, can usually rely on centralized planning and coordination by the respective ministries of higher education, which also adapt the distant study programmes to the requirements of the economic system. Sometimes central institutes have been established to prepare and distribute the necessary teaching and study material and to examine problems of teaching at a distance for the benefit of all universities.

INTEGRATION INTO THE HIERARCHY OF THE UNIVERSITY

The way in which distance education is integrated into the hierarchy of the university sheds some light on its relative institutional importance.

As has already been mentioned, in *western* countries distance education is usually organized by a section of the department of university extension or adult education. As these departments lack the academic reputation and the weight and power of the classical faculties or departments, this organizational structure is bound to be detrimental to the healthy development of distance education. The same can be said about universities which cooperate with correspondence colleges outside the university by using their course material as, for instance, the University of Lund. There, distance education is even less integrated. An extreme form of this non-integration of distance education can be found when the university limits itself to conducting final examinations only and relies on private correspondence colleges for the teaching of the courses. For a very long time the University of London was a good example of this approach.

In *eastern* European countries the organizational structure of distance education provides that most professors, deans and rectors of the universities have to be responsible for their distant students in the same way as for their day students. Quite often the universities even have special pro-rectors for distance study. In this way, distance education is fully integrated not only into the general teaching programme, but also into the hierarchy of the university.

A total integration is achieved in seventeen higher educational institutions in the USSR and in China. There, the entire faculty of the college caters exclusively for distant students. If we want to find out what a similar set-up would look like in a western country, we need only examine the University of South Africa, where there is a whole university which takes care of distant students only.

METHODS OF TEACHING AND LEARNING

There are also fundamental differences between the two models of distance education with regard to the methods of teaching and learning employed. A first structural difference can be derived from the fact that western correspondence schools have contributed considerable experience to the development of printed teaching material. It was taken over by universities and adapted to their special purposes. Over the last hundred years private correspondence colleges have accumulated special knowledge of how to teach at a distance, which could easily be systematized into a methodology of teaching by writing. However, the value of this methodology should not be assessed as being higher than that of traditional methodologies for face-to-face teaching based on common sense, pragmatic approaches and didactic recipes. Nevertheless, wherever western universities insist on a careful development of written special materials for distance study courses and on a regular correspondence between teacher and student, they profit by these early experiences.

Eastern European models of distance education, however, are not related to this tradition. Consequently, little or no attention is paid to the development of special teaching and learning material and to the regular, individual correction of test papers. Mostly, these elements are substituted by regular consultation periods at weekends, and by yearly seminars of several weeks' length. This may be considered as an adjustment of forms of traditional university study to the conditions of distant students. It was made under the unfortunate socio-economic conditions of the time after World War II. Hence, many measures were dictated by sheer need. The students were urged to work in full-time employment and to study at the university at the same time. The universities had to rely on the professors and the further teaching staff as well as on the infrastructure at hand. They used the same curricula and the same text-books which were provided for the day students. Hence, one could define the eastern model of distance education as a system of administrative measures which enable the universities to cater for considerable numbers of additional students who were expected to study mainly at home. This, of course, means that the eastern model is not derived from any elaborated concept in which the elements of self-study, regional consultation periods and yearly seminars at the university are carefully related to one another. Gerhard Dietze (1965: 155), a leading expert in distance education at the University of Dresden, deplores, for instance, the fact that 'the general scientific concept of distance education is inadequate and that, so far, its crucial components and their interactions in view of optimal learning conditions have not yet been analysed at all'. And Andrej Kamiač, a Czechoslovakian expert, explained that in his country distance education was introduced and developed by the administration of the universities and not by experts in teaching methodology.

TECHNOLOGICAL MODEL OF DISTANCE EDUCATION

Reports from the United States, Sweden and Japan, and the planning papers of the Open University in Great Britain, show that at present a third model of distance education is becoming discernible. It is characterized by the calculated use of modern technical media – for instance, television, radio, computer and telephone, as well as audio and video tapes. This development changes the structure of the teaching and learning process to such a great extent that it seems to be justified to speak of a new form of distance education, which I should like to call for the time being the 'technological model'.

The structural change can be seen immediately if one realizes that the use of these technical media confronts the teachers with new and difficult problems, as the contents of teaching and the teaching functions have to be redistributed if they change from the use of predominantly one medium – the correspondence course – to bi- or multimedia teaching activities. The new technical media force them to objectify longer sequences of their teaching. Careful, time-consuming and expensive preparations have now become inevitable. All the problems of planning the teaching–learning process, especially the division of labour between the teachers and media experts, and the organization and control of learning activities, assume a new importance.

Fortunately, the new model of distance study can profit from the 'technological turn' in the methodology of teaching (Flechsig 1969) which can at present be identified – mainly as a consequence of experiments with programmed learning. Today, it is easier to recognize the characteristic outlines of the emerging new model of distance education and to further its progressive elements than it would have been only a few years ago, because the newly developed 'educational technology' already provides us with a number of categories necessary for analysing and describing it.

Such assistance, though, cannot be expected from an educational technology which regards itself as the technical or instrumental side of the teaching–learning process only and attempts to reinforce it. Rather, we will have to look out for an educational technology which concentrates on the use of scientific methods and procedures for the planning, development and evaluation of teaching-learning projects. A. A. Lumsdaine (1964), who described such an educational technology for the first time, said that it depends on the scientific disciplines related to it in the same way as, for instance, the technology of engineering depends on physics and the technology of medicine on biology. In short, the technological turn in the methodology of teaching and learning means that those processes are to be explored and manipulated which can help to influence the learning situation.

Flechsig has pointed out that the technological turn in the methodology of teaching is brought about in five phases. In the first phase, the technical medium is used to simulate the teacher, in the second phase this approach is given up and teaching techniques are developed in a rational way, which are optimized in the third phase. In the fourth phase, teaching techniques are coordinated with the help of the systems approach, and in the last phase the development work is based on curriculum research and the duplication of teaching techniques.

It is important to investigate how the western and eastern models of distance education relate to these phases, and what the possible features of the coming technological model of distance education will be....

If we analyse the relationship of distance education to the five phases of the technological development we can conclude that it had a remarkable affinity to some of these phases long before this concept was developed. And, on the other hand, we can identify several features which do not yet correspond to these phases. In other words, distance education is partly a forerunner of educational technology and in part still lacks the specific technological development.

Such a partial delay need not concern or discourage distance education experts. It can already be considered to be remarkable progress that we are now able to explain accurately how a project of distance study can be improved as the technological model displays the standards of future developments in distance education. Only ten years ago the improvement of projects of distance education took place more or less arbitrarily, at best based on conjectures or according to the principle of trial and error. Even if money was available, one could not really identify the critical factors in the system of distance education which needed purposeful changes. The real contribution of the new educational technology is that now things have changed. It provides us with a system of scientific instruments and procedures which enable us to improve distance education systematically and also verify the outcomes. Even more: if we match a given project of distance education with the five phases of the technological turn its structural advantages and deficits become clearly visible. This is a very favourable precondition for slowly raising the development of distance education to higher levels of accomplishment.

An additional advantage of the new technological model of distance education is that the techniques of planning, designing and optimizing projects in distance education can be communicated because of their scientific nature. This will be favourable for the further development of distance study at university level.

Which of the three models of distance education will become dominant? I believe that the western and eastern models will continue for a considerable time, as they have already become a matter of routine and have also become a tradition. The technological model is much more demanding, as special experts, very expensive media and organizational systems will be required. For this reason, only a slow development can be predicted. In the long run, however, this model will permeate all endeavours of teaching at a distance at university level.

REFERENCES

Dietze, G. (1965) 'Die Bedeutung des Fern- und Abendstudiums im Rahmen des einheitlichen sozialistischen Bildungssystems', in *Epistolodidaktika* 3: 152–6.

Flechsig, K-H. (1969) *Die technologische Wende in der Didaktik*, Konstanzer Universitätsreden 23, Konstanz: Universitätsverlag.

Lumsdaine, A. A. (1964) 'Educational technology, programmed learning, and instructional science', in E. R. Hilgard (ed.) *Theories of Learning and Instruction*, Chicago: University of Chicago Press.

Part II
Analysis

4 Didactic analysis (1972)

Peters did postgraduate research on distance education at the University of Tübingen in the early 1970s and was awarded a doctorate in 1972. The thesis was published in 1973 as *Die didaktische Struktur des Fernunterrichts. Untersuchungen zu einer industrialisierten Form des Lehrens und Lernens* (The didactical structure of distance education: research into a more industrialized form of teaching and learning (328 pages)). The book relates distance education to relevant sociological, philosophical and educational findings in Germany. This extract (pages 51 to 107 in the original) sets out to contrast and compare distance education with all other forms of indirect or mediated teaching to show what is characteristic of this new form of education produced by industrial technology.

Distance teaching has been ignored by the science of didactics for an astonishingly long time. Up to the present, it has hardly been mentioned at all in articles on the form and the methods to be used for instruction, let alone been contemplated as a possibility, or analysed with regard to its particular characteristics. Didactic compendia do in fact point out in a few short paragraphs, under the title 'Forms of instruction', that alongside the immediate (direct) method there is also an intermediate (indirect) form of instruction (Huber 1965: 146; Stöcker 1966: 165), but are silent with regard to the existence of distance teaching, which should really have its place here in any systematic discussion. This is particularly strange as this form of instruction is now more than 120 years old, and it can be estimated that in Germany alone several million people have acquired knowledge and gained qualifications using this method.

Further proof of the neglect of distance teaching is supplied by Berthold Michael (1963). In his extensive study entitled *Self-Education* in School he deals in great detail with the *Institutio Oratoria* of Quintilian (died around AD 90), but fails to mention distance teaching at all, although this form of instruction has played a considerable role – in instruction in schools as well – in the United States, Canada and Australia, and in the last decade above all in the United Kingdom and Sweden in the form of supervised correspondence instruction. This is an example of how the historicizing pedagogical viewpoint is drawn more to a form of instruction obtaining in the ancient world than to a contemporary form, in particular if the latter requires looking beyond the borders of one's own country.

The reservations of didacticians regarding distance teaching are difficult to explain with any clarity. The understanding of the new form of instruction may well on the one hand have been made more difficult by ideological handicaps, which in modern theories of education have come into being since the *Sturm-und-Drang* period, the Romantic period and the popularity of the theories of reform pedagogics – namely, that the spoken word was preferred to the written word. This meant that the role of the written word was undervalued, in particular when its great importance for the handing down of culture is taken into account. On the other hand, the principal reservations, to which Günther Dohmen (1967: 14) referred in connection with distance studying, may have stopped didacticians from becoming interested in distance teaching: the too pragmatic form of acquiring knowledge, the lack of a personal relationship between instructor and student, and the isolating style of distance instruction, which is 'inimical to any sense of community'. Finally, the still insecure status of distance teaching, and its image, which is greatly affected by commercial abuse, may have caused didacticians to exclude this form of instruction from their studies.

A further reason for the reservations shown by educational scientists may possibly result from the fact that even those didacticians who might have attempted to free themselves from the ideological conceptions referred to above and to put the principal reservations to one side for the moment, in order to observe and to interpret this form of instruction as objectively as possible, would probably have encountered great difficulties. This is because distance teaching, as will be shown, is extremely difficult to fit into the usual methods and systems of instruction. The history of instruction does not contain any theoretical approaches or drafts with which the phenomenon of distance teaching might be explained. It would appear that this method has escaped any analysis which shows its characteristic constitutive structural elements in the correct relationship to its

Didactic analysis

concomitant phenomena. Until today, distance teaching has remained a didactic *terra incognita*.

In this chapter, a first systematic exploration of this unknown territory is to be carried out with the help of didactic analysis. In order to prevent misunderstanding, it must be stressed immediately that the following pages do not contain an analysis of an example of a concrete lesson, but of a certain form of instruction. The analysis will not therefore relate to particular topics of lessons and their respective educational contents, but will concern itself rather with recognizing in the totality of the phenomenon of distance instruction some formal elements which show proof of structural similarity or concordance with other, better-known forms of didactic instruction.

Even an initial, rather superficial, examination shows that distance instruction may be understood as a combination and integration of several teaching processes, some of which have a long history. These include:

- instruction by letter;
- instruction using printed material;
- teaching using periodicals;
- instruction using teaching, learning and working aids;
- audiovisual lessons;
- instruction with mass media;
- programmed instruction and
- computer-aided instruction.
  Distance instruction also appears to be characterized by
- the social forms of person-to-person teaching and independent work, and
- the form in which the courses are presented.

Each of these ten didactic elements has therefore things in common with distance education of a theoretical or a practical nature. It should thus be relatively simple to gain first insights into distance education if certain factors of effectiveness of these didactic structures are described from the perspective of how they play a role in distance teaching and how far even formal elements of the indirect teaching forms illustrated can be found in distance teaching.

The representation of the didactic elements referred to is divided where possible into the following sections:

1 designation of the didactic element;
2 naming its didactically relevant structural characteristics;

3 sketching the part which this didactic element played, is still playing or will play;
4 naming the structural characteristics which it has in common with distance education.

The sketches of the individual teaching processes, which in some cases also take the historic dimension into account, have a twofold purpose as far as the object under examination is concerned. On the one hand, the purpose is to illustrate that the didactic elements shown have obviously proved themselves outside the field of distance education; and on the other hand the fact is to be called to mind that some older teaching and learning experiences have been absorbed by the distance education system.

INSTRUCTION USING WRITING

One of the roots of the distance education system may well be the early experience that with the help of written notes a person is able to pass on linguistically coded information to another person and can thus have an educational and instructional effect on this person. This type of process uses the advantages of writing, with the help of which the restrictions of time and space can be overcome. Writing enables a teacher to reach students who are unable at certain times to come and listen to him directly.

Because of their particular structural relationship to distance education, two forms of instruction by letter are to be examined more closely here: the instructional exchange of letters, and the written interaction between teacher and student in classroom teaching.

The instructional exchange of letters is a special form of written correspondence which is used by persons who are separated from one another to exchange information of a private, business or official nature. For the context of the study it is important to stress the following six didactic features of the instructional exchange of letters. First, the instructional exchange of letters was regarded early on as a substitute for instructional conversation, and this led to corresponding simulations. Secondly, a letter is addressed accordingly to a particular person or a particular group of persons, which has an effect on its style and in particular on its tone. Thirdly, the writer usually writes as much as the person to whom the letter is addressed can read at one sitting (this can be seen in particular in German, where 'letter' (*Brief*) comes from the Latin *breve* (short, brief); in other words the writer does not write a treatise or a book,

Didactic analysis 61

and this brings out the idea of measuring or dispensing). Fourthly, the instructive exchange of letters is based on the pattern of delayed dialogue. The writer assumes that the addressee will react to his letter, and he himself then reacts to the addressee's reply. This means, fifthly, that both become conscious that each single letter is a link in a chain of letters. In order to maintain the delayed dialogue, the letter writer sometimes attempts, sixthly, to provoke a reaction from his partner.

Examples of the instructive exchange of letters have been familiar since classical antiquity; for example, the letters of Plato and Epicurus to their students, and Cicero's extensive correspondence. Sometimes letters were even used as a form of illustration for philosophic discussions (such as Seneca's *Epistolae Morales*).

In this context reference is usually made to the letters of the Apostle Paul which he sent for concrete reasons to individual early Christian communities. They contain not only theoretical discussions of basic questions of dogma, but also an interpretation and development of Christ's message. The letter in this case became a medium for disseminating and strengthening the Christian faith, and was later to be developed into a preferred means for a detailed, comprehensive religious ministry (Simmel and Stählin 1957: 292). Calvin's letters, with which he instructed his followers in the reformed communities which had sprung up in nearly all European countries, probably had a similar effect. He handed out advice, issued orders and instructed them in individual questions of faith and discipline (Zeeden 1967: 229). Ignatius Loyola also had to carry out a worldwide correspondence as a result of the spread of the Jesuit Order. This correspondence, too, became a means of pastoral care and spiritual instruction (Zeeden 1967: 229).

The extent of the influence on the spread of humanist ideals which Erasmus, for example, exercised in his correspondence with the *homines literati* in Europe is so great that it can hardly be assessed. Erasmus corresponded with the most important men of his time in the field of politics, art, literature, science and religion. The humanist's correspondence overcame the distances, which at that time were considerable, and united the correspondents living in various countries into a 'scholars' republic'.

In the case of distance education, structural similarities or accordances with instructive exchanges of letters can be shown in the following points:

- The principle of the relationship to the addressee, the techniques

of delayed dialogue, of measuring out, of ordering in series, and provoking replies: these techniques were developed further here.
- In most distance education institutes today correspondence takes place between teacher and student as a supplement to work with printed material, in particular when students come across difficulties which they are unable to solve with the means available to them. The written answers of the distance teacher to the written questions of the distance student are important examples of instruction by letter. In addition, the letters of encouragement which many distance education institutes send to those students who have failed to send in their solutions to the set problems should be mentioned. Behind instruction by letter can also be found educational intentions, in particular when an attempt is made to motivate the students to further work with the help of letters and to influence their work attitudes.
- The dominant form today of instruction by letter is without a doubt the drawing up of teaching letters and written instructions for study. The pattern of the 'writing teacher', which has taken the place of the 'talking teacher', today still determines distance teaching in practice, in spite of all the technological procedures for the development of teaching material. In spite of certain similarities, the teacher's work differs from that of those authors who, for example, write textbooks or instructive articles for periodicals. The reason for this is probably that the writing teachers originally wished to simulate the talking teachers, and their aim was to convert oral instruction into instruction by letter, a motive which is not close to the hearts of the authors of textbooks or articles for periodicals.

In addition to this, distance education probably has another close relationship with the instructive exchange of letters which would have to be explained in context with its coming into being. The hypothesis for this is as follows: if there were also important cultural historical examples for the effect of correspondence, as shown above, if it can be assumed that this correspondence can be used not only for passing on information and behavioural rules, but can also have an instructive effect on the reader in the religious and scientific field, if his disposition for this is strong enough, the step towards distance education on a written basis must have seemed obvious as a demand for instruction and training came into being which could not be covered by direct instruction. How strong the domination of the concept of an exchange of letters was in the establishment

Didactic analysis 63

of distance education systems can be seen from the names which were given to these systems at the time: in English, 'correspondence instruction'; in French '*télé-enseignement par correspondance*', in Spanish '*ensensanza por correspondencia*', in Danish and Swedish '*correspondens-undervisning*', '*brevkurs*' and '*brevskole*'. In Germany in the 1850s, Gustav Langenscheidt published *Lehrbriefe* for the '*brieflichen Sprachunterricht für das Selbststudium Erwachsener*' (teaching letters for language instruction by letter for adults to teach themselves). Shortly before the turn of the century, Bonness and Hachfeld developed 'individual instruction by letter'. At the same time, Karnack founded his 'teach yourself by letter operation' (Sommer 1965: 29). And when, seven years ago, the first teachers in West Germany approached the problems of distance education, it was significant that they also called it 'Instruction by letter' (Flitner 1964: 3) or 'Distance instruction by letter' (Wenke 1964: 57), although in practice distance education had in the meantime moved away from the original form of correspondence. Hermann Röhrs (1969) still speaks of 'instruction by letter' in his book *Allgemeine Erziehungswissenschaft*.

It is difficult to find an explanation of why the concept of instruction by letter or correspondence lessons still dominates in discussions on distance education. We can only assume that the long tradition of the transmission of information by means of letters and the utilization of the advantages of a rational postal delivery system have left a deep impression on people. The technology behind this is accepted and internalized to a great extent, whereas the technology of the transmission of information using the new technical media still has to create a correspondingly secure place in man's consciousness. Behind the choice of this designation for distance education and the persistent holding to terms such as 'distance teaching letter' lies perhaps the idea that something of the personal relationship and the personal tone, which, for example, often characterizes correspondence between relatives or friends, may be brought into the written form of instruction between teacher and students, and thus to some extent balance out the loss of the direct personal contact between them.

The instructive exchange of letters of the type referred to was sometimes seen as a 'precursor of the institutionalized distance education system' (Graff 1964: 33; Delling 1966: 211). The following analyses of distance teaching will show, however, that modern distance teaching has many important new structural features which are missing in an individual exchange of letters. For this reason, this assumption cannot be followed. All that we may suppose is that the tradition of the instructive exchange of letters played a part in the introduction of the distance education systems, a part which would still have to be examined and determined in more detail. This tradition was carried on in the distance teaching systems with which we are familiar merely as one component among many.

The written interaction between the teacher and the student in classroom instruction is an element of direct teaching which up to now has hardly been touched on by didacticians, if we ignore Jürgen Henningsen's conception of corrections as 'teaching by means of the written word' (1969: 173). Even teachers in the classrooms are often not aware that an important trace of teaching by writing is embedded in their traditional teaching methods.

The didactically important elements of this form of written instruction result from an analysis of teaching behaviour by the correction of written work. The teacher informs students, usually in writing, of the mistakes they have made. But not only this, he also gives the student an assessment and evaluation of the work, which are often extended into long commentaries. It is now important that the student as an individual reacts to the corrections. The student replies in writing to the teacher's comments by writing a 'corrected version' of their work. In this way, three important teaching functions – information, assessment of achievement and counselling – are taken in part from direct instruction and 'passed on' by means of the written word; that is, a technical medium – the sheet of paper – comes between the teacher and the student.

This written interaction between the teacher and the student in classroom-based instruction has proved itself over a long period, and is unquestioned because it provides an individualized approach to the students.

Examples of this form of written lesson can be found in everyday practice. All work with notes, all written work done in the class, and, in principle, all homework corrected by the teacher is the start of a written interaction between teacher and taught, which can be comprehensive and detailed, in particular in the case of the assessment of essays. Over a period of time sick children often have their lessons reduced to written homework which the teacher corrects, and this itself is a temporary form of distance education.

Distance education can basically be regarded as an extension of this indirect classroom communication. By developing this element of direct teaching, distance education strengthened its inherent tendency towards individualization, which meant that distance teaching was usually conceived as an individual lesson for one person.

Correction of work as 'teaching by means of the written word' has become one of the standard techniques of correspondence education and is often a factor of modern multimedia distance education systems. Along with a personal exchange of letters it is the second possibility for indirect interaction between the teacher and the taught, and thus for individualization.

By using the advantages of the written word as in the instructive exchange of letters, distance education has at the same time to put up with the mistrust which has always existed with regard to the written form of language and, in particular, with regard to the written form of teaching. Plato, in his comparison of oral and written teaching, observed that written work was 'mute and lacking willpower', that it could 'neither reply nor defend itself' and that for this reason the spiritual content was guaranteed in the spoken word only. This alone would ensure 'the correct transmission of the thought to the student'; this alone was able 'to explain and to correct directly'. Plato was willing to grant the written version the status of a 'support for the memory' only (cf. Weisgerber 1961: 17). It may well have become significant for the image of distance education that this and similar attitudes can still be encountered today.

INSTRUCTION USING PRINTED MATERIAL

Instruction using the help of printed material may be regarded as the second root of the distance education system. Printed material includes, among other things, brochures, pamphlets, books, textbooks and encyclopaedias.

The new factor in the case of instruction using printed material lies in the possibility of simultaneously reaching a large number of addressees who are widely scattered. As a consequence of the invention of printing, the large-scale production and distribution of texts was placed at the service of education. It is important to note that this implied the linking of instruction to the work of guilds, so that it became a commodity.

History has several impressive examples for teaching using printed material.

The new ideas of the Reformation were spread with great rapidity and almost revolutionary effect using printed material. For example, Luther worked using many of his own writings – and, what was new, addressing a wide reading public in 'lively, popular and often coarse language' (Lortz and Iserloh 1969: 49). Because of the invention of printing, all those who could read were able to study Luther's own translation of the Bible. Printing was even more clearly used in the service of instruction by Ignatius Loyola. His famous *Exercitia spiritualia* (Spiritual exercises), which he used in order to teach in a forceful manner how a pious life is to be led, had an 'unparalleled universal effect' (Zeeden 1967: 123). It is possible that this was the most effective textbook in modern Europe.

The catechisms published by Luther and Canisius were also products of the printing press, which were to start and influence learning processes for a large number of readers. The size of the possible circle of readers caused the authors to differentiate the learning process according to the circle of addressees. Canisius wrote one catechism for the people, another for academically educated people and yet another especially for the clergy, while Luther's Great Catechism was planned for the clergy, and the Small Catechism for the people. However, it has to be said that in Luther's Small Catechism the questions and answers did not have a teaching function, but, aimed at simplifying the act of listening to pupils repeating the texts, were an aid to recapitulation. For the purposes of this study it is particularly significant here that in this way a function which a priest would normally have to exercise could now, with the help of the printed material, be passed on to the head of the house.

In the following age of reason the greatest example of an intention to use the assistance of printed material to pass on knowledge is probably the *Encyclopédie ou Dictionnaire raisonné des sciences, des arts et des métiers* (1751–80) published by Diderot and the *Encyclopédistes*.

In the case of handbooks and textbooks the systematic division of the contents is to provide the student with assistance for the acquisition of knowledge. Often, the presentation is carefully calculated with the student in mind and developed methodically. Printed material has become more abundant and more important in schools and universities, in the form of lexicons, guidelines, handbooks and textbooks, and today it is no longer possible to contemplate teaching without it. Textbooks were probably able to achieve such an important position in instruction because they carried out a number of teaching functions, and therefore to a certain extent assumed the position of the teacher. This was possible because their methodical construction followed that of oral forms of teaching. Jürgen Henningsen (1970: 183) has pointed out the extent to which forms of presentation used in direct instruction were transferred to textbooks:

Didactic analysis 67

Each of the methodical means of oral instruction aimed at direct communication has its counterpart in teaching by means of the written word. The 'aim' of a lesson corresponds to the title or the chapter heading of a textbook; the extent of their variations ranges from notatory indications to journalistic headlines in nonfiction books with the paedagogical function of creating excitement and stimulating expectations. 'Access' and 'pegs' are just as important to the author of textbooks as they are to the teacher: they represent an introductory connection between the knowledge provided by the addressee and the knowledge to be passed on. The 'example' plays a similar part for the textbook as it does in oral teaching; problems of the construction, division and the arrangement of the material are familiar to the textbook, as are summaries, control functions and repeating. All forms of organization of oral teaching have been simulated by textbooks, with greater or lesser amounts of success, for example the teacher's lecture, the process developed through questions, the dialogue between teacher and pupils, the committed and the free discussion.

As a result of this adaptation for the purposes of instruction, printed material in the form of textbooks has had a considerable influence on lessons. The degree of its influence is shown by a remark made by Otto Willmann (1957: 586) that a lesson can be construed as 'the staging of the textbook'. The polemic designation 'book school' used by the reform pedagogists shows how much books were the focal points of lessons. There has probably not been very much change here up to the present day; the number of textbooks used has grown, and certain textbooks definitely influence teaching in our schools to a greater extent (in the sense of standardization) than curricula and official guidelines. An attempt was made in the United States to compensate for the often unsatisfactory level of training of teachers with the assistance of particularly carefully and expensively developed textbooks. In particular, in addition to the individual textbooks, children were offered workbooks which allowed them to work through the course contents without the help of the teacher. In this case, the functions of the teacher were more or less deliberately restricted and worked into the printed material in the form of didactic 'pegs' and processes.

Parallel to the development of textbooks, a series of teach-yourself books came into existence which went even further in the transfer of teaching functions to printed material and attempted to dispense completely with the teacher in the learning process. Books of this kind were published as early as the fifteenth, sixteenth and seventeenth centuries because, particularly in the towns, the necessity of learning arithmetic and reading grew faster than it could be satisfied in the schools of the time. The printed material was therefore used here with the declared intention of instructing adults outside the school system.

Berthold Michael (1963: 124–34) reports on the efforts of arithmeticians in the fifteenth century to write self-teaching arithmetic books. He furnishes proof that Petzensteiner wanted to instruct adults in arithmetic through self-teaching with his book dated 1483. There were similar books at the time from Boschenstein and Adam Riese. He reports on Valentin Ickelsamer's attempt to use printed texts to give an opportunity to learn to read, whereby, if we read between the lines, the quotations show that the hidden motive was possibly to pass on the art of reading to those who were handicapped by their background. Ickelsamer wanted to show how 'a man might learn to read himself' so that 'everyman .... might come to the correct origins of reading ... and if he might be a woodcutter' or a 'shepherd in the fields'.

The *Orbis sensualium pictus* by Johannes Amos Comenius, published in 1658, may also be regarded as a teach-yourself book, as this was a grammar book, picture dictionary and teaching aid in one. More than any other writer, Comenius recognized the possibilities of printed material for self-teaching. In his *Didactica magna* (1947: 100) he addressed in 1657 the problem of how it might be possible 'for all to be taught from the same book'. In the face of the large numbers of pupils using the books, he demanded that books should 'all be written carefully and so that they are easily understood', and that they should comply with his own rules for simplicity, soundness and time-saving. In this he stressed the importance of presenting the material 'in a popular manner' so that 'everything easily becomes clear to the pupils even without a teacher, and serves to enlighten them' (1947: 101). Comenius argued: 'It makes no difference to the pupils whether the teacher has himself drawn up the material for instruction, or whether another has done this beforehand (in a book)' (1947: 100). He also requested that books should be written in the form of conversations, so that the pupil could be led as familiarly and as naturally as in the classroom. Comenius himself experienced the effect of printed material of this kind. He achieved fame for his textbook *Janua linguata reserata*, which was published in 1631, and was translated into twelve European and four Asian languages (Lindner 1947: XIV). And in his *Pampaedia* (1960: 147) he demanded specifically that material represented in books might not only be 'easily understood' in the classroom, but that it might also serve the purposes of self-education outside school. His reasons for this were as follows:

> If there should be any people who do not have an opportunity to learn in ordinary schools, they should (with the help of the little books be able) to compensate with diligence and perseverance for this deprivation – if they are only able to read – and by penetrating the whole themselves reach the same goal. In this way, autodidacts would only be differentiated from those who had been taught in schools by the fact that the latter would be fully educated and certain of their knowledge, whereas the former would be marked by a certain insecurity. However, they would have in common the fact that they both know everything which is useful to them.

This quotation reflects not only Comenius' optimism that with printed material everything can be taught to everyone, but also his assumption that the self-teaching method was much inferior to oral teaching. This evaluation has obviously been retained until the present day and influences attitudes towards the many teach-yourself books of a popular and scientific nature which are published in Germany and Britain, and in the United States.

After printed material had come to play a dominant role in direct teaching, and experience with teach-yourself books had been gathered, it was only natural that distance teaching used this medium from the start and in the first place. From this it is understandable that a number of important distance teaching schools have developed from publishing houses. Even today there are distance teaching institutes which are simply departments of publishing companies. Tried and tested series of teaching letters were printed, and served as a foundation for individual distance teaching courses. This incorporation of printed material had the following consequences for the didactic structure of the developing distance teaching system:

- The tradition of a democratization of knowledge, which was introduced after the invention of printing, was taken over by the distance teaching system and continued. By making large groups of students independent of time and space, many people were able to acquire knowledge who had previously been prevented from doing so. For very many years distance teaching was

regarded as the only possibility for overcoming educational barriers of a class, regional, religious and racial nature.
- As a result of the change from a single addressee to the largest possible numbers of potential students, the language of the teaching texts had to be so designed that every unnecessary difficulty was avoided. This basic methodological rule, derived from experiences gained from teaching with the first mass media, is still today taken nowhere as seriously as in practical distance teaching, which has thus taken up and is continuing Luther's and Comenius' endeavours referred to above to achieve a popular and easily understood written language. In the United States, similar efforts at USAFI, the forces' distance teaching school in Madison, Wisconsin, led to the empirical determination of different reading levels among the servicemen taking part in distance teaching. In this way it was possible to differentiate the distance teaching courses according to the reading capabilities of the addressees, similarly to the differences made by Luther and Loyola in their catechisms.
- Texts used for teaching which were prepared for printing and which were able to reach a large number of addressees were now much more carefully worked out than any individual instructive letter. By making printed material the basis of a distance course, the start was given for course development, in which the teacher carefully 'prepares', in Comenius' use of the word, the contents of the lesson before the lesson begins. The use of printed matter thus lengthens and intensifies the phase of preparing lessons. This aspect was to become a characteristic feature of the new form of teaching.
- An opportunity was offered to distance teaching of taking over from textbooks, methods of representation and didactic 'pegs' which already aimed at the simulation of a teacher, and to develop these further for its own purposes.
- In contrast to face-to-face teaching, the printing of the contents of a distance education course stabilized the teaching and rendered it immune to the variable conditions of the classroom; for example, lessons being cancelled, interruptions caused by illness or unplanned deviations from the content by the teacher.
- In the case of experienced and advanced participants in distance teaching, the particular technique of knowledge transfer using printed material makes itself felt: within a given unit of time they are able to extract much more from the printed material than even the fastest teacher or lecturer could pass on.

Didactic analysis 71

These advantages may have led to printed material becoming much more frequently used in distance teaching, in place of the educational exchange of letters and also maintaining its ground in the face of other modern technical teaching media.

TEACHING BY MEANS OF PERIODICALS

An ancillary form of transmitting knowledge by means of printed material consists of those magazines and newspapers which are employed to instruct the readers, to shape their taste or to educate them in the direction of certain goals.

The main difference between the book and the periodical is above all the frequency of publication and, in part, the fact of delivery. In this way a new category of the transmission of knowledge becomes important, which an American sociologist described many years ago as 'dissemination or accessibility for all types of people' (Cooley 1909: 61), and which an American communications expert described as 'physical availability' (Swanson 1954: 51). For the dissemination of knowledge it is extremely important to know whether the interested person has to go to the next town to buy printed material, or whether this is delivered regularly to their house. For this reason, book clubs and paperback publishers have attempted to increase the degree of availability of their products. Another characteristic of periodicals is that in each case a series of uniform publications follows the same aims, and that with the series a defined, relatively homogeneous group of persons is addressed. The texts are selected more and more for their effect on the reader; namely, in the sense that from many articles usually only those are selected which best comply with a number of criteria, such as topicality, interest or addressing the reader's personal requirements. The tone is adjusted much more to the intended circle of readers than is the case with the neutral style of treatment found in books. Publishers hope to find some sort of resonance among the readers which manifests itself in the form of written replies. From this arose the institution of the readers' letters. A determined effort is made to generate in the readers the feeling of belonging together, which leads to the formation of communities (as with *Der Spiegel* readers). Very often, emotional contacts are created between reader and newspaper or magazine which express themselves in the form of particular loyalty and cherished reading habits.

In order to be able to achieve the effects referred to, a report by a journalist or an author commissioned to write the report will be edited by a specialist, who, for example, will formulate forceful headlines, shorten or simplify the text where necessary, whereby the specialist will probably follow the old journalistic rule of offering as much information in as few words as possible. Illustrations and graphic representations will be commissioned and the placing and design of the contribution will be determined. This means that behind every article in a periodical can be found the efforts of several differently trained experts. The contributions in the periodical will then often remain anonymous.

The increased availability of periodicals referred to above is sometimes augmented even further by publishers aiming at extending the circle of readers – that is, increasing the circulation – because this ensures that profits are maximized. In contrast to the sale of books in bookshops, periodicals also have a special form of active advertising which is aimed at gaining subscribers.

Max Weber (1911: 42) stressed in his article 'On the sociology of newspapers' that the press is 'necessarily... a capitalist, private business' with a growing demand for capital, therefore the problem arises as to whether the increasing demand for capital means 'an increasing monopoly of those companies already in business'. It is obvious that the effects of commercialization on the process of the transmission of knowledge have been greater here than has been the case with the craft trade of the book printer or with the bookseller.

With printed works which appear regularly there are concise examples of the instructive transmission of knowledge. The oldest periodical of this kind was the almanac. Otto Willmann (1957: 588) regarded this as an 'important vehicle... for the education of the people'.

At the beginning of the eighteenth century initial experiences were gathered with newspapers and magazines with an instructive content; these were, above all, the moral weeklies, which spread throughout Europe and were based on Richard Steele's *Tatler* (1709–11), Richard Addison's *Spectator* (1711–12) and the successor, the *Guardian* (1713). In Germany, the numbers of this type of weekly rose from fifty to more than 1,200 (Koszyk and Pruys 1969: 391). In accordance with the strong didactic tendencies of the Enlightenment, these moral weeklies were not only aimed at entertainment, but above all at education, in that they transmitted knowledge in an appropriate form and served the cause of moral education. The newspaper the *Guardian* was aimed, for example, mainly at education and instruction in domestic matters. The readers were presented with a wise guardian who had taken up the education of the children of a deceased friend by giving the widow practical advice and informing her of many interesting facts. The addressees were members of the middle classes. However, the language of the moral weeklies was kept so easily understandable and popular that – as in the case of the *Guardian* – the women and young persons in the families involved were able to make use of the paper.

From these beginnings, in the last 250 years an extensive newspaper press has developed, and in Germany alone there are more than 6,000 titles registered today. The readers are mainly persons who form relatively homogeneous groups because they have the same or similar interests. For example, there are specialist newspapers which are aimed at the regular instruction of their readers in a particular, mainly specialized, field of knowledge. Newspapers for professional or occupational groups pass on information with the intention above all of gaining members for the representation of particular interests and to promote their integration in the respective organizations. Similar objectives are pursued by newspapers which are supported by members of churches, sects and political groups, where there is always the passing on of information and at the same time an attempt to alter opinions, to express interests and to canvas for the representation of these interests.

If the instructive effect of newspapers and magazines cannot in general be proved empirically, it is obvious to everyone that before the introduction of radio and television a mass public was informed constantly by means of periodicals, and that this information was passed on in many fields, in politics, science, literature and the arts. The increasing circulations indicate that this effect has not lessened. 'In our education we are all in debt to the press. What we have added in the form of general knowledge to the knowledge learned in school, comes to the greatest extent from reading newspapers', wrote Wilhelm Bauer (1914: 256), the cultural and newspaper historian, at the beginning of the century.

Distance teaching has the following structural similarities with the periodicals of the type referred to. As we know, many distance teaching schools work by sending their students a teaching letter at regular intervals, usually monthly. There are even companies which restrict their activities to the regular delivery of series of instructive works to which the student has subscribed. In addition, the idea of establishing a connection between distance education and newspapers and magazines seems even more obvious when we remember that the largest American distance education institute, International

Correspondence Schools, grew out of a newspaper in which miners were informed regularly about safety regulations in the pits, and that in Algeria, some years after independence, distance courses were printed in the daily press because the number of available schools was much too small. In addition to this, large distance teaching schools often have a house magazine which is part of each distance course.

There are further parallels to the production of periodicals in that in distance education as well the authors usually remain anonymous, and that the tone and style of the representation is adjusted much more to the circle of addressees than is the case with an instructive book. Often readers' letters are used didactically, like those published in newspapers and magazines, in that they are drawn to the attention of other participants in the course, and these are given an opportunity of giving their views and thus taking part in a written discussion on problems discussed in the distance course. Distance education schools also often attempt to give their students, who are usually isolated from one another, a feeling of belonging and of loyalty to their own distance school.

Finally, the path taken by the 'raw manuscript' of an author in the course of its processing for use in distance education is very similar to the corresponding editorial processing and arrangement of texts in periodicals. Here, as well, experts with different backgrounds work together. However, there are naturally other criteria for the selection of topics and the design of the texts.

Parallels can be seen most clearly in the attempts of commercially operated schools in particular to increase the accessibility of lessons by means of advertising and even by using sales representatives. Instead of subscribers, distance students are gained. There are many distance schools which can bring more than 100,000 students to order one of their courses. The circulation is increased, so to speak. As in the case of newspaper publishers, an increasing demand for capital is making itself felt in distance schools, as is the trend towards monopolization.

INSTRUCTION BY MEANS OF TEACHING AIDS, LEARNING AIDS AND LEARNING MATERIALS

One of the arguments in popular criticism of the methods of distance education most often heard states that teaching without the continuous presence of the teacher is really not possible at all. But this argument is in contradiction to a series of didactic efforts, which are regarded as progressive, to get away from the continuous presence of the teacher in the classroom, so that pupils are given an opportunity of working relatively independently. These efforts include all those attempts to dispense wholly or partially with the direct influence of the teacher on the pupils by using teaching aids, learning aids and working aids.

Teaching aids are used typically to strengthen certain functions of the teacher – for example, illustration and demonstration – and when they take over this function, such as when plants, minerals, animals, people, artefacts or illustrations of these are shown, the teacher retreats behind the object in certain phases of the teaching process, because the pupil has an opportunity of interacting directly with the object shown.

The removal of the teacher can be seen to an even greater extent with learning aids, which each pupil uses for the solution of construction problems or experiments. These are suitable for guiding the work of the pupil over long stretches of the learning process. In the case of learning materials the independence of the pupil goes even further. 'Learning aids lead the pupil away from the direct guidance of the teacher towards free and independent learning in which the didactic plan of the teacher becomes indirectly effective' (Bischofs 1970: 71).

Freyhoff (1968: col. 570) differentiates four learning aids which make clear the trend towards an increasing detachment from the person of the teacher. With the help of games children gather their first independent scholastic experiences and gain important basic insights. The drill aids make learning by heart and acquiring skills easier. Learning aids such as nature and science books and schoolbooks lead pupils to new insights and to develop their mental abilities. And finally, work instructions and work sheets induce pupils to 'grapple independently' with the contents of courses, as well as guiding them towards the independent use of works of reference and other aids.

Some characteristic examples show how the intention to remove the pupil from dependence on the teacher by means of materials has become stronger in this century. The corresponding school reform movements are connected with names such as Hugo Gaudig and Otto Scheibner, Maria Montessori, Frederic Burk, Carleton W. Washburne, Helen Parkhurst and Henry Clinton Morrison. In the sense of the 'activity school movement', the aim was followed in Germany of achieving the self-education of the pupils in lessons by means of self-action or spontaneity. Hugo Gaudig and Otto Scheibner attempted to realize in an increasing degree 'the independence of pupils and at the same time the withdrawal of the teacher' (Michael 1963: 248). Scheibner structured pupils' independent work by demanding that they formulated the working objectives themselves, then selected the necessary working aids with which they would reach the objective by taking a path they would also select themselves, and keeping to independent working steps (Scheibner 1955: 37).

Maria Montessori developed games and learning materials which were made available to the pupils in a special room. Each pupil selected something at will and then occupied himself with it quite freely. Where possible the material is such that the pupils can see for themselves whether a task has been solved or not. This self-teaching material served the aim openly of granting the pupil more freedom. In 1912, Frederic Burk developed written courses with colleagues in the San Francisco Normal School which were to enable the pupils to work through the curriculum at their own pace and with a minimum of assistance from the teacher. His self-instructional bulletins, which were developed for six school subjects, were in great demand all over the United States and in other countries as well, and were distributed at cost. They reached a circulation of 100,000. At first the bulletins supplemented certain textbooks, but later they were developed into independent written courses themselves (Saettler 1968: 63).

Carleton W. Washburne worked in the 1920s in Winnetka, Illinois, with prepared working material (worksheets and workbooks) which initiated the pupils' work and guided it, and steered the pupil towards an assessment of his or her own performance and even to keeping accounts of achievements (Washburne and Marland 1963). In the same period, Helen Parkhurst was teaching in the Dalton High School, in Dalton, Massachusetts, using self-instructing material. The individual pupils were given weekly and monthly plans for their work together with written instructions (assignments). They then entered into an agreement with the teacher regarding work on the assignment. The pupils found the work material necessary for this in the individual subject rooms. Using the written instructions, each pupil worked independently at his or her own pace, whereby the teacher's assistance was only called for when a pupil encountered difficulties. A new assignment was not handed out until the first had been completed (Parkhurst 1922). The Dalton Plan thus worked with the model of the 'Work aid course' (Gabele 1968: 24). In the 1920s and 1930s, Henry Clinton Morrison made schoolwork easier by subdividing classroom work into units for which he developed special guide sheets which the pupils used to work for themselves (Morrison 1931).

Experiments of this nature are at present increasing once again, because it is hoped that with the help of the work materials the subjects taught can be increased and at the same time a differentiation in the actual lesson itself can be achieved. For example, the students in the Miami Springs Junior High School have access at any time to the school's work-rooms where they go through a defined amount of work with the help of resource units and continuous progress packages (Jenkins 1971: 61) which the teachers in the school have prepared.

At present, lessons using teaching, learning and work aids are being stressed again in the context of curriculum reform. For example, multi-media teaching packages are being developed in which the course of the learning process is planned and prepared exactly down to the last detail. In the United States these teaching packages have even been used to compensate for the unsatisfactory educational standards of many of the teachers. Significantly, these materials were known in the profession as 'teacher-proof'. In lessons using these materials the teacher is pushed into a marginal position from which interference in the learning process is in part unwanted, so that the teacher now only has an organizational and custodial function. In the case of the Swedish IML Project (IML = individualized maths lessons), pupils in the 3rd, 4th and 5th forms worked through the whole of the maths syllabus using working materials which were found in three levels of difficulty. The teaching texts for this independent work were developed by a distance teaching school according to aspects of the didactics of distance teaching. The role of the teachers was restricted to occasional individual or group counselling, and to registering tests (cf. Marklund 1971: 63).

In the development series, programmed instruction thus represents a final stage, in that optimization of the programmes even dispenses with the teacher's remaining functions – correcting tests and counselling. In the process of the increasing substitution of functions of the teacher by specially developed teaching, learning and work aids an extreme position has thus been reached which will be the subject of special observation.

In the case of instruction using teaching, learning and work aids, the structural similarity with distance education lies in the following points, if the graduations indicated are taken into consideration:

- In both types of instruction the materials have to be prepared before use with regard to reaching defined instruction objectives. In the case of working aids as well as with the distance course, the time and care spent on this can be much greater than with preparation for oral lessons. Preparation may also include testing the material. With the preparation of many of the working aids referred to, the development work for distance teaching courses is already invested in the core.
- Teaching, learning and in particular working aids enable the student, as with a distance teaching course, to work without the constant presence of the teacher. In spite of this, the student in both cases is not without guidance from the teacher. This guidance is, however, indirect, and can in certain circumstances be much stronger than in face-to-face instruction, because the latter is not usually planned in such great detail beforehand.
- Both types of lesson enable the student to work according to his or her own learning pace.
- The following teaching functions may be assigned equally to the didactic materials and the distance teaching course: motivating, arousing and controlling attention, representing course contents, drill, transfer, control, assessing and registering achievements. However, in both cases the material has to be constituted in such a way that students can take over some functions themselves which the teacher would normally exercise in direct instruction.
- In both types of instruction the previously much more extensive activity of the teacher which dominated the teaching and learning process is restricted to functions such as those of a stimulator, a diagnostician and an administrator (Husén 1971: 186).

The structural similarity of distance teaching with free work according to the Dalton method is the most obvious. These two teaching methods come into contact as follows: the students work according to written instructions. Contact with the teacher is only taken up when the student encounters difficulties when solving the task they have been given. Students test themselves and register their own progress. All instructions and work aids have to be developed, tested and produced before the student can start work. Lessons are individual lessons.

AUDIOVISUAL LESSONS

Lessons using audiovisual media have also contributed to a restricted extent to the development of newer forms of distance teaching. These media are, for example, photos, slides, films, slides with synchronized commentary, records and tapes.

As with teaching using learning aids, teaching using audiovisual media is mediated teaching; that is a teacher working with these media communicates indirectly with the pupils. Even though advocates of audiovisual teaching often claim that this method simply serves the methodical processing, the enlivening and reinforcement of the teaching event and is not a substitute for the teacher (for example, Brudny 1970: 87), these media do in fact take over certain teaching functions for a shorter or longer period. For example, while an instructional film is being shown, or slides with synchronized commentary, the teacher retreats behind the technical transmission of the contents of the lesson.

In place of the teacher there is a teaching action which is constructed and determined with the assistance of the audiovisual media. As with printed material it is therefore possible to reproduce it as often as desired and to transmit it everywhere. The new factor with regard to the media which have been referred to up to now is that the contents of the lessons are no longer symbolically transmitted by means of the printed word, but that the voice of the teacher and his – moving – picture can influence the students, in so far as this is required by the objectives of the course and the circumstances; above all, however, that the 'universal capacity for topics' (Heimann and Schultz 1967: 18) of picture and film is brought into the lesson.

Although there has been a tendency among teachers from the start (in the United States from about 1918, in Germany from around 1934) until the present to ignore the indirect form of teaching which has been made possible by the use of audiovisual media, there is no real need to list examples of attempts to pass on knowledge in this way, as there is such an abundance of this type of teaching material in the catalogues of the film and slide agencies and teaching aid companies that it is difficult to gain an overview. All that need be done here is to point to the concentrated effects which emanated from projects which were based almost exclusively on audiovisual material. The teaching films, for example, which were developed and produced by the Minnesota Second Language Association of America together with the Center of Applied

Linguistics and the Teaching Film Custodians, have played a considerable role in the training of language teachers and in particular have promoted the introduction of the oral approach. The film series La Familia Fernandez, which consists of fifty-four film lessons, fifty-four series of slides and fifty-four training tapes, has also had a lasting modernizing effect on American language teaching as well, as it introduced the visual-audio-lingual method, which forced the teacher to give up the traditional reading and translation method.

A structural relationship between audiovisual teaching and distance teaching is in principle to be found in the fact that audiovisual teaching is basically also 'distance' teaching, and this is always the case when the teaching effect of certain materials is not intended to come from the teacher in the class, but from other persons at another time and in another place, where the learning objectives, topics, methods and sequencing are already determined down to the last detail. This structural affinity may have led to many distance education courses in fact using audiovisual materials. In particular, drawings, illustrations, maps, overhead projectors, slides and films, as well as records and tapes, are often integrated into distance teaching.

The two types of teaching also have the following points of contact:

- there has been an increase in the importance of development work;
- whereas teaching and working aids were often prepared by individual teachers or teaching staff, the more demanding audiovisual materials and the distance courses are usually prepared and produced by experts in this field;
- central agencies are usually established for the production, storage and distribution of teaching material. Because of the similarity of the tasks involved, in American universities the distance teaching departments and the audiovisual departments are often interlocked organizationally.

With the advantage of universal capacity for topics and with the integration of audiovisual methods, distance education takes over the structural disadvantage of restricted availability and accessibility. This disadvantage stems from the requirements that, in order to use audiovisual materials, technical appliances often have to be purchased, set up and started, and this is not always possible for the distance student.

COMMUNICATION OF KNOWLEDGE BY MEANS OF RADIO AND TELEVISION

An important element of present-day distance education are the experiences gained with the communication of knowledge by means of radio and television. With the development of audio and video cassettes and their manufacture, conditions have been created in addition for these elements to determine the structure of distance teaching to a much greater extent in the future.

As with printed materials and periodicals, radio and television are mass media and are able to reach very high numbers of participants in teaching events, because the communication of knowledge can take place over considerable distances. As in the case of printed matter, these media are only suitable for one-way communications, which in the case of their utilization for teaching purposes has led to the establishment of additional feedback mechanisms, such as listeners' letters or telephone calls. The new element as against these other media is the opportunity for the teacher to teach at the same time as the students learn. This simultaneous effect had been lost as a result of the utilization of the instructive letter and printed matter in distance education. In this point the original state can in part be established again with the help of electronic media. What is also new is the live effect which creates in the student the illusion of being there, and creates an even greater feeling of authenticity than a film. It is in fact this live effect which again and again leads to radio and television being regarded as instruments which enable students to be present during a direct lesson which is actually taking place. Instruction by means of radio and television is obviously always threatened by the feeling of satisfaction with this kind of minimal solution. The station effect (Heinrichs 1971: 259) binds students emotionally to *their* radio or television station, whereby an effect is achieved which is similar to the formation of communities of readers of newspapers and magazines referred to above. Attention must also be drawn to the theatrical potential (Heimann 1965: 21) of these media which allow the teacher to give a stage setting to suitable course contents.

Since 1924, when the first European schools broadcast took place in the form of a radio talk from Hamburg in English, and the following years, when many universities and colleges in the United States established their own radio stations and many 'schools of the air' were founded, many remarkable models for the use of radio for instruction purposes have been developed. From the academic radio talk, such as those broadcast by the RIAS-Funkuniversität, which have now reached their sixty-eighth series, sprang above all the Quadriga-Funkkolleg, initiated by the Hessische Rundfunk, which can now be regarded as the most advanced form of the communication of knowledge by radio.

In 1950 the first education television station started transmitting in the United States, and there are now more than 100 stations of this kind there. In 1959, the most extensive schools broadcasting system in the world was established in Tokyo. In Germany, the Third Programmes took up the task of communicating knowledge at a high level. The Bayerische Rundfunk has had a permanent schools broadcasting system since 1964, and North Rhine-Westphalia since 1969. In the educational programmes of the Bayerische Rundfunk the communication of knowledge has been influenced most through television. Along with informative programmes there are also pure teaching programmes, such as Telekolleg, course programmes, programmes for apprentice training and further vocational training, university television and the Teletechnikum.

The structural correspondence between traditional distance teaching on the basis of printed material and the communication of knowledge using radio and television is easily recognizable. In both processes, a relatively homogeneous audience is reached over distances from a central position. In both cases it is a question not of directly but of indirectly communicated knowledge, in fact, knowledge communicated with the help of technical media. This type of lesson is characterized by the periodicity of its occurrence, careful and detailed preliminary planning, addressing defined groups, and the reproducibility of the teaching behaviour.

These correspondences led at an early stage to attempts to combine both processes for communicating knowledge. In a first stage, experts for distance education attempted to integrate the new media in part into the distance teaching system (Wedemeyer and Childs 1961: 45), while radio and television often took over elements of distance teaching when they produced educational programmes. Examples of this are the radio programmes which were developed in Australia in collaboration with the distance schools (School of the Air), and radio and television programmes for schools and other educational programmes which are accompanied by written material. Certain forms of Japanese distance education may be regarded as the second stage of combination in which the whole course is offered with the help of television as well as with that of printed material, so that the type and the duration of the combination of the two learning processes is left to the student. A third stage is reached by those large-scale educational projects which were established in the sixties through the collaboration of governments and television companies in Italy, Great Britain, Sweden, Poland, West Germany, Canada and Brazil (Multi Media Systems 1970). In these cases forms of integration were in part consciously aimed for. Starting from the experience gained with these projects, the Open University in Great Britain at present uses radio and television on a regular basis along with printed material as media for university education.

TEACHING USING PROGRAMMED LEARNING

Present-day, and future distance teaching probably even more so, is influenced by the principles of programmed learning, as these principles caused a change in the development of didactic thinking which was to have a considerable effect on the theory and practice of distance teaching. 'Teaching programmes' in this context are to be understood not only as programmed printed material, which is found most often and with which the parallels appear obvious from the type of stimuli, but also programmed tapes, films and teaching machines.

With the increasing use of teaching programmes the following structural elements are formed in the field of indirect teaching:

- the consistent orientation of the lessons to learning objectives;
- the testing of the lesson with the objective of predicting the learning success;
- the application of findings and methods from the empirical behavioural sciences, which has led, among other things, to the programming technique of small steps, feedback, and above all to a differentiated control of the answering attitudes.

With these structural elements it was possible to let the learning process run independently of all direct influences of a teacher in person, and to develop completely new strategies of indirect teaching.

In spite of the many difficulties which result from the partial incompatibility of technologically constructed teaching systems such as programmed learning with the traditional school systems, an overview from Glaser (1969) shows that the teaching programmes played a definite part in teaching and training as early as the middle of the 1960s and are, it appears, gaining in importance, in spite of many disappointments. For example, the number of pupils in Texas taking part in programmed teaching increased in 1961 to 1965 from 381 to 81,236. Surveys carried out in 1962 and 1963 showed that the percentage of primary and secondary schools in the surveys which used programmed learning had increased in a single year from 11.4 per cent to 36.36 per cent. In addition to this, in 1964 there were fifteen faculties of medicine using programmes in their regular teaching schedules. In industry the new teaching method spread even more rapidly. Of 277 large companies, 30 per cent had taken programmed learning into their regular training systems by 1965. In 1963 it was found that 382 teaching programmes were in use in American federal agencies. There is also a survey published in 1966 which stated that programmed learning had spread to a great extent in the armed forces, and, for example, had been introduced in twenty-four naval training centres. In West Germany, 213 German language teaching programmes were registered in January 1970 by the Pädagogische Zentrum in Berlin. Klaus Weltner (1972) reported that about 1,000 teaching programmes were available, of which several had already reached a circulation of over 100,000.

With the rise of programmed instruction, a number of similarities led several distance educationists (see, for example, Larsson 1965: 66) to the judgement that distance education had observed the principles of programmed instruction from the very beginning. The following common structural features also speak in favour of this judgement:

- The students work as individuals.
- Time, place and rate of learning can be determined to a great extent by the student, which – in these points – can lead to an individualization of the teaching process.
- The course contents are measured out and sequenced before the start of the learning process. While distance teaching measures out with the help of the teaching letter unit and the organization of the layout (for example, by means of short paragraphs), programmed teaching works above all with the help of frames.
- Testing and constant revision are possible, and usual, in both systems.
- The self-test assignments in distance teaching are in principle designed so that after a lesson has been presented students can check whether they have reached the objective. To do this, they are given the correct result, and this corresponds to the feedback (knowledge of results) in the teaching programmes. In both sys-

tems, therefore, there is a periodic strengthening of the learning attitudes.

However, the new criteria of relativity to learning aims, of the empirical control of success and of the systematic control of the learning process with the help of emphasis and intensification go so much further than these common features that it hardly seems justified to regard programmed instruction, with Ake Bjerstedt (in Larsson 1965: 66), merely as a 'rationalized form of correspondence instruction'. Something entirely new has been added, and this new characteristic will be significant for the development of distance education.

It is true here as well that the points of contact referred to have led to the integration of teaching programmes in distance education and to partial programming of distance teaching courses respectively. Hermods, the Swedish distance teaching school, has developed, for example, an auxiliary lessons programme for a mathematics course which is to be used to eliminate any difficulties of comprehension which might occur. In 1965, twelve out of sixty-two American universities polled used programmed instruction on distance education courses (Kempfer 1965). In 1964, programmed material was used in distance education courses in secondary schools (Sjogren 1964). Teaching programmes are also planned for the AIM project of the University of Wisconsin for the development of a multimedia distance education system, as well as in the UNRA/UNESCO distance education courses for Beirut. If there has not as yet been any further integration of teaching programmes in distance education, this has probably been caused not so much by the didactic difficulties as by the high costs which organizers of distance teaching courses do not regard as being appropriate, above all when comparative empirical studies have shown that the efficacy of the programmes is not higher than that of distance teaching courses (Larsson 1965: 67).

COMPUTER-AIDED INSTRUCTION

In conclusion, attention is drawn to computer-aided instruction. Here the learning process is either guided by a computer from start to finish on the basis of a program, or aided, in that individual teaching functions are carried out by a computer.

In contrast with learning using teaching programmes, computer-aided instruction has the advantage that the branching which is necessary for the individualization of learning can be much more differentiated. This is possible because the computer can compare thousands of data in a second, and therefore from an accumulated repertoire of tasks can rapidly assign those tasks which are appropriate to the type of answer given in each case, as well as to certain characteristics of the student and of the learning situation. In this way the computer is able to generate learning incentives which can be derived from the whole stored answering behaviour of the student, and as a consequence enable many different learning paths to be followed when new teaching contents are offered. Thus forms of the adjustment of the teaching process to the individual learning process (Klotz 1970: 256) are achieved in a way which is impossible elsewhere, even in direct teaching itself.

The computer is able to carry out the following functions specific to the medium:

- enablement of instantaneous dialogue as a result of two-way communication;
- enablement of a practically unlimited drill and applications capacity;
- integration, coordination and synchronization of forms of presentation in an interconnected media system – for example, learning with printed material, slides, tapes, films and so on;
- evaluation during the learning process, in a more differentiated and more exacting form. For example, evaluation can relate particularly to learning objectives determined by the contents and to psychological learning objectives such as learning pace, duration of retention and extent of transfer achieved. Above all, special learning results can be drawn in from courses which were worked through some time before, in order to test how knowledge, once acquired, is applied in new learning situations.

According to Lawrence M. Stolurow (1969: 273), computer-aided instruction as practised at present is at the level of technological development which corresponds to the trials carried out by the Wright brothers in the history of aviation. The didactic potential of this type of instruction has not been recognized, according to Stolurow. He goes on to sketch a concept for the future application of a computer in instruction, whereby he differentiates between the following five forms:

- problem-solving mode;
- drill and practice mode;
- answering set questions (inquiry mode);

- counselling the pupil with regard to the learning path (tutorial mode);
- development, compilation and presentation of teaching material for the individual pupil (author mode).

In Europe, experiments have been carried out using some models of computer-aided instruction; namely, in France since 1967, the Netherlands since 1968 and in West Germany, where the coordinating agency and the application of EDP in the educational system was established in 1968, and the project 'EDP facilities as an aid for teaching and learning' began in 1969 in the Technical University in Aachen with the support of the Federal Ministry of Education and Science. Corresponding experiments in the United States were started much earlier, and the number of experiments is much larger (Atkinson and Wilson 1969; Bushnell and Allen 1967). The Office of Education in Washington has already had several extensive surveys carried out on the possibility of establishing large, central computer systems which will work on the time-sharing process and which will be available to large school districts with 500,000 children (Stone 1968; Lewis 1968). In general, however, the use of computers is still restricted today to the following tasks which they are able to solve much better than other media because of their absolutely reliable memory, which can also be extremely large, and the rapidity with which they are able to carry out logical operations:

- development of constant review of a file with data on the students;
- construction of a timetable;
- registration of relevant learning activities;
- evaluation and analysis of tests;
- issue of achievement reports (certificates) for individual pupils, for groups and for all pupils together;
- provision of data for counselling purposes.

Computer-aided instruction is 'distance' instruction because here as well teachers program the learning process beforehand elsewhere. In addition, computer-aided instruction often takes place with the help of terminals which are connected to the computer by means of a telephone line (teleprocessing systems). As a result, a large number of students, scattered over a large area, can take part in computer-aided instruction. The number of students being looked after at the same time can be increased even further if the students are not dependent on direct access to a terminal, but can post their learning results on marking sheets to the central computer.

In addition to this, computer-aided instruction has the following structural characteristics in common with distance education, where the correspondences with the didactic structure of programmed learning are not repeated here:

- there is delayed and instantaneous dialogue with the teaching system;
- study counselling is carried out on the basis of registered data;
- following the evaluation of tests, individualized recommendations for further learning are often sent.

The degree of mutuality of these structural features can be characterized by being referred to as functions which are necessary in the case of distance education, but which are usually performed by tutors. In the case of computer-aided instruction, the exercise of the same functions is automated on the basis of prior, extremely careful programing. This means in part that it is at the same time considerably intensified and above all carried out in each case following the evaluation of relevant data.

In distance education the computer is used in the main for drill and examination purposes. This was done first of all, and to a very great extent, in the distance courses of the Extension Course Institute of the Air University of the US Air Force (Peters 1968: 1275; Birtwistle 1966), in which the answers to revision questions, which refer to larger sections, are marked by the airmen on special sheets which are then sent to the institute. There the sheets are read mechanically and evaluated by computers. The airman then received a postcard on which are marked the questions which were answered correctly and the sections which have to be worked through again. Only after the airman has made sure of the success of his learning efforts by means of several programed drills of this nature will he register for an examination, which is then carried out in the same manner, with the difference that the sheets are filled in under the supervision of an officer.

In the Open University as well, computers are used above all for the evaluation of tests. In West Germany, computer-aided testing proved itself for the first time on a large scale in the Quadriga-Funkkolleg Educational Science (Gross *et al.* 1971; Gallus 1971), after the final examination for technical calculations in the *Land* distance teaching school for hotels and catering had been checked by computer (Brand 1968).

INDIVIDUAL TUITION

As distance education makes use in the main of printed material for self-instruction which can be copied as often as required and sent everywhere, there arose the possibility that each student could work alone. In this way a type of instruction was revived which had almost been lost completely, if one disregards coaching and cramming. The degree to which the form of individual tuition has been pushed out of the consciousness of didacticians can be seen in the fact that it is not mentioned at all in the compendia from Huber (1965) and Stöcker (1966), and that classroom instruction is regarded as a sort of uniform standard (Drechsler 1967: 147).

Individual tuition is often regarded as the optimum social form of instruction in so far as the teachers can apply themselves with undivided attention to the control of the learning process, and the pupils are not hindered in their learning progress by faster or slower learners or by group dynamic disadvantages and the resulting emotional disturbances. Willmann (1957: 585) stressed that individual tuition strengthened 'the eye for individuality' and that 'the combination of objective and subjective factors' could be controlled carefully down to the last detail: 'In comparison with the methods of a talented private tutor, classroom instruction can appear to be mediocre work'.

The original pattern for individual tuition appears to be the discussion between teacher and pupil, the instructive dialogue, which was probably a considerable advance on the instructive monologue. This instructive dialogue can take many forms:

- the imitation of the teacher by repeating what he has said;
- instruction, tuition;
- advice, counselling;
- the inquisitorially developing explanation of an object for instruction.

As the most important structural characteristic it should be stressed that in individual tuition the communication of knowledge is combined with an original situation which plays an important part even independently of this purpose: communicative action, whose external forms appear to be pre-structured by the respective level of development of a society, and which plays an important part in the communication of culture.

The pattern of individual tuition is concretized in many forms. This chapter will refer only to the examples of instruction by the comptroller of the household in the feudal system and private tutors respectively, tuition based on the tutorial system and the counselling system.

Tuition from the comptroller of the household, a function which developed from that of the comptroller of the armoury, and later from private tutors, cultivated the individual care of the children of noble families, and later of those of rich patrician families. According to Reble (1968: 242), this system of tuition was differentiated deliberately from schools open to all because the latter were regarded as de-individualizing. Reble stressed the 'wholly individualistic pedagogical reference' of this type of tuition and its 'stress on the care of individuality'. The tuition was integrated in and subjected to personal educational care. Individual tuition by the comptroller of the household or a private tutor had a great effect on educational thought into the twentieth century, because a number of famous educators (such as Basedow, Dinter, Schleiermacher, Herbart and Berthold Otto) had themselves worked for many years in this capacity. Rousseau's *Emile* also showed how great was the domination of the conception of individual tuition. In Herbart's theory of didactics the classroom always appeared as an extension of the individual, standing opposite the teacher. In Berthold Otto's *The Private Tutor*, the conception of individualizing teaching was integrated into the educational reform movement. And fundamental categories of humanistic didactics, such as personal reference or the educational relationship, always related to the pupil; in other words, in tuition they were related to the individual pupil. Categories such as 'encounter' (Bollnow 1959) and the 'dialogue or familiar relationship' (Buber 1964) were also derived from this type of one-on-one situation.

The tutorial system is traditional in English universities. There each student (undergraduate) is assigned to a tutor who supervises the student's studies as well as his general behaviour. Each student works alone, but the timetable, achievements and any difficulties which arise are discussed with the tutor. If the student has any difficulties with the university administration, the tutor acts as a mediator.

The counselling system is a fixed component in the American educational and training system and has been introduced not only in primary and secondary schools, but also in colleges and universities. This system provides for individual talks with trained and specialized teachers with reference to decisions regarding the school or vocational career, personal problems or the development of suitable techniques for studying.

How far can a connection be seen between distance education and the above forms of personal, individual tuition? When a teaching text is compiled, the authors do not normally have an imaginary class and its reactions in mind. The distance teacher imagines an individual pupil and attempts – anticipating the pupil's probable reactions – to map a defined learning path for him. Stimuli are worked into the text which the teacher would normally give to individual pupils in order to motivate them, to control their attention, to prepare them for difficulties, to give them prompts and assignments, and finally to inform them whether the results of the work are correct. In this way teaching techniques are fixed into the texts for use in distance teaching which are not those of a class teacher, but rather those of a private tutor. This means that in texts for distance teaching 'the prince's tutor is simulated, not the corporal's instructions to the troops', as Flechsig (1969: 11) said with regard to teaching programmes.

The instructive exchange of letters, which takes place in connection with the correction of work assigned and when special learning difficulties occur, leads to a dialogue between the student and the teacher correcting the work, which in fact can have the advantages of individualization referred to by Willmann. The need of the student, and the possibility for the teacher, to make a concentrated, steady examination of the difficulties referred to by the student create favourable conditions for the establishment of personal relationship. The same applies to instructive correspondence using tapes (Schmidt-Sommer and Peters 1971). Many distance teaching schools and institutes of distance higher education offer their students a system of study counselling which uses written, telephone and oral communications.

The structural proximity to the tutor is found in part here just as with the teacher correcting the written work, in that both tutor and corrector are not at the same time teachers. The counselling relationship can be much less partial than with a teacher who has teaching, examining and advising functions. Distance teaching thus takes over individual functions which are usually only exercised by the private tutor, the university tutor and the counsellor, and in doing so develops the forms referred to. An analysis of these forms of individual tuition would show that they also enable the various types of interaction of instructive dialogue, such as imitation, instruction/tuition, counselling and the inquisitorially developed examination of a subject to take place.

INDEPENDENT STUDY

As participants in distance teaching are not normally part of a group of learners, but work through the teaching letters alone, the didactic assessment of distance teaching is also important from the point of view of independent work for which school pedagogics has developed some traditional patterns.

Independent work is a social form of instruction in which the teacher retreats and no longer influences the student's work by means of direct social interaction, but only by means of assigning work and giving instructions. Sometimes the teacher uses certain prepared material in order to stimulate independent work, to control it and to evaluate it.

In school, independent work has always played a role which has not been given enough attention simply because of the dominance of class instruction. Before the introduction of instruction in class age groups, each pupil worked for themselves, even though, seen from outside, they formed a group with others. From time to time the teacher would hear pupils' lessons individually. In rural schools this type of independent work was common for many years after the introduction of classes according to age groups, as teachers in these schools had to give lessons there to several departments with pupils of various ages and levels of achievement. While the teacher was teaching one department orally, the other pupils would have to solve written problems. As this work was essentially quiet work, each pupil was basically on their own. However, this form of independent work was seldom used for new contents, but instead for drills, repeat work and applications of material already learnt, and the introduction of new contents for lessons was reserved for the teacher. This led Stöcker (1966: 170) to differentiate solely between preparatory, processing and continuing independent work, whereas he described the elaborating type of independent work as a didactic novelty. He wrote, 'according to traditional views... only direct instruction is entitled to the task of elaborating'. But then according to the new opinions, independent work could now become the core of instruction by believing the pupil capable 'of independently acquiring knowledge and skills' (p. 173). Independent work is also very common in schools which are heavily streamed. For example, as a result of organizational difficulties there is the almost daily problem in large schools of 'keeping classes busy'. Pupils are often required to occupy themselves. In the case of written examinations, care is taken that each pupil works alone, even if here the reason is to prevent cheating. Also the annual project report is a form of independent work steered by the teacher. Similar conditions apply to homework, which is also usually done in the form of independent work. The content of this work is closely connected with oral tuition, whereas the study period in American schools, which usually takes place in the reading room of the school library, may also be used for working on freely selected topics.

While widespread 'quiet work' and 'occupying' classes led to forms of independent work which were regarded in the main as emergency solutions, as a result of the efforts of reform pedagogics independent work was given a new didactic status. The aim now was the independence of the pupil, who was to be liberated from the domination of the teacher in the classroom and from the spoonfeeding of traditional teacher's questions. Hugo Gaudig (1929: 151) demanded, for example, that each pupil should acquire an appropriate working technique in order to be able to work on a self-active basis. However, in the context of free intellectual self-activity, Gaudig stressed self-drive, self-power, the self-chosen paths and the freely selected objectives so emphatically that the type of independent work he was aiming for was considerably set apart from that of distance education, because here the objectives and the path of instruction are laid down to a much greater extent than in lessons in the learning schools against which Gaudig was struggling. Similar statements can be made on the concept of independent work in other directions of the work school movement.

In contrast, in the case of reform educationists outside Germany, independent work developed more strongly in the direction of prepared and guided activities of the pupil because of the stronger stress placed on individual pedagogical aspects; this was in particular the case with Maria Montessori, Carleton W. Washburne and Helen Parkhurst, whose experiments have already been referred to in the discussion of instruction using teaching, learning and work aids. At present, many aspects of these educationists are once again topical in the concept of independent study in the United States (Beggs and Buffie 1969).

The forms of independent work referred to above have the following points of contact with the didactic structure of distance teaching:

- The work of the individual pupil is set in motion and finally controlled by a teacher. It is therefore not a form of autodidactics.
- Pupils often use printed material (learning or working aids) in their independent work which has been specially prepared for this purpose.
- The work is structured by the solution of problems.
- Pupils are able to work at their own learning pace. In some forms of independent work, such as homework and the annual topic, pupils determine the time and the place for their work as well.
- If pupils encounter difficulties, they can turn to the competent teacher.

INSTRUCTION IN COURSE FORM

As distance teaching is usually offered in the form of courses, a further structural relationship of this type of instruction with an important methodical aspect of direct school and adult education can be established.

The course is a form of communication of knowledge and skills in which a fixed and foreseeable amount of work is presented in a defined period in graduated learning steps, one after the other. These learning steps are defined teaching units which in themselves are relatively independent, but are in fact connected with one another and are offered in a calculated sequence. An important aspect of the course is the reference to a group of addressees. Courses differ from a systematic representation of knowledge in that their aim is to point out to the student the most suitable way (hence the word 'course') to gain the contents offered and to achieve the objectives. According to K-H. Schwager (1958: 112), a course is always pre-planned and is therefore fixed in advance. The contents are offered in such a way that each course unit, where possible, builds on earlier courses and also prepares for later courses. On the whole, courses serve the objective of 'being able to ensure successful learning in the field involved through special course construction'. The course is 'the core of all scheduled instruction' and is thus an 'essential factor in the school'.

In the history of education forms of courses can be traced back to lessons in the early Middle Ages, when the classical teaching system was taken over on the foundation of Christian schools. Many great educationists have taken part in the further development of courses; for example, Comenius, A. H. Francke, Rousseau, Pestalozzi, Fröbel, Herbart, Ziller, Rein and Berthold Otto.

In West Germany, courses have not played any great role in teaching practice in primary and secondary schools, in contrast to the United States, for example. On the contrary, courses stand out from the usual form of classroom instruction through their detailed planning and defined methodological structure. In spite of this, various courses are structured in teaching in these schools; for instance, reading courses, or advanced specialist courses. As pupils from different classes are often able to take part in these courses, the original class community is broken up, which means that the chances for much stronger subject-related instruction may be greater. Many events in adult education have the character of courses. The advantage of the course is that potential addressees can be informed relatively clearly of the contents which will be communicated, and how much time they will have to spend on the course. The course system gives the students in addition the possibility of choosing between several course offers. The course form has become established in training systems for the armed forces and political parties, as well as for associations, in particular sports associations, probably because of its pronounced pragmatic-utilitarian objectives.

With the technique of communicating teaching contents in course form, distance education is following a long tradition and widespread practice of direct teaching methods. As distance courses usually have to be produced before the first student can work with them, the course character is often much more marked here: pre-planning and determining is done on a much greater scale than in direct teaching. The topic is delineated, the teaching letters form the course units, which are relatively restricted but which are connected with one another, and this is strengthened by cross-references. The distance course is not only set apart from the textbook with regard to its tone but also with regard to its construction and to its much closer relationship to a circle of addressees. It could be assumed that many distance teaching institutions seek to compensate by means of a careful construction of the courses for the lack of a teacher's presence, which is regarded as a disadvantage.

FINDINGS

The above analyses of distance education on the basis of a comparison with eight other forms of indirect teaching and learning, as well as with two social forms and an organizational form of direct teaching, lead to the identification of a very large number of didactic elements which, each taken separately, are well known in the field

96 *Analysis*

of education. These elements are shown in the table below (pp. 98–102). The characteristics shown in this overview are not themselves complete, neither in regard to the didactic forms from which they are derived, nor for distance teaching itself, as only those concurrences and similarities of these didactic forms with distance teaching which are obvious were listed. This process leads to repetitions, but these can be of use to the purposes of the study in so far as they make continuous structural features of indirect teaching on the whole visible. An initial attempt at a definition could lead to the following:

> Distance education is a form of indirect instruction: instruction which is communicated by technical media such as letters, printed material, teaching, learning and working aids, audiovisual teaching aids, radio, television and computers, and which is made up of didactic elements as shown in the table.

Interpretation

An analysis of the didactic elements displayed shows that these can be arranged by and large in the following three categories: didactic features, principles and elements of form.

Didactic features

If we look at the feature fields and observe various accumulations of features, three main features can be recognized which are evidently constructive in the case of distance education. First, planning and preparation are essential conditions for the materialization of the teaching and learning process: from instructive correspondence to programing for computer-aided instruction, there are many degrees with regard to personal, temporal, financial and material expense, as well as the type, extent and differentiation of this work. In contrast to traditional direct teaching, however, there is a minimum level of planning and preparation which has to be adhered to.

Secondly, tasks for the teacher are transferred to a technical medium, or to several connected technical media: with the help of didactic manipulations, the behaviour of the student can be 'remote-controlled' using these media, among other things by addressee-related, regular, periodic amounts of learning which are divided into easily controllable units, arranged according to didactic criteria and structured by means of tasks.

Thirdly, a defined amount and a special form of activity on the part of the students is a pre-condition for the prepared learning process actually taking place: students have to take decisions on the place of learning, the time at which learning is to be carried out, the duration, how to measure progress and (in part) learning strategies, and how to take over the responsibility for the concrete course of the learning process. Independence here thus means much more than in direct teaching, and it also means different things.

Didactic principles

In the first place is the principle of individualization which is introduced by the various forms of indirect teaching and learning with very different degrees of comprehension of the term itself (for example, showing understanding of the student's inclinations, interests and personality in the case of instructive correspondence, determination of the pace of learning by the student in the case of programmed learning, taking prior knowledge, capabilities and response behaviour into account in computer-aided instruction).

The principle of democratization of the communication of knowledge, in the way in which this has been traditionally formed in connection with books and periodicals, makes itself felt to a greater extent in that distance education is in fact suitable for breaking down barriers of a social, religious, ethnic and institutional nature, even though all restricting conditions which conflict with this have to be reflected on at the same time.

The principle of reference to the student takes very different forms from instructive correspondence to computer dialogue.

The principle of self-instruction or self-study may have an autodidactic touch for many, but what is meant by these terms is, from the initial examples, that the student deals independently with the didactic material. This principle is close to the principle of independent study, which plays an important role in the American school system. Significantly, correspondence study and independent study are used here in part as synonyms. In Germany the principle of self-instruction is closely related to that of self-activating taken from the work school movement. This concept has not been taken over by the theory of distance education because of the tension associated with educational reforms. At present it seems that in distance education as well the principle of self-instruction is being developed further into a principle of learner-guided and learner-controlled instruction.

Table. Didactic characteristics and formal elements which distance teaching has in common with other types of indirect teaching

Didactic elements	Distance education	
a) *Other forms of indirect instruction*	Didactically relevant characteristics in which distance teaching corresponds with the didactic elements in the left-hand column	Form elements taken over or harmonizing
Written instruction: Instructive correspondence Written interaction between teacher and pupil in classroom system	• Speech and tone are related to individual addressees • Answers are provoked • Delayed dialogue (two-way communication) • Metering • Individual instruction • Principle of individualization • Time and place for learning can be determined within limits by the pupil	Personal correspondence Written tuition from tutors Written correction of assigned work
Instruction using printed material	• Mass reproduction of material • Democratization of communication of knowledge • Preparation phase lengthened and intensified • Economy of representation: more contents communicated per unit than with oral lessons • Lessons stabilized: presentation of contents is independent of imponderables of school life • Development of a language style suitable for large groups of addressees • Binding to trade and commerce (commercialization)	Representation of distance courses in printed form Distance courses supported by textbooks and supplemented by literature

Teaching using periodicals	• Periodicity of delivery • Increased availability and accessibility by delivery • Series of uniform publications • Relatively homogeneous circle of addressees • 'Formation of communities' • Editorial processing of the contributions by specialists • Deliberate selection and arrangement of the contributions according to defined criteria • Language and tone related to a defined group of addressees • Increased commercialization: circulation increased by acquiring 'subscribers'	Monthly delivery of teaching letters 'Readers' letters' Magazines for distance students
Instruction using teaching, learning and study aids	• Work with the materials has to be didactically prepared (indirect teaching) • A number of teaching functions are transferred to the material • Independent examination of the student with the material is necessary • Teaching behaviour has a distance effect with the help of the materials: the teaching and learning processes are determined by their distribution • Presence of a teacher is to a great extent restricted or is not necessary • The role of the teacher is altered: he becomes a stimulator, a diagnostician, an administrator • Mainly individual instruction, but group instruction possible • Influences from the teaching aids industry in so far as it produces learning, teaching and work aids	Written instructions for studying Sheets for solving tasks and for assigned work Work sheets Works of reference Teaching packages Counselling from the teacher on request

(continued overleaf)

Audiovisual teaching	• Detailed and expensive development work necessary • Professionals must take part in the development work and are drawn from several technical divisions • Large-scale financial investment required • Institutionalization for the purposes of production, storage and distribution • Instruction over great distances with a large number of students possible, using film, synchronized slides, tapes • Freedom to choose the place and time of learning restricted by necessity of apparatus	Use of photos, slides, overhead projection, film strips, tapes, records and films
Communication of knowledge using radio and television	• Long-term detailed planning and development work required • Large apparatus with work-sharing cooperating specialists must be available • Spatial distances crossed from one point, so that a 'dispersed' public is reached • Egalitarian instruction because of the ubiquity of the presentation • Periodicity of the presentation (fixed learning times) • Construction on montage principle and context model • One-way communication	Teaching broadcasts on radio in distance education media combinations Teaching broadcasts in television in distance education in media combination
Instruction using programmed learning	• Detailed and expensive development and pilot phase • Metering and sequencing of contents • Periodic strengthening of learning attitudes • Student determines time, place and pace of learning, therefore large number of addressees possible • Individual instruction	Distance courses are in part programmed or are based on teaching programmes

Computer-aided instruction	• Reaches large number of dispersed addressees • Delayed and instantaneous dialogue between teaching system and student possible (two-way communication) • Counselling on the basis of registered data • Individualization	Computer-aided drills
		Computer-aided tests
		Computer-aided counselling
b) *Social forms*		
Individual tuition	• Individualization • Undesirable group dynamic effects are avoided (e.g. the roles of 'scapegoat' or 'outsider')	Individual forms of address in teaching by correspondence
		Individual counselling (consultation) possible using letters, telephone or exchange of tapes, or face to face
		Discussions with a 'travelling teacher' who visits the distance students

(*continued overleaf*)

| Independent study | • The teacher withdraws to a great extent from the teaching and learning process
• The student's work is initiated, controlled and structured by assigned work
• Work is often 'remote-controlled' by didactic material
• Teacher is prepared to intervene on request when difficulties occur
• Principle of 'self-activation'
• Principle of 'independent study' | Individuals working through teaching letters and literature; 'independent study'

Student draws up own plan of work and controls own observance of plan |

(c) *Forms of presentation*

| Instruction in the form of courses | • Easily visible amount of work presented in graded learning stages one after the other
• Instruction consists of relatively independent units which are still combined with one another
• Sequence of contents not based on system of knowledge but didactically calculated
• Regularity
• Principle of anticipation and referral (interconnections)
• Principle of learner orientation | Presentation of teaching contents in the form of distance 'courses' |

Didactic form elements

The twenty-seven form elements shown in the table above, which have been taken over from other forms of indirect teaching and learning, or which harmonize with corresponding elements of these forms, show a composite picture of distance teaching and its particular opportunities for forming variants. Distance teaching courses can be constructed which use only one of these form elements or which combine several form elements with one another (the classical form of correspondence education – printed distance courses, correspondence with the tutor, counselling), or which integrate a large number of these form elements into a system (the Telekolleg). Most existing distance teaching systems can be illustrated with the help of the didactic form elements shown here, if interlayered events taken from direct teaching are ignored.

REFERENCES

Atkinson, R. C. and Wilson, H. A. (eds) (1969) *Computer Assisted Instruction*, New York: Academic Press.

Bauer, W. (1914) 'Die öffentliche Meinung und ihre geschichtlichen Grundlagen', in A. Silbermann (ed.) *Reader Massenkommunikation*, Bielefeld: Bertelsmann, 1969, pp. 42–67.

Beggs, D. W. and Buffie, E. C. (1969) *Independent Study*, Bloomington, London: Indiana University Press.

Birtwistle, O. G. (1966) 'US Air Force correspondence education program', in *The Home Study Review*, 6 (Summer): 25–32.

Bischofs, J. (1970) 'Arbeitsmittel', in *Lexikon der Pädagogik*, Freiburg: Herder, vol. I, p. 70.

Bollnow, O. F. (1959) *Existenzphilosophie und Pädagogik*, Stuttgart: Urban-Taschenbuch.

Brand, P. (1968) 'Computer wertet Schlusstest für "Fachrechnen" aus', in *IBM-Nachrichten*, 18, vol. 187: 23–9.

Brudny, W. (1970) 'Audio-visuelle Unterrichtsmittel', in *Lexikon der Pädagogik*, Freiburg: Herder, vol. I: pp. 86–8.

Buber, M. (1964) 'Uber das Erzieherische', in *Reden über Erziehung*, Heidelberg: Quelle & Meyer.

Bushnell, D. D. and Allen, D. W. (eds) (1967) *The Computer in American Education*, New York: Wiley.

Comenius, J. A. (1947) *Grosse Unterrichtslehre*, Berlin: Volk & Wissen.

—— (1960) *Pampaedia*, Heidelberg: Quelle & Meyer.

Cooley, C. H. (1909) 'Social organization', in A. Silbermann (ed.) *Reader Massenkommunikation*, Gütersloh: Bertelsmann, 1969, pp. 18–25.

Delling, M. (1966) 'Versuch der Grundlegung zu einer allgemeinen Fernunterrichtstheorie', in *Epistolodidaktika*, 2 (4): 209–26.

Dohmen, G. (1967) *Das Fernstudium. Ein neues pädagogisches Forschungs- und Entwicklungsfeld*, Heidelberg: Quelle & Meyer.

Drechsler, J. (1967) *Bildungstheorie und Prinzipienlehre der Didaktik*, Heidelberg: Quelle & Meyer.
Flechsig, K. H. (1969) 'Die technologische Wendung in der Didaktik', in G. Hess (ed.) *Konstanzer Unterrichtsreden Nr. 23*, Konstanz: Universitätsverlag.
Flitner, W. (1964) 'Grundfragen der Didaktik des Fernunterrichts', in *Epistolodidaktika*, 1 (1): 2–8.
Freyhoff, U. (1968) 'Lehr-, Lern- und Arbeitsmittel', in Grothoff and Stallmann (eds) *Pädagogisches Lexikon*, Stuttgart: Kreuz-Verlag, p. 567.
Gabele, P. (1968) *Arbeitsmittel und Lehrprogramme*, Stuttgart: Klett.
Gallus, L. (1971) 'Computerunterstützte Übungs- und Prüfungssysteme', in *IBM-Nachrichten*, vols. 202–5, Sindelfingen: IBM, pp. 29–35.
Gaudig, H. (1929) *Freie geistige Schularbeit in Theorie und Praxis*, Breslau: Hirt.
Glaser, R. (1969) 'The Design and Programming of Instruction', in *The Schools and the Challenge of Innovation*, CED Supplementary Paper 28, New York: Committee of Economic Development, pp. 156–215.
Graff, K. (1964) 'Briefwechsel und soziale Distanz', in *Epistolodidaktika*, 1 (1): 30–5.
Gross, M., Allinger, U., Busch, H. G. and Rütter, T. (1971) 'Computerunterstützte Prüfungen beim Fernstudium im Medienverbund', in *IBM-Nachrichten*, Sonderdruck, vols. 202–5, Sindelfingen: IBM, pp. 22–8.
Heimann, P. (1965) 'Überlegungen zu einem deutschen Bildungs- und Schulfernsehen', in *Jugend, Film, Fernsehen*, 1 (1): 12–24.
Heimann, P. and Schultz, W. (1967) 'Zur Bildungsrelevanz des Fernsehens', in Müller, G. (ed.) *Schul- und Studienfernsehen*, Weinheim: Beltz.
Heinrichs, H. (1971) 'Schulfernsehen', in H. Heinrichs (ed.) *Lexikon der audio-visuellen Bildungsmittel*, Munich: Kösel, pp. 256–60.
Henningsen, J. (1969) 'Zur Geschichte des Fernstudiums', in E. Prokop and G. M. Rückriem (eds) *Erwachsenenbildung, Grundlagen und Modelle*, Weinheim: Beltz, pp. 167–83.
—— (1970) 'Lehrbuch', in W. Horney, J. P. Ruppert and W. Schultze (eds) *Pädagogisches Lexikon*, Gütersloh: Bertelsmann, pp. 182–4.
Huber, F. (1965) *Allgemeine Unterrichtslehre*, Heilbronn: Klinkhardt.
Husén, T. (1971) 'Können Hilfsmittel den Lehrer ersetzen?' in A. Schuller (ed.) *Lehrerrolle im Wandel*, Weinheim: Beltz, pp. 186–7.
Jenkins, J. (1971) 'Die Innovationspraxis in der Miami Springs Senior High School', in A. Schuller (ed.) *Lehrerrolle im Wandel*, Weinheim: Beltz, pp. 61–2.
Kempfer, H. (1965) *Programmed Instruction in Correspondence Education, Symposium on Programmed Instruction in Correspondence Courses*, Annual Convention of the National Society for Programmed Instruction, Philadelphia, 7 May.
Klotz, G. R. (1970) 'Computer-unterstützter Unterricht', in *Lexikon der Pädagogik*, Freiburg: Herder, I, pp. 256–7.
Koszyk, K. and Pruys, K. H. (1969) *Wörterbuch zur Publizistik*, Munich: dtv.
Larsson, H. (1965) 'Programmed instruction in correspondence study', in *CEC (European Council for Education by Correspondence) Congress*, Malmö, Yearbook, pp. 64–9.

Lewis, D. G. (1968) 'Centralized computer systems', in Aerospace Education Foundation (ed.) *Technology and Innovation in Education*, Washington, DC: Praeger, pp. 78–84.
Lindner, J. (1947) 'Einleitung zur grossen Unterrichtslehre von J. A. Comenius', in J. A. Comenius, *Grosse Unterrichtslehre*, Berlin: Volk & Wissen.
Lortz, J. and Iserloh, E. (1969) *Kleine Reformationsgeschichte*, Freiburg: Herder.
Marklund, S. (1971) 'Das IMU-Projekt: Ein System für den individualisierten Mathematikunterricht', in A. Schuller (ed.) *Lehrerrolle im Wandel*, Weinheim: Beltz, pp. 63–7.
Michael, B. (1963) *Selbstbildung im Schulunterricht*, Weinheim: Beltz.
Morrison, H. C. (1931) *The Practice of Teaching in the Secondary School*, Chicago: University of Chicago Press.
Multi Media Systems (1970) *Internationales Kompendium. Analyse von 11 Projekten kombinierter Unterrichtssysteme aus 8 Ländern*, Internationales Zentralinstitut für das Jugend- und Bildungsfernsehen (ed.), Munich: IZJB.
Parkhurst, H. (1922) *Education on the Dalton Plan*, London: Bell & Sons.
Peters, O. (1968) *Das Hochschulfernstudium*, Weinheim: Beltz.
Reble, A. (1968) 'Geschichte der Pädagogik', in *Pädagogisches Lexikon*, Stuttgart: Kreuz.
Röhrs, H. (1969) *Allgemeine Erziehungswissenschaft*, Weinheim: Beltz.
Saettler, P. (1968) *A History of Instructional Technology*, New York: McGraw-Hill.
Scheibner, O. (1955) 'Der Arbeitsvorgang', in *Die Arbeitsschule in Idee und Gestaltung*, Heidelberg: Quelle & Meyer.
Schmidt-Sommer, J. and Peters, O. (1971) 'Zur Tonbandkorrespondenz beim Fernstudium im Medienverbund', in G. Dohmen and O. Peters (eds) *Hochschulunterricht im Medienverbund*, Heidelberg: Verlagsgemeinschaft VRMV, part 2, pp. 68–72.
Schwager, K-H. (1958) *Wesen und Formen des Lehrgangs im Schulunterricht*, Weinheim: Beltz.
Simmel, O. and Stählin, R. (1957) *Christliche Religion*, Frankfurt on Main: Fischer.
Sjogren, D. P. (1964) *Programmed Materials in High School Correspondence Courses*, Cooperative Research Program of the US Office of Education, Lincoln, Nebr: University of Nebraska.
Sommer, K-H. (1965) *Der Fernunterricht. Seine Wirklichkeit und Problematik unter besonderer Berücksichtigung des berufsbezogenen 'Briefunterrichts' in der Bundesrepublik Deutschland*, Cologne: Institut für Berufserziehung im Handwerk.
Stöcker, K. (1966) *Neuzeitliche Unterrichtsgestaltung*, Munich: Ehrenwirt.
Stolurow, L. M. (1969) 'Computer-assisted instruction', in Committee for Economic Development (ed.) *The Schools and the Challenge of Innovation*, New York: CED, pp. 270–319.
Stone, J. C. (1968) 'The information sciences requirement', in Aerospace Education Foundation (ed.) *Technology and Innovation in Education*, Washington, DC: Praeger, pp. 85–90.
Swanson, C. E. (1954) 'Procedures and effects of the printed media', in N. B. Henry (ed.) *Man, Media and Education: the Fifty-Third Yearbook of*

the *National Society for the Study of Education*, Part II, Chicago: University of Chicago Press, pp. 129–91.

Washburne, C. W. and Marland, S. P. (1963) *Winetka: The History and Significance of an Educational Experiment*, Englewood Cliffs, NJ: Prentice-Hall.

Weber, M. (1911) 'Zur Soziologie des Zeitungswesens', in *Verhandlungen des ersten deutschen Soziologentages in Frankfurt 1910*, Tübingen: Mohr, p. 42.

Wedemeyer, C. and Childs, G. (1981) *New Perspectives of University Correspondence Study*, Chicago: Center for the Study of Liberal Arts.

Weisgerber, L. (1961) *Der Buchstabe und der Geist*, Mannheim: Dudenverlag.

Weltner, K. (1972) *Bildungstechnologie in der BRD im öffentlichen Bereich*, paper presented to the 10th Symposium of the Programmed Learning Association, Berlin, April 4.

Wenke, H. (1964) 'Der Fernunterricht – kritisch beleuchtet', in *Epistolodidaktika*, 1 (2): 57–60.

Willmann, O. (1957) *Didaktik als Bildungslehre*, Freiburg: Herder.

Zeeden, E. W. (1967) *Das Zeitalter der Gegenreformation*, Freiburg: Herder.

5 Distance education and industrial production: a comparative interpretation in outline (1967)

Peters' first theoretical analysis of distance education was published as a 45-page monograph in 1967 entitled *Das Fernstudium an Universitäten und Hochschulen: didaktische Struktur und vergleichende Interpretation: ein Beitrag zur Theorie der Fernlehre* (Distance education at universities and higher education institutions: didactical structure and comparative analysis – a contribution to the theory of distance teaching). The second half of this monograph is translated here and is also to be found in D. Sewart, D. Keegan and B. Holmberg (eds) (1983) *Distance Education: International Perspectives*, London and New York: Croom Helm/Routledge, pp. 95–113.

The more one attempts to grasp and explain the phenomenon of distance teaching, and especially the more one tries to identify the particular educational opportunities distinguishing this form of teaching from other forms of imparting academic knowledge, the clearer it becomes that the conventional range of educational terminology is not sufficiently comprehensive. Distance study represents facts new to education in several aspects. Compared with other forms of study it was novel in the form in which it made its first breakthrough over ninety years ago. With even greater justification it can be called novel in its present form in which it is currently spreading throughout the world, contributing towards the discovery of the educational opportunities provided by the modern media, such as radio and television. It is, above all, novel and pointing towards the future when it makes use of electronic data-processing equipment and wide-band cable transmission techniques. It is no coincidence that university study at a distance, in its early form of correspondence teaching, began its development only about 130 years ago, as it requires conditions that only existed from then on.

One necessity, for example, is a relatively fast and regular postal and transport service. The first railway lines and the first correspondence schools were established around the same time. When one further realizes how much technical support distance teaching establishments need nowadays in order to cater effectively for large groups of students, it becomes clear that distance study is a form of study complementary to our industrial and technological age. Lectures, seminars and practice sessions, on the other hand, have developed from forms of teaching derived from ancient rhetoric and were practised at medieval universities; the colloquium originates from the dialogic teaching methods of the humanistic era (Hausmann 1959:153). These forms of teaching have changed little in their basic structure since the beginning of the nineteenth century. They proved almost completely resistant to combination with technical support facilities. In this context they can therefore be described as pre-industrial forms of study.

On account of these differences, distance study can only be described and analysed to a limited extent using traditional educational terms. They are not wholly adequate for this new form of study. This is understandable in so far as these terms developed from pre-industrial forms of teaching. If one applies them to distance study one will think in conventional concepts. To emphasize the point, one looks at a new form of study from an old perspective and has one's view of the essential structural characteristics distorted.

Industrialization is the symbol of a new epoch in the development of man fundamentally different from all previous epochs. It is without example in history, above all, on account of the basic changes in most spheres of human existence. Academic teaching alone seems to have remained largely unscathed by industrialization – with the exception of distance study, for this form of study is remarkably consistent with the principles and tendencies of industrialization. For this reason, experimentally, structural elements, concepts and principles derived from the theories of industrial production are used here to interpret the distance study phenomenon. This does not mean that the teaching and learning processes occurring in distance study are equated with processes in industrial production. The comparison is purely heuristic.

A comparison of this kind between a form of teaching and processes from another sphere of life is legitimate and not without example in the history of educational theory. Amos Comenius, the 'founder and virtuoso of the method of parallel comparison' (Hausmann 1959: 68) in his *Didactica Magna*, for example, com-

Distance education and industrial production 109

pared the 'art of teaching' in unusual detail with the art of printing, also a technical process. Theodor Litt identified the nature of pedagogic thinking by comparing it with artistic creativity, technology and the processes of growth (Litt 1958: 83). In the sixties, experiments were carried out which tried to explain the teaching and learning processes using the technical model of the feedback control system, in order to find approaches to a 'cybernetic pedagogy' (Frank 1965). Most impressive, however, was the achievement of Gottfried Hausmann who, in 1959, condensed the analogy between the dramatic arts and education into a 'dramaturgy of teaching'. In it he interprets the educational structure of teaching and learning processes in detail using the terms and principles of the dramatic art in the theatre. Paul Heimann saw the merit of this comprehensive and detailed comparison in the possibility that 'it might give rise to a complete revision of our teaching and learning models' (Heimann 1962: 421).

Furthermore, it may not be without significance for this planned interpretation that for another important aspect of university or college work, namely research, comparisons with the production process already exist. In 1919, Max Weber defined structural similarities between research institutes and capitalistic organizations (Weber 1951: 566) and, in 1924, Helmut Plessner pointed out that the 'mechanization, methodization and depersonalization of the manufacturing process equally dominate the production of economic as well as cultural goods' (Plessner 1924: 407). The following comparison between distance study and the industrial production process will prove similar consistencies.

From the start, distance study has a special relationship with the industrial production process in so far as the production of study materials in itself is an industrial process built into the whole teaching process as a constituent part, quite unlike the production of textbooks, for example. In the case of commercial distance teaching establishments the further question of selling the printed or otherwise duplicated study units adds calculations of applied economics to the teaching process. Even the distance teaching departments of government-financed universities are not entirely free from these considerations. It would be interesting to examine how far these facts have already influenced the structure of distance teaching.

In order to facilitate the discovery of further relationships between distance teaching and the production process, the following structural changes – essentially brought about by industrialization – in the development of the production of goods should be noted:

Analysis

1 According to the principle of rationalization, individual work as was traditional in the craftsmen's trades changes at an early stage to a production based on the division of labour (e.g., in factories), and this later leads to the development of assembly lines and mass production.
2 Work processes initially characterized by the use of tools are increasingly restructured by mechanization and, later, automation.
3 In detail, these changes lead to the following results:
- The preparatory phase becomes increasingly important.
- Success depends, among other things, on systematic planning and organization. Scientific measures of control are needed.
- Work processes must be formalized and products standardized.
- The production process is objectified.
- Each developmental step towards increased mechanization leads to changes in the function of those involved in the production process.
- Small concerns are no longer able to raise the investment needed for developmental work and technical equipment. A strong tendency towards concentration and centralization becomes noticeable.

The terms used in business studies to describe these facts will be outlined briefly and – where possible – applied to distance teaching.

RATIONALIZATION

By rationalization we mean all 'methodical' (that is, rationally guided) 'measures' with the purpose of achieving 'output with a comparatively (compared to earlier situations) lower input of power, time and money'. Scientific discoveries should 'be evaluated for practical use in such a way as to achieve the best possible results in view of the continually necessary development and redevelopment of economic and technical processes' (Seischab and Schwantag 1960: col. 4530).

Applied to the practical example of the production process this means that 'the entire production line, from raw material to end product, is carefully analysed to allow each single work process to be planned so as to make the most effective contribution possible towards achieving clearly formulated business tasks (Buckingham 1963: 24).

Georges Friedmann emphasizes that this is a dynamic process aiming at continuous improvement in quality through 'continuous progress in the study of materials, accuracy and precision' (Friedmann 1952: 203). Rationalization of this type has only started to develop with increasing industrialization at the end of the nineteenth century (Seischab and Schwantag 1960: col. 4531).

Management science holds that the reason for the considerable obstacles to rationalization lies in human nature itself, because 'human inadequacy inhibits the motivation to gain unprejudiced views and the willingness to act according to rational convictions' (Seischab and Schwantag 1960: col. 4530). Further obstacles are considered to be tradition, convention, habits and fashion.

In education, a rationalizing way of thinking is nothing new. In a general form, it influences the reasoning for numerous educational decisions. For example, the introduction of lectures to larger groups of students, the use of printed books and the specialization of university lecturers were considerable steps towards the rationalization of the academic teaching process. Every university teacher will, when planning a lecture, choose those subjects that will best help him or her to fulfil the purpose of that particular lecture. In distance teaching, however, ways of thinking, attitudes and procedures can be found which only established themselves in the wake of an increased rationalization in the industrialization of production processes. The characteristic details are, among others, as follows:

1 In distance study the teaching process is based on the division of labour and detached from the person of the university lecturer. It is therefore independent from a subjectively determined teaching situation, thus eliminating part of the earlier mentioned obstacles to rationalization. The division of labour and the objectification of the teaching process allow each work process to be planned in such a way that clearly formulated teaching objectives are achieved in the most effective manner. Specialists may be responsible for a limited area in each phase.
2 The use of technical equipment (duplicating machines, organization systems, transporting devices) makes it possible to convey the knowledge, ability and teaching skills of a university lecturer, by means of the detached objectivity of a distance study course of constant quality, to a theoretically unlimited number of students. The rationalization effect of mass production becomes apparent here.
3 The rigorous application of organizational principles and means saves teachers as well as students unnecessary effort.
4 At some of the newer distance teaching establishments, modern

means of technical support, such as film, television and electronic data-processing installations, have replaced teaching staff in certain areas of their work, in particular, in the fields of giving information and assessing performance.
5 Students work through a course which has been tested prior to going to print. This prevents misunderstandings and stops students from going in the wrong direction.
6 The quality of a distance study course can be improved, because its effectiveness can be monitored at any time by scientific methods.

If the number of students required in a society outgrows the number of university teachers available, rational thinking should be able to find ways and means of changing teaching methods in such a way that the teaching resources of the university teachers available are used to the best effect, quantitatively as well as qualitatively. Distance study can be regarded as a result of such endeavours.

THE DIVISION OF LABOUR

The division of labour has played an important role in the sociological theories of the last 100 years (Durkheim: 1986; Schmoller: 1985). Applied to the production process it means that the work is split in the sense of 'dividing one complete work process into a number of elementary procedures' (König 1958: 27), as described by Adam Smith at an early stage (Smith 1776). With an extensive division of labour 'training periods become shorter, more people are able to carry out the work and wages can be lowered (König 1958: 27).

A result of the advanced division of labour is increased specialization. The following statement, by Adam Smith in 1776, applies to everyone involved in a production process where a division of labour exists:

> Men are much more likely to discover easier and readier methods of attaining any object, when the whole attention of their minds is directed towards that single object than when it is dissipated among a great variety of things. It is naturally to be expected therefore that some one or other of those who are employed in each particular branch of labour should soon find out easier and readier methods of performing their own particular work, whenever the nature of it admits of such improvement (Smith 1963: 110).

Just as the division of labour is a precondition for the mechanization of work processes and for industrialization as a whole, it has made university study at a distance possible. The division of labour is the main prerequisite for the advantages of this new form of teaching to become effective. The principle of the division of labour is thus a constituent element of distance teaching.

The 'complete work process', which is split in distance teaching, consists of the teaching activity of the university lecturer: namely, the entirety of the measures he takes in order to initiate and guide learning processes in students. Initially, the two basic functions of the university teacher, that of conveying information and that of counselling, were allocated as separate responsibilities in distance teaching departments of universities or colleges. Both functions, above all however that of transmitting information, are now even further divided. If, for example, the number of students enrolled on a distance study course is high, regular assessment of performance is not carried out by those academics who developed the course. The recording of results is the responsibility of yet another unit; and the development of the course itself is divided into numerous phases, in each of which experts in particular fields are active.

This specialization may bring the following advantages:

- Materials required for the development of the distance study course can be assembled by leading experts in the specialist fields concerned.
- Having completed the manuscript, the author can then be freed from the time-consuming processes of exact source references and of lecturing.
- Educationists and experienced practitioners of distance teaching are able to revise the manuscripts of study units in order to make the planned teaching process more effective.
- Colleagues from the 'academic middle tier' may be involved in the correction of exercises carried out by students. There are cases where even senior students have taken over such tasks, especially where they are concentrating on marking the exercises from a limited number of correspondence units. As in the industrial manufacturing process, the level of previous training may be lower on account of the division of labour and, as there, 'more people are able to carry out the work'. Since with extensive specialization of this type the number of scripts one university teacher is able to mark may be much higher, this process is also cheaper.

MECHANIZATION

Mechanization means the use of machines in a work process (Buckingham 1963: 17). These machines replace the work done by the muscles of men or animals. In part they even take over elements of brain work. There are varying degrees of mechanization. The pre-industrial stage is characterized mainly by craftwork making use of tools. The first level of industrialization was reached with the use of 'dependent machines'. The second level of industrialization led to mass production as a result of the use of 'semi-independent machines' and assembly lines. Finally, the third level of industrialization is characterized by the spread of automation (with automatic control or feedback). The changes occurring at each level are so great that, in this context, one author has spoken about a first, second and third technical or industrial revolution (Buckingham 1963: 17).

In order to stay with this analogy, distance study could be ascribed to the industrial levels, as it cannot take place without the use of machines. Duplicating machines and transport systems are prerequisites, and later forms of distance teaching have the additional facilities of modern means of communication and electronic data-processing installations.

In contrast, when considering the framework of conventional study, one cannot help thinking that its forms of teaching belong to the pre-industrial level. There the university teacher is comparable to a craftsman as he uses 'tools' (pictures, objects, books), without these changing the structure of the teaching process to any considerable degree.

ASSEMBLY LINE

Buckingham referred to the importance of the assembly-line principle in connection with the use of machines. Both these factors, among others, had made mass production possible (Buckingham 1963: 20). Assembly-line work is characterized by the fact that the worker remains at his place of work whilst the workpieces travel past him.

The formal similarity between distance teaching and the production process becomes particularly noticeable here. In the development of the distance study course the manuscript is passed from one area of responsibility to another and specific changes are made at each stage. The study units are printed on a large scale, stored, sent to the distance learner, who completes them, sent to the script marker who checks the work, and finally submitted to the administration, where the performance of the distance learner and the effort of the script marker (to calculate fees) are recorded. The rationalization effect achieved by the fact that many university teachers and thousands of students do not have to meet in one place in order to participate in teaching events is at least the same as that which a car manufacturer tries to achieve when, instead of sending the worker to the vehicle to be built, he transports the necessary parts to the worker. In both cases – the production process as well as distance teaching – time, energy and money are saved.

MASS PRODUCTION

In modern sociology the term 'mass trend' has rid itself of its negative cultural connotation, making it a largely neutral expression (König 1958: 171). Mass trend nowadays merely denotes a structural characteristic of an advanced industrial society and indicates 'that in a pure consumer society such as ours, the rise in the standard of living is due purely to the fact that industry produces certain consumer goods and commodities in large quantities, thus making them generally accessible' (König 1958: 171).

Mass production is by its nature only possible where there is a sufficiently large 'mass of consumers'. This, in turn, requires an efficient transport system providing a connection between producer and consumer who, as is typical in today's system, are geographically distant. In order to work profitably, producers need to research consumer requirements and find standards acceptable to all consumers for their products. They must continually improve their goods (aim at perfection), as each shortcoming is multiplied by the number of items produced.

If one equally rids the term 'consumer' of its negative cultural connotation, one can speak of the student as a 'consumer of academic education'. Quite obviously, 'demand' outstrips 'supply' at universities and colleges, and this had led to the large-scale operation at our universities and colleges. As traditional forms of academic teaching originally envisaged small groups of students, and today's practice of applying methods designed for small groups to large groups must be seen as a perversion of an educational concept (for example, lecture rooms with loudspeaker connection), one can understand it if various governments see distance teaching, on account of its similarity with the mass-production process, as a means of providing very large groups of students more adequately with academic teaching than conventional methods would allow.

Indeed, the multiplication effect achieved by technology and the postal delivery system means that the university teacher and the distance learner – like producer and consumer – no longer need to live in the same geographical location.

From an economic point of view, the production of distance study courses represents mass production. Apart from reasons of profitability, the large number of courses produced forces distance teaching organizations to analyse the requirements of potential distance learners far more carefully than in conventional teaching and to improve the quality of the courses. For example, in the USSR the Public Accounts Authority complained at one time that too many students dropped out of distance study, and it is suspected that this might have been the reason that led to an examination of the study materials. Most American distance study courses are revised and reissued at regular intervals (every one to four years). As American universities charge fees to cover the greatest part of the budget allocated to distance teaching departments, the quality of distance study courses must not be allowed to deteriorate. When, on account of mass production, the University of California has more distance study courses to offer than there is demand for them, it occasionally places advertisements for students in newspapers.

Statistics prove that the number of graduates in areas without a university is lower than in areas near universities. It is possible that, according to the principle of mass production, distance teaching will one day equalize the opportunities to study, just as industrial mass production has assimilated consumer patterns in town and country. Analogous to the increase in the standard of living, this would make a general increase in the level of education possible, which might not otherwise have been achieved.

PREPARATORY WORK

In a production situation where a division of labour prevails, economy, quality and speed of the work processes depend on the right type of preparation. This is necessary in industries producing a variety of articles and needs to be carried out by senior specialist staff in special departments (thinking departments), as workers, foremen and masters involved in the production process lack the necessary knowledge and experience. During the preparatory stages one determines how workers, machines and materials can usefully relate to one another during each phase of the production process. In addition, there are developmental and constructional tasks. The more thorough the preparation, the less is a successful production process dependent on the particular abilities of the workers involved. Consequently, workers can easily be exchanged. Normally, considerably larger sums of investment are required for preparatory work than was the case previously in the manufacture of goods.

As distance teaching institutions have to develop a great variety of distance teaching courses, the comparison with a firm producing a variety of goods comes to mind. In distance teaching too success depends decisively on a 'preparatory phase'. It concerns the development of the distance study course involving experts in the various specialist fields with qualifications also often higher than those of other teachers involved in distance study. Here, too, each section of the course can be carefully planned. The use of technical support and a suitable combination of this with individual contributions from distance tutors and advisers play an important role here. Compared to university teachers in conventional study, who are responsible for the entire teaching process, distance tutors and advisers are more easily exchangeable on account of the thorough preparatory work. Finally, the development of distance study courses also requires investment to an extent that has never before been considered at establishments of higher education.

The separation of preparatory work and individual instruction and the distribution of these functions among several persons is a particularly clear example of analogy with the production process.

PLANNING

An essential element of preparation is planning, which needs to be far more comprehensive and detailed in the industrial manufacturing process than in manual production, as it requires the coordination of many interacting factors. By planning we mean that 'system of decisions which determines an operation prior to it being carried out' (Seischab and Schwantag 1960: col. 4341). In more detail this means that 'all measures necessary for the economical execution of an order – from placement to delivery – must be introduced according to plan' (Seischab and Schwantag 1960: col. 1742).

Management science distinguishes two methods of planning. Effective planning consists of choosing the most advantageous of several alternatives and forecasting the future development of data.

Contingency planning is applied where market situations suddenly change (Seischab and Schwantag 1960: col. 4348).

In the developmental phase of a distance study course planning plays an important role, as the contents of correspondence units, from the first to the last, must be determined in detail, adjusted in relation to each other and represented in a predetermined number of correspondence units. Where distance study is supplemented by residential weeks on campus or weekend seminars, planning becomes even more important; these supplementary teaching events are not intended to repeat academic contents already offered, nor have an 'enrichment' function, but should be structurally integrated in the distance study course. When combining distance teaching with other media, one has to consider carefully which type of contents suits what medium. Finally, where computers are used in distance study, preparatory planning is most advanced and demands by far the greatest expenditure, as the teaching activity of the computers needs to be programmed.

In all these efforts to predetermine and arrange the course of teaching processes as far as possible, we are dealing with effective planning. Intervention by advisers and tutors during the course of distance study, however, is regarded as contingency planning, which supplements effective planning.

ORGANIZATION

Planning largely concerns itself with the organization of the production cycle. In organizational management terms, organization means 'creating general or permanent arrangements for purpose-orientated activity' (Mayntz 1963: 86). As a consequence of the division of labour, the production process has to be rationally ordered according to organizational principles and with specially developed organizational means, since 'the continuous interacting of numerous people towards a specific purpose requires organization' (Mayntz 1963: 7). Furthermore, productivity depends on the type and degree of organization. Distinguished from organization are improvisation (preliminary and provisional regulations) and disposition (special regulations) (Kosiol 1959: 18).

In distance study, likewise, there is an immediate connection between the effectiveness of the teaching method and rational organization. Organization, for example, makes it possible for students to receive exactly predetermined documents at appointed times, for an appropriate university teacher to be immediately available for each assignment sent in, for consultations to take place at fixed locations at fixed times, or for examinations to be held, or for counsellors to inform themselves at any time of the progress of a student or a group of students. Organization becomes easier in large distance teaching establishments, as trained personnel and modern means of organization are available. These enable them to supplement the organization of distance teaching with improvisation and disposition.

The importance of organization in distance teaching can be assessed by the fact that it is often difficult to distinguish between the operational (technical) organization of distance study and the methodical organization of the actual academic contents.

SCIENTIFIC CONTROL METHODS

In recent decades the principles of scientific management have made a gradual breakthrough. According to them work processes are analysed systematically, particularly by time studies, and in accordance with the results obtained from measurements and empirical data the work processes are tested and controlled in their elementary details in a planned way, in order to increase productivity, all the time making the best possible use of working time and the staff available (Seischab and Schwantag 1960: col. 1055). Frederick Winslow Taylor describes this process as the application of scientific engineering techniques to management (McConnel 1966: 268). In distance teaching, similar tendencies can be shown. For example, some distance teaching institutions commission experts to analyse scientifically the success of their courses. Michael Young (1965: 37) outlines the educational function of the research techniques applied by remarking that they replace the eyes and ears of academics in face-to-face teaching: they register students' reaction to the distance study course and aim at improving its effectiveness accordingly. These research techniques are not only used to determine the effectiveness of the course for individual students, but – and this is even more important – its effectiveness for the whole group of students involved. With its efforts to measure the success of a teaching method, distance teaching has doubtless introduced a hitherto neglected aspect into university teaching.

FORMALIZATION

On account of the division of labour and mechanization in the manufacturing process there is a much greater need to predetermine the various phases formally than in manual production. It is only the emphasis on formality which makes the cooperation of all those involved in the production process possible, as each of them has to rely on previous work having been carried out according to plan. Most activities and interactions in an industrial set-up must therefore be determined according to agreed rules (Mayntz 1963: 86).

In distance study, likewise, all the points in the cycle, from student to distance teaching establishment to the academics allocated, must be determined exactly. Communication is standardized by the use of forms. Authors of correspondence units are recommended to consider the incorporation of standard formalized aspects that have proved to be of advantage. Lecturers marking assignments also work to standard guidelines. Assessment is, in parts, largely formalized through the frequent use of multiple choice questions, where the student only has to place a cross against the right answer. In the most modern forms of distance teaching, formalization goes as far as students marking the results of their learning on a punchcard in coded form, and this is then input to a computer.

STANDARDIZATION

It is characteristic of a production situation involving the division of labour and high technology that manufacture is limited to a number of types of one product, in order to make these more suitable for their purpose, cheaper to produce and easier to replace. Georges Friedmann (1952: 394) pointed out that this does not at all represent a threat of dullness and uniformity. On the contrary, the elementary parts produced could be combined in extremely diverse ways.

The application of the principle of the division of labour and the use of machines, as well as the duplication of correspondence units in often large numbers, force distance teaching institutions likewise to adopt a greater degree of standardization than is required in conventional teaching. Not only is the format of the correspondence units standardized, so also is the stationery for written communication between student and lecturer, and the organizational support, as well as each single phase of the teaching process, and even the academic contents.

Whereas the academic giving a conventional lecture may indulge in an interesting deviation, because he sees educational advantages in this at a particular time with a certain group of students, the distance study lecturer has to be aware that he is, when writing a correspondence unit, addressing such a large group of students that situation-dependent improvisation becomes impossible. Instead he has to find a standard adequate, as far as possible, for every student admitted to the distance study course in question. This is achieved by developing a model for the course, perfecting it through the involvement of several experts and then approximating it to the required standard by testing it on a representative group of students before printing large numbers of copies. Just as the production of a branded article can only remain economical if its quality is continuously adapted to the constant needs of a large group of consumers, a distance teaching institution has to standardize the academic contents of its courses in such a way that it can be sure they appeal to all distance learners as equally as possible. The adaptation to any number of students, however large, forces the lecturer more strongly than in conventional study to consider the necessary standard that is, at the same time, realistic for as many students as possible.

Consequently, the choice of contents of a distance study course is less likely to be a reflection of the particular interests of an academic giving conventional lectures, than of the objective requirements of the total course profile.

CHANGE OF FUNCTION

On account of the division of labour and the use of various types of machines, the function of the worker in the production process has changed considerably. Whereas it was typical for the craftsman to plan the production of a piece of work as well as acquire the necessary materials, carry out the work and finally sell the finished piece of work himself, industrialization led to a more marked functional differentiation. When preparatory work and selling became separate from production and, within these three phases, many individual functions were allocated to different individuals, a loss of function naturally occurred for each single worker. On the other hand, new roles were created and new achievements became possible. For example, 'in jobs where, due to mechanization, the processing of the material has been taken out of the worker's hand, speed and energy of execution are no longer required; they have been replaced by accuracy and diligence; the work no longer shows quantitative but qualitative criteria' (Friedmann 1952: 389).

As a result of the division of labour, the function of the lecturer teaching at a distance also changes. The original role of provider of knowledge in the form of the lecturer is split into that of study unit author and that of marker; the role of counsellor is allocated to a particular person or position. Frequently, the original role of lecturer is reduced to that of a consultant whose involvement in distance teaching manifests itself in periodically recurrent contributions. In order to ensure the effectiveness of the four functions mentioned, numerous support functions of an operational-technical type are particularly important, as, without them, distance study could not take place.

As tutors and consultants have largely been relieved of the task of conveying course matter, they are able to devote themselves to a considerable degree to more demanding tasks, such as aiding motivation, providing individual support, structuring course contents for students, identifying problems, establishing connections and so on. Here, too, a loss of function is compensated for by a gain in function whereby, at the same time, an otherwise almost unattainable level of quality can be achieved.

OBJECTIFICATION

The more the production process is determined by machines and organizational principles, the more it loses its subjective element which used to determine craftsmen's work to a considerable degree. Hermann Schmidt (1966: 133) pointed out that this process already started when man began to substitute tools provided by nature, such as hands, fists and teeth, with tools taken from his surroundings. Objectification was not possible until the item to be objectified had become the subject of reflection.

Considering that, since Frederick Winslow Taylor, there has been a changeover to analysing each single phase of the industrial production process with scientific means and to organizing purposefully the contribution of workers and machines accordingly, it becomes clear what a high degree of objectification has been achieved. This development has found a climax in automated production where man's involvement in the course of the production process has largely been eliminated.

In this respect too, the relationship between distance study and conventional study is the same as between industrial production

Distance education and industrial production 123

and mechanical fabrication. The university lecturer who lectures from his chair or leads a seminar discussion has the freedom and the opportunity to allow his subjectivity to influence his way of teaching: he is free to decide how and how much to prepare, he determines his own academic aims and methods and is able to change them spontaneously during a lecture, whereby not all the changes in his teaching method need to be reflected. In distance teaching, however, most teaching functions are objectified as they are determined by the distance study courses as well as technical means. Only in written communications with the distance learner or possibly in a consultation or the brief additional face-to-face events on campus has the teacher some individual scope left for subjectively determined variants in his teaching method. In cases where a computer is used in distance study, even this opportunity is limited further.

The advantages of objectifying the teaching process in the form of a distance study course lie in the fact that the teaching process can then be reproduced, thus making it available at any time and, above all, that it can be manipulated. Without objectification distance study courses could not take place anywhere and at any time and be continuously improved.

The objectification of teaching practice in distance study is of particular importance in societies where, on account of an hierarchic structure of universities and colleges, the function of the provider of knowledge is combined in many academics with that of a holder of very great authority. As a result of this the relationship between student and lecturer is similar to that of subordinate and superior. As distance study has largely been freed from subjectivity, the process of providing knowledge is hardly affected by situations of this kind. In this context, distance study is particularly suitable for the further education of adults.

CONCENTRATION AND CENTRALIZATION

The investment required for mechanized mass production involving the division of labour has led to large industrial concerns with a concentration of capital, a frequently centralized administration, and a market that is not seldom monopolized.

In this context it is significant that some distance teaching establishments cater for very large groups of students. The largest universities teaching at a distance in the USSR and in South Africa have over 40,000 students, and the Open University in England has more than 70,000. Each of these three establishments – as well as their Spanish equivalent – caters for the national demand. Obviously, a minimum number of students is necessary to make the technical installations and the establishment of an efficient organization feasible. Economically, it is therefore more worthwhile to create a large central distance study establishment rather than ten or twenty small regional institutions. Just as the industrial markets for certain products have long expanded beyond narrow regional frontiers, such centralized distance teaching establishments must cross the traditional areas of the responsibility of universities and the educational administration.

If all the said principles of distance teaching are rigorously applied, monopoly-like prestige positions in teaching activity are created for leading experts in various disciplines. Just as no record producer would use a mediocre singer when he can engage a Fischer-Dieskau, a distance teaching institution has to try and gain the best lecturers in their field for the development of its distance study courses. Just as in industry, however, one must ensure that such monopoly-like positions do not hinder free competition.

The possible consequences of a rigorous concentration and centralization of distance teaching were hinted at, for the first time in 1966, in a memorandum from the British government concerning the then proposed University of the Air (British Government 1966). In future, universities would no longer pursue the same objectives in all subjects, but specialize in some disciplines and cater for the national requirements for distance study in these.

SUMMARY

From the above comparisons the following conclusions in relation to distance teaching may be drawn:

1 The structure of distance teaching is determined to a considerable degree by the principles of industrialization, in particular by those of rationalization, division of labour and mass production.
2 The teaching process is gradually restructured through increasing mechanization and automation.
3 These changes are the reason for the following structural characteristics to have emerged:
    - the development of distance study courses is just as important as the preparatory work taking place prior to the production process;

- the effectiveness of the teaching process is particularly dependent on planning and organization;
- courses must be formalized and expectations from students standardized;
- the teaching process is largely objectified;
- the function of academics teaching at a distance has changed considerably *vis-à-vis* university teachers in conventional teaching;
- distance study can only be economical with a concentration of the available resources and a centralized administration.

The result of this comparative interpretation permits the addition to recent explanations of distance study based on traditional educational concepts of a definition which is apt to point to the specific characteristics of the new forms of teaching and learning, thus structurally separating them from conventional forms of teaching and learning. This definition is as follows:

Distance study is a rationalized method – involving the division of labour – of providing knowledge which, as a result of applying the principles of industrial organization as well as the extensive use of technology, thus facilitating the reproduction of objective teaching activity in any numbers, allows a large number of students to participate in university study simultaneously, regardless of their place of residence and occupation.

This definition shows that, within the complex overall distance teaching activity, one area has been exposed to investigation which had regularly been omitted from traditional didactic analyses. Contrary to other attempts at definitions, new concepts are used here to describe new facts.

It was not a purpose of this comparative interpretation to pass judgements on the industrial structures which have been shown to apply to distance teaching. Presumably, the striking advantages of these structures, from a point of view of educational policy and organization, are also connected with important educational disadvantages. This question has yet to be discussed. In this context it will merely be hinted that it must be disadvantageous to a society if the developments outlined here have not been, or have not been fully, recognized, or are even denied. Such deep structural changes in academic teaching merit everyone's attention, no matter what hopes or fears are connected with them. If society's awareness lags behind the speedily developing technological and industrial opportunities, this is bound to lead to painful malfunctions, even in the area of academic teaching. They can be detected and remedied more easily, when the industrial structures characteristic of distance teaching are recognized and taken account of when the appropriate educational decisions are taken.

REFERENCES

British Government (1966) *A University of the Air*. Presented to Parliament by the Secretary of State for Education and Science by command of Her Majesty. London: Her Majesty's Stationery Office.

Buckingham, W. (1963) *Automation und Gesellschaft*, Frankfurt on Main: Fischer.

Durkheim, E. (1986) *De la division du travail social*, Paris: Quadrige PUF.

Frank, H. (1965) *Kybernetische Grundlagen des Lernens und Lehrens*, Stuttgart: Klett.

Friedmann, G. (1952) *Der Mensch in der mechanisierten Produktion*, Köln: Bund-Verlag.

Hausmann, G. (1959) *Didaktik als Dramaturgie des Unterrichts*, Heidelberg: Quelle & Meyer.

Heimann, P. (1962) 'Didaktik als Theorie und Lehre' in *Die deutsche Schule*, 54 (9): 407–27.

König, R. (1958) *Soziologie*, Frankfurt on Main: Fischer.

Kosiol, E. (1959) 'Grundlagen und Methoden der Organisationsforschung', quoted from R. Mayntz (1963) *Soziologie der Organisation*, Reinbek: Rowohlt, p. 86.

Litt, T. (1958) *Führen und Wachsenlassen. Das Wesen des pädagogischen Denkens*, Stuttgart: Klett.

McConnel, J. W. (1966) 'Scientific management', in H. F. Pratt Fairchild, *Dictionary of Sociology and Related Sciences*, Totowa, NJ: Littlefield-Adams, p. 268.

Mayntz, R. (1963) *Soziologie der Organisation*, Reinbek: Rowohlt.

Plessner, H. (1924) 'Zur Soziologie der modernen Forschung und ihrer Organisation in der deutschen Universität', in M. Scheler (ed.) *Versuche zu einer Soziologie des Wissens*, Munich, pp. 407–24; quoted from H. Schelsky (1963) *Einsamkeit und Freiheit*, Reinbek: Rowohlt, p. 192.

Schmidt, H. (1966) 'Objektivierung', in L. Englert *et al* (eds) *Lexikon der kybernetischen Pädagogik und der Programmierten Instruktion*, Quickborn: Schnelle.

Schmoller, G. von (1985) 'Das Wesen der Arbeitsteilung und der sozialen Klassenbildung', in W. Fielder and R. Karl (eds) *Gustav Schmoller, Kleine Schriften zur Wirtschaftsgeschichte, Wirtschaftstheorie und Wirtschaftspolitik*, Leipzig: Zentralantiquariat der DDR, pp. 199–226.

Seischab, H. and Schwantag, K. (eds) (1960) *Handwörterbuch der Betriebswirtschaft*, Stuttgart: Poeschel.

Smith, A. (1776) *An Inquiry into the Nature and Causes of the Wealth of Nations*, London.

——(1963) 'The division of labour', in A. D. Lewis (ed.) *Of Men and Machines*, New York: Dutton, pp. 110–13.

Weber, M. (1951) 'Wissenschaft als Beruf', in *Gesammelte Aufsätze zur Wissenschaftslehre*, Tübingen, pp. 566–97; quoted from H. Schelsky (1963) *Einsamkeit und Freiheit*, Reinbek: Rowohlt, p. 192.

Young, M. (1965) 'Towards an Open University', in *The Home Study Journal*, 6(1): 3–10, 30–8.

6 Distance education: a historical, sociological and anthropological interpretation (1973)

The 1973 book has five different approaches to the analysis of distance education: (1) didactic analysis, (2) didactic structure, (3) comparative analysis, (4) relationship to educational technology, and (5) historical, sociological and anthropological dimensions. The sections on didactic structure – taken from the Heimann-Schultz Berlin (Hamburg) School of Didactics – and on educational technology are not reproduced here. Chapters 4 and 5 of this book give the didactic and comparative analyses and this chapter (pages 258 to 308 in the original) translates the final section on distance edcuation as a historical and sociological phenomenon.

The description of distance education as a form of industrialized education will, among other things, be criticized as public opinion is still influenced by anti-technical, or more generally, anti-industrial emotions which emerged in the context of the critique of our modern culture. Herder, Goethe, Schiller, Hölderlin, and above all Humboldt had already set the tone of this critical movement, as Theodor Litt (1959) has shown. These authors deplored the dismembering of man, his alienation from nature, his self-destruction, his radical isolation and his atrophy – all these being the consequences of the industrialization of society. 'The gospel of humanity cannot be separated from the critique of modern culture,' summarized Litt (1959: 39). In the second part of the nineteenth century critics of culture such as Ruskin, Hildebrandt, Nietzsche and Langbehn opposed industrialization, arguing mainly that it mechanizes and functionalizes man.

Hans Scheuerl (1970: 134) has described the damage done to man by industrialization as set forth by critics of culture. According to these critics there is a fear that 'original individuality will decline in a mass culture' and will be standardized to mere functional

A cross-disciplinary interpretation 129

efficiency, that 'the imitation, the mass production will make the deeper layers of soul waste away', that stressing external values will result in the loss of interior values, that a materialistic attitude towards life will alienate man from spiritual contents and their requirements. Altogether, these critics believed that 'the originally wholesome nature' of man is not enriched by the artificiality of civilizatory achievements but 'alienated, endangered and suffocated'.

These attacks of the critics of culture have become especially important as their fundamental attitude was mediated by the youth and school reform movements and had strong effects on the theory and practice of education in the first half of our century. The attitude of several generations of teachers towards technical achievements, the mechanization of instruction, and, therefore, towards distance education as well was influenced by their critique of culture.

In spite of this, the return to the critique of culture in order to find out the reasons for the reservations of present-day educationists to distance education seems to be a little inadequate at first glance. First of all, a critical discussion of distance education has not yet started on a scientific level. And secondly, we have learnt that the opposition towards other forms of industrialized education, such as programmed learning and cybernetic pedagogy, has been less strong than was expected. In the meantime, one is often prepared to view industrialization as an irreversible process. Nevertheless, it must still be supposed that the attitude of former critics of culture was handed down by the movement of neohumanistic education and is still potent in the educational world of today, even if it is mainly found below the level of scientific discussion. This may be the reason for the widespread scepticism, lack of interest and even disdain for distance education. As evidence for this are the critics who readily concede that industrialization is, indeed, an irrevocable development, but at the same time consider it dangerous and disastrous. Judgements of this kind can be heard from modern critics of culture in the conservative camp to the anti-authoritarian and progressive Marxist camp – where they are growing in numbers. A conservative example is Wilhelm Flitner (1967: 327), who thinks that the 'spirit of industrialization' dominates our life. According to him, the more profound authors predict 'not paradise, but hell on earth' as a consequence of an intensified industrialization and rationalization. Progressive Marxist examples are mainly the attacks on the cultural industry by Theodor W. Adorno (1967: 60), on the consciousness industry by Hans Magnus Enzensberger (1963) and Herbert Marcuse's description of the consequences of advanced industrialization on man (1969: 161).

There is no doubt that many of the arguments set forth by critics of culture in three different historical periods apply also to industrialized education. One is, for instance, in line with the critics of culture of the second part of the nineteenth century when saying that the original individuality of the teacher and also of the students cannot express itself and is even lost over long periods of the teaching–learning process because of the use of technical media and of fixed goals and procedures of instruction. Teachers and students do not meet as fully developed individuals, but only as reduced and specialized functionaries. Distance education produces neither funny teaching characters nor notoriously annoying types of students, as is often the case in face-to-face instruction. The systems of distance education are, it is true, 'standardized in order to raise their functionality', and 'production in series', 'mechanization', and 'functionalization' are their important structural traits. Finally, it should be mentioned that the motivation of many distant students derives from a 'materialistic attitude towards life' – that is, that they strive to improve their conditions of life by obtaining higher qualifications. While this attitude may be a general one in our time, it seems, however, to be typical in a special sense for distant students.

When we consider new arguments – for instance, those of Jochen Kaltschmid (1965: 135), who has proved again in a profound analysis that 'the apparatus, the technicalization, mechanization, division of labour and organization' are all elements of the process of rationalization which shape the existence of man, and that the consequences of this rationalization are that our world is 'dominated by purposes', that we lose our 'inwardness', the 'immediacy of life' and the unity of our psychological faculties – then, of course, we have to see that these consequences, indeed, are very likely to be reinforced by industrialized education. In fact, its rationalized systems of teaching and learning are, as we have seen, structured in such a way that the purposes – the defined teaching goals – are achieved in the best way, the 'inwardness' of the students and the teachers, which is normally preserved by their personal interaction, is more or less lost by the objectivation of teaching behaviour, the splitting up of teaching and learning functions, and by the use of technical media. Also, the 'closeness to life' of instruction is, naturally, reduced a great deal. Teachers and students are no longer involved as whole human beings. And the unity of our psychic faculties is broken up.

There are also many current arguments about the incompatibility of technical developments and education which are often emotive and relate to the concept of industrialized education, as this form of education is – as we have shown – a result of the general process of technicalizing of society. Ludwig Heieck (1969: 21) has discussed some of these arguments. According to him, education gives way to the functionalist thinking in terms of expediency in our technical age and abandons man. He says: 'Education derives from history. It is determined by the view that man is a historic being. Technical progress, however, is ahistoric. Instruction and education, therefore, have not participated in technical progress as they have felt threatened by it.' And he concludes: 'If man abandons himself to the world of materialistic objects, if he delivers his humanity to the functionality of set purposes – then he dehumanizes himself.'

If this treatise shows that distance education has developed – so to speak unnoticeably – as industrialized education during the last 120 years, and if, over and above, it is maintained that this model of education will be of great importance for tackling important educational tasks at present and in the future, then it is necessary to comment on the reservations voiced by those critics of culture as they would otherwise underline that such a concept will be questionable, if not dangerous. The problem cannot be solved in the theoretical framework used so far in other chapters of this book. We have to face the same situation which was characterized by Paul Heimann (1961: 6), when he defended his contention that 'film, radio, and television are the powerful educational institutions of the present'. The objections raised to their educational use in the past also apply to distance education, especially when it employs such mass media. According to Heimann, these critics were afraid of 'the furtherance of a receptive learning behaviour, an educational and instructional impressionism, the emergence of a dangerous conformism, the immobilization of creative imagination, the artificial increase of optical and acoustical stimuli, the reduction of primary experiences in favour of secondary experiences, the depersonalization, the mechanization of the relation between teacher and taught, and the levelling out of individual instruction'. Heimann emphasized that these objections must by no means be trivialized, as some of them contain important arguments of educational philosophy. On the other hand, his reflections led to the conclusion that these objections can scarcely be refuted on the level of pure educational thinking. Therefore, he offered arguments dealing with problems of intellectual history and sociology.

132 Analysis

In this chapter a similar avenue is followed in order to invalidate possible objections of cultural critics to distance education or other forms of industrialized education. The discussion will have four different starting points. First, the interpretation of a model of the historical development of instruction is to clarify whether distance education really distinguishes itself structurally to such a great extent from traditional education that the teacher and the students are placed in an entirely new existential situation which is not in line with the general historic trend and which must be considered as a development which fundamentally fails to reach the goal of humanity. Secondly, a number of socio-cultural preconditions of distance education and developments in the history of ideas are dealt with, in order to find out whether the objections of the critics of culture remain feasible. Thirdly, it will be proved by comparing traditional instruction in the classroom with distance education that it integrates into the process of general change of social subsystems and into the present inevitable development of society, whereby many of the norms defended by the critics of culture appear to be unreal. Fourthly, distance education is interpreted in anthropological terms. It is to be expected that dealing with it in such a way will result in further general arguments for judging the objections of the critics of culture.

HISTORICAL INTERPRETATION

If we consider the context of the origin of distance education not in a concrete socio-economic, but in a more general, far-reaching sense, then a new dimension emerges for the understanding of distance education. In order to achieve this it is, however, necessary to describe some structural elements of historical forms of instruction. If we interpret sources of ancient Indian and Egyptian education (Keay 1950; Brunner 1957) their earliest forms can be characterized by the following six aspects:

1 Usually, only a few people belonging to the ruling religious and political class participated (*elitist aspect*).
2 The imparting of knowledge and skills was mostly connected to the performance of priestly functions (*sacral aspect*).
3 The instruction was connected to special forms of the domination of the teacher who exercised his power over the student (*hierarchical aspect*).
4 The instruction took place in small groups (*familial aspect*).

5 No technical media were used (*personal aspect*).
6 The nature of the instruction was determined by an individual teacher, a fixed place, and a fixed time (*aspect of traditional ties*).

If one relates this initial situation of instruction to our distance education today, a historical model of instruction can be constructed which shows that instruction has fundamentally changed in a development of several thousand years. The dimensions of this change can be determined by the following extreme parameters: the elitist instruction becomes egalitarian, its sacral contents and procedures become profane, the government of the teacher is substituted by the self-government of the student, the intimate group becomes a larger and less intimate group or even an anonymous mass of students, the personal interaction between teacher and students becomes mechanized and automated, and the traditional ties of instruction to a special teacher, a special place and a special time are removed.

It is evident that developments have taken place in the dimensions referred to whereby it is not necessary to consider their division into periods or their delays in certain cultural areas. The entire extent of these changes could be demonstrated on a bipolar scale. Distance education would arrive at the extremes in all cases. However, if one also assesses the present instruction in classrooms it becomes apparent that this form of education has not developed accordingly. A closer examination will show that there is a correlation between the different stages of development and the extent to which principles of industrialization have been applied in each case.

1 Analogously to the historical process of the democratization of political power, which passed through several stages, there was also a process of continued democratizing of teaching and learning and of knowledge. One can even – parallel to the political development – distinguish priestly-aristocratic, bourgeois and democratic forms of teaching and learning and of knowledge. Whereas in the beginning of the cultural development only small groups handed down their knowledge, which was often kept secret, to the chosen ones, now a phase is reached in which in many countries of the world knowledge is in principle accessible by everyone, whereby traditional ethnic, religious, social and regional boundaries, which still make education a privilege to many, can be surmounted – due to the availability of industrialized education. The latest and most convincing steps in this direction have been taken by the Open University

in the United Kingdom. But also the extension of the TV-College in Chicago and the plans for a University of the Air in Japan must be mentioned here. Before this, distance education techniques had been used in many universities and technical colleges of the socialist countries in eastern Europe in order to enable workers to raise their qualification by acquiring a higher education while working for a living (Peters 1968: 199–245).

Consequently, in many countries educational politicians consider distance education as a means for equalizing educational opportunities. Such a way of thinking, it is true, overlooks the enormous socio-cultural barriers on the way to education and surely underestimates the real difficulties. Nevertheless, it must be admitted that distance education provides at least necessary technical and organizational preconditions for a universal admission to continued and higher education. An analysis of statistics about distance education reveals that millions of distant students do indeed profit from this industrialized way of education. Often enough it offers them the only way towards the desired education as all other ways are barred by lack of funds or by other circumstances.

Comparison with the conditions under which face-to-face-instruction takes place in the schools of the Federal Republic of Germany as well as in those of other countries can be used to show that we are dealing with school systems organized according to class structures in which access to secondary schools and universities remains restricted, so that people continue to suffer from the inequality of educational opportunities. Ralf Dahrendorf (1965: 87), in his analysis of the society of the Federal Republic of Germany, has called this continued inequality a scandal.

2 The sacral character of instruction can be related to the fact that at the beginning of our cultural development the knowledge and skills which were handed down from one generation to the other were priestly wisdom and ritual ceremonies. Only later were the various scientific disciplines differentiated from the knowledge of the priests. In ancient Babylon the priests were physicians and teachers in one person. The Indian Veda consisted at first of hymns, prayers, wordings and proverbs which were important in sacrificial ceremonies. Only later varying systems of interpretation and research approaches developed out of them and disciplines like law, logic and dogmatics branched off. The Egyptian priest caste also imparted collections of hymns as part of the holy literature. There again, the scientific disciplines could emancipate themselves from

mythical ideas and ritual reinforcements only later. This applied, of course, to the respective instruction as well.

In the beginning, however, the forms of instruction corresponded to sacral contents. Everything we still can learn shows us that the priest-teacher was venerated by the students and that the instruction and examinations were permeated by a ceremonial solemnity. Keay (1950: 40) reports, for instance, how the opening ceremony of the instruction of Brahmins proceeded:

> The student had to grasp with his right hand the left hand of the teacher – leaving, however, his thumb free – and to speak the words: 'Venerable Sir, recite!' In doing this he had to direct his eyes and his mind to the teacher. He must touch his head three times with kusa-grass and hold his breath for the space of fifteen moments. Then he had to sit down on the kusa-grass, the tips of which had to be bent in such a way that they point to the east. Then, five mystical words must be spoken. Another part of the daily ceremony was that the student embraced the feet of the teacher before and after the beginning of the instruction.

These activities were, as Keay explained, considered to be of great importance as they were to impress the students by 'their mysterious holiness'.

It is obvious that most forms of our present instruction have left those sacral origins far behind them, of course. However, on looking more carefully one can see that the process of secularization has not yet ceased everywhere. As distance education is mainly dependent on indirect interaction and communication it has, so to speak, completed its secularization. The interaction between teacher and student is objectified by rational teaching techniques and the use of technical media to such a degree that even relicts of archaic attitudes are no longer possible. In instructional face-to-face situations, however, one can still find them. In fact, rudiments of an originally sacred teaching–learning behaviour can be identified in the following circumstances:

- teachers – be they in the classroom or lecture hall – see themselves as the source of knowledge;
- the teacher dominates the students verbally in such a way that the intended dialogue between the student and the teacher is still a monologue (Tausch 1960), a situation which is structurally similar to that of a priest in the pulpit preaching to the faithful;

- the students rise from their seats when the teacher enters or leaves the classroom;
- there are ceremonial greetings and forms of dismissal;
- the teacher – for example, in English public schools and colleges – still wears a gown which recalls a clergyman's vestments;
- the school continues to stick to certain rituals as, for instance, prayers at the beginning of the school day or hymns and other ceremonies during inauguration and graduation;
- school celebrations assume a special significance in the educational process.

These and other aspects of face-to-face instruction have been handed down by tradition. In distance education, however, this tradition is discontinued because of the technological revolution in the methodology of teaching. The original communicative stance of teachers and students is substituted by a technologically mediated interaction between the two of them. The process of secularization could, therefore, go further than in face-to-face teaching.

3 Under the aspect of hierarchy it can be stated that the structure of all early forms of instruction was characterized by the fact that the teacher assumed the role of the old man, the father, which was connected with wisdom, authority and power. His power derived often from the knowledge of the power bringing formulas and from his knowledge of the tradition (van de Leeuw 1956: 545). But above all, it was derived from the power of God. *Hieros* means 'holy'. Accordingly, a hierarchy was originally a 'holy rule'.

The students, who also waited on their teachers, were expected to respect and venerate them. Brunner (1957: 63) reports on ancient Egyptian education how the power of the teachers resulted in the punishment of the students. The students were subjected to corporal punishment, were put in the stocks, threatened, admonished, but never praised.

In the Middle Ages the status symbol of the teacher was, typically enough, a rod, which he was to hold upright, as may be seen in contemporary pictures (Fuchs 1969: 96, 98). Sometimes, the teacher was supported in his punishing activities by the *locatus*, a school janitor who also carried a rod as a token of his dignity, but – for hierarchical reasons – with the tip facing downwards (Fuchs 1969: 96). Generally, people were of the opinion that, for instance, in the education of artisans as well as of knights, learning and serving went together (Reble 1968: 1087). The master–servant relationship which was constituted during the training ceased only when the apprentice was formally released from this relationship after having qualified as a journeyman.

The development which started off with the student who was ruled and maltreated in the ways described comes to an end with a student who is able to identify his learning needs and who decides himself which learning goals he wishes to reach and in which way (Rademacker 1969: 41) or with the university student who applies the concept of learning by researching (Huber 1970). Both approaches orientate themselves to the model of the self-determined and self-governing student. Both of them advocate domination-free learning.

There are several reasons why distance education has developed structural approaches for forms of learning which are free from teacher dominance and the influence of the teacher's authority and why, hence, distance education would have its place at the end of this dimension:

- The increased availability and accessibility of distance education enables the learner for the first time to check through the learning material of a number of respective courses and make decisions himself when selecting one of them. The necessary qualification for doing so may still be lacking with most learners as, so far, usually other persons have decided what is to be studied and when and where the studying will take place. It can, however, be acquired with the help of systems of distance education and their counselling services.
- Normally, the teacher is not physically present when the student learns. He effects his learning only indirectly. In the same way as in the political sector the personal power of the king was objectified as soon as his personal exercising of power was substituted by the indirect exercising of power with the help of written documents which then led to bureaucracy, the personal interaction between teacher and student became objectified by the written word and the use of other media. Thus a scope of independence and freedom came into being, which, indeed, is used and appreciated by the students.
- The student takes over the control of the time, the frequency and the duration of his learning.
- Very often adults begin to study a course in distance education by their own free decision. In such cases, the relation between the teacher and the student is entirely different from the corresponding relationship in the traditional and institutionalized

schools, where the teacher is usually the representative of the power which makes students attend the school and even controls their learning behaviour and school life.

However, the simple fact that a student learns relatively independently does not allow the conclusion that distance education already gives rise to absolutely dominance-free learning. In particular, if distance education is organized as a part of compulsory general education – as, for instance, in Australia, Canada and the United States, with the military services or in vocational training – repressive effects of those who have the power are not removed, but only distributed in another way and sublimated. Their power cannot be done away with simply by replacing face-to-face instruction by distance education.

In spite of this, it must be stressed that the objectivation of learning processes offers more scope for independent learning than instruction tied to special teachers in special situations. Above all, it enables the critical cooperation of students when instruction is evaluated even if this happens only in a representative form. When, for instance, selected students are members of the course team their influence upon the intended teaching–learning process can be increased. Here, dominance-free learning might, indeed, have more scope for its development in distance edcuation than in face-to-face instruction. At the extreme point of this dimension one can place learners who identify their learning goal themselves, select and handle the respective system of industrialized teaching expertly, and also control the outcomes of their learning themselves.

Obviously, face-to-face instruction is still far from this extreme point, as the learning process is often not only influenced by the teachers' dominance and predilections, as A. and R. Tausch (1965) have shown so impressively in their research on the language behaviour of teachers and students, but also by traditional and institutional constraints. Criteria of repressive teaching behaviour are: corporal punishment of pupils which is still preserved in many primary schools, various forms of disciplinary action at secondary schools, and sending down from universities. In these cases the teaching–learning process is still connected to the process of disciplining the students. The double meaning of 'discipline' is, indeed, telling and applicable even today.

4 The social pattern of instruction was originally modelled after the social interaction in the family. Keay and Brunner agree in that in ancient times instruction began in the family on the basis of the

father–son relationship. In ancient Egypt a teacher and a student were even called father and son (Brunner 1957: 31). If the student belonged to another family, he was, nevertheless, integrated into the teacher's family. Obviously, teaching started in the intimacy of a father–son relationship and in the form of private tuition.

Thinking in ideal types, one can assume that there was an initial period in which private tuition dominated; for instance, when a priest introduced his successor into the procedures of secret sacral ceremonies, or when children of aristocratic families were carefully prepared for their future role in society. Our knowledge from history shows us that the subsequent periods must have been characterized by the following communication structures between teacher and students:

- group instruction;
- classroom instruction;
- large group instruction;
- instruction of mass audience.

It must be added that each period continued to exist and could even assume new importance in later periods. The changes, however, which came to pass when one period replaced the other must have been considerable, and were, obviously, caused by certain societal necessities. Brunner (1957: 14), for instance, reported that in ancient Egypt private tuition changed to classroom instruction as early as the beginning of the second millennium – that is, at a time when a rigid administration was established and a technically and ethically well-educated civil service was highly valued. The ability to rationalize instruction with the help of better organization is obviously a precondition for proceeding from one period to the next one.

If one asks how distance education relates to these periods, and especially distance education in the multimedia form which has developed during the last fifteen years and which has already integrated radio and television, the answer can only be that it belongs to the final period. The extreme of mass education has been reached fully. Some projects of this kind provided tuition for groups counted in tens of thousands and even a hundred thousand students – for instance, the Quadriga-Funkkolleg in the Federal Republic of Germany and the Television Course 'Introduction into Computer Science' in Japan where 700,000 students ordered the accompanying textbooks (Nishimoto 1971: 113). The traditional instruction in the classroom, however, originated at a very early period. It is, strictly speaking, still closely attached to individual instruction, as classroom instruction is basically often still merely an extended and schematized individual instruction – if one disregards the many efforts to change it into group instruction. Educational theorists, who stressed the individuality of the single pupil, Locke, Rousseau, Herbart, Weniger, Bollnow and Buber may have supported this practice. The traditional teaching and learning behaviours are obviously so stable that they resist the use of technical media and the application of principles of industrialization. The communicative structure of traditional instruction in the classroom depends on a limited number of students. Probably 120 students would be the largest possible number in a lecture hall. A radical new approach was needed to overcome this limitation and to make possible the instruction of large and extremely large groups of students which appeared when the general level of education had to be raised as a consequence of industrialization. Distance education is such an approach.

5 The archaic forms of imparting knowledge and skills could be characterized with regard to their media structure by the negative statement that they functioned without any technical medium. This means that the teachers relied on the medium of the words spoken directly to the student. Whether the teacher was a medicine man, a prophet, a shaman or a priest, he or she always communicated knowledge orally.

The oral teaching of those priest-teachers must, however, not be understood in a modern (that means more or less abstract) sense, as the words were not yet isolated from their original context. For a long time it remained part of the redeeming actions of the priest. The student experienced his speaking as his action. This means that the student not only took in the words, but was also included in the actions. This alone shows why the students had to be taken into the teacher's house. And it becomes clear why the spoken language could not just be substituted by written language at that time as this would certainly have reduced the global context of those actions.

Therefore, the spoken language of the early forms of instruction was, so to speak, only a medial *pars pro toto*. It was connected to the personality of the teacher – who was considered to be a medium himself. The ancient Greek prophets, for instance, were required to go into ecstasy when they spoke, which excluded all their individual qualities and their personality. Prophets were 'a tool of power', 'full of God' (enthusiast), and 'empty of himself'. The prophet became 'a mouthpiece of God' (van de Leeuw 1956: 244).

Oral instruction consisted of the teacher's saying a text and the student's repeating it. A comprehensive and reliable memory was required for both of them. This oral form of instruction prevailed after writing and reading had been introduced. In ancient India they were used first for commercial and trading purposes, and it took a long time before they were accepted by the teachers. Keay (1950: 33) assumes that the texts were considered to be too holy to be handed down in writing. Teachers might have also been afraid that such written texts could be used by unauthorized persons. He reports that in India the old forms of instruction have been preserved longest and have remained unchanged. The Veda are still handed down orally today, although they are, of course, also available in print. And it is not unusual that students succeed in learning whole textbooks by heart. Even in ancient Egypt with its comparatively more advanced written culture, memorizing was the student's main activity. The teachings were all learnt by heart although they were also available in writing (Keay 1950: 41).

The historical development in this dimension led to an increased use of technical media and a decreased physical presence of the teacher in the teaching–learning process. Clay tablets, wax tablets, papyrus, parchment, paper and later screen, loudspeaker and computer were placed between teacher and student in order to profit from their mediating functions. Distance education, especially in its form of integrated multimedia systems, will again have to be placed at the present end of this line of development. With regard to the decreased importance of the physical presence of the teacher it is surpassed only by programmed instruction.

Traditional face-to-face instruction, however, must be classed with an earlier stage of this development, especially when the teacher and his spoken words dominate. In spite of the use of technical media such as paper, books, blackboards, pictures or even film, the basic communicative structure has not detached itself from the original oral form of instruction.

6 Linking instruction to a special place is also of sacral origin. If a place had proved to be holy, because the effects of the divine power were repeated there, it became a 'special place' (van de Leeuw 1956: 446). This could be a grove, a grotto, but also a house or a temple. Obviously, temples were the first places where the priests accumulated wisdom, and, hence, the first places of instruction.

Just as there was – in archaic thinking – no idea of a homogeneous space, there was also no idea of a uniform time. Rather, each time had its own significance. This suggests that the early forms of instruction did not take place at fixed times in the sense of an abstract regularity. This became possible only after a first and very important phase of rationalizing in which it was considered to be possible to isolate time from its close connection to traditional places and actions which up to then were experienced as a global unit. Such an abstracting of traditional places and times became necessary when, as in ancient Egypt, one teacher had to teach several students or even larger groups of students at a time. In such a situation he was compelled to invent group instruction. It was characterized by a certain regularity and by the unity of place, time and persons. In fact, this structural unity was to become a traditional constant of all face-to-face instruction to this day.

In a second phase of rationalizing the teaching–learning process, this unity of place, time and persons disintegrated as a consequence of the application of principles of industrialization. This means that a long tradition, which had so far shaped the ideas of theorists of teaching and learning, was discontinued. The significance of this break in the tradition of instruction may be indicated by a parallel in the arts: when dramatic presentations on the stage were substituted by dramatic presentations in film, space lost its static condition, and time its continuity. In distance education as well, the unit of place and time, constitutive of face-to-face instruction, as has been shown, ceases to exist. As the teaching is objectified in the form of course material or educational film, several teachers who live far apart from each other and from the students can impart their knowledge one after the other, or even simultaneously, and in a sequence quite different from face-to-face teaching. Time as well is taken out of the context of traditional instruction. The course team can manipulate the stimuli and thus organize the presentation according to new ideas of the dramaturgy of teaching, and the students are free to develop their own learning strategy by fixing their individual times of study. Seen in this way, the break of tradition mentioned appears to be a singular event in the history of instruction.

If one assesses the described stages of development of face-to-face instruction and distance education in this sixth dimension, one cannot but see that face-to-face instruction has – on the whole – not come further than the special conditions of group instruction in ancient Egypt; that is, instruction with fixed times and places and persons. Distance education, however, developed considerably further by becoming largely independent from these ties. This opens up new perspectives which have not yet been noticed and new problems which have not yet been tackled by experts of the methodology of teaching and learning.

The six lines of development show clearly that distance education is a form of instruction which reached the final stages in each dimension only because it applied principles of industrialization. This can be specified as follows.

Distance education can be *egalitarian*, as the application of technical media overcomes some of the traditional barriers to educational opportunity. These media enable schools and universities to extend their instructional systems in such a way that every capable citizen can profit from learning if they wish – even after their school or college years. In the present historical-economic situation of highly industrialized societies the increased availability and accessibility of education thus assumes a special importance, as the further democratizing of society will increase the educational needs of all citizens considerably. More and more of them will lay claim to their human right of education. It is safe to say that such an increased demand of education can only be satisfied with the help of industrialized forms of education.

Distance education provides for instruction in which teaching and learning have been *secularized* to a high degree, as the relation between teacher and students has been isolated from its traditional social context and objectified. Teacher and students do not interact as persons in their totality, but as special teaching and learning functions which operate only in order to reach the defined goals. The numinous, however, needs the social context in order to be able to express itself.

Distance education enables and facilitates *instruction without repressive actions* in the sense that arbitrary acts of teachers – as well as of students – are cut out as technical mediation and the required division of labour have objectified instruction. If there are institutional or direct dependencies, as, for instance, in the military services and in vocational training, they will be less effective for the same reasons.

Distance education is a form of instruction which is capable of catering for great numbers of students and even *mass audiences*. Such a form of instruction would be impossible without the techniques of industrial mass production and without the help of mass media and the computer.

Distance education is principally mediated instruction. It cannot take place without the help of *technical media*. Without the mechanization of the presentation of the contents of instruction and of the feedback activities it would not be possible to start, optimize and control it.

Distance education has *cut the three bonds which tie face-to-face instruction to special places, special times and special persons.* The industrial approach of objectifying teaching and learning behaviour and of storing, transporting and reproducing it was the required precondition for this. It has made distance education the most accessible and flexible form of teaching and learning.

On the whole, and with regard to the objections of the cultural critics referred to at the beginning, the interpretation of the historic model of instruction results in the conclusion that the tradition of instruction has not been disturbed or even neutralized by the advent of industrialized education. On the contrary, it subsequently developed along the lines of development in the history of instruction. Distance education is, therefore, not something entirely new, different and strange in the world of education. It cannot be placed beside face-to-face teaching, but rather belongs to the hitherto final stage of the developments of instruction, as it has overtaken face-to-face teaching on the six lines of development, in part even considerably and distinctly. This means that distance education is, structurally speaking, ahead of face-to-face teaching. Clearly, this is the result of its industrialization.

SOCIO-CULTURAL AND INTELLECTUAL PRECONDITIONS

In this section the hypothesis to be established and substantiated is that distance education can be assigned to the era of industrialization not only because of the availability of the necessary material and technical conditions, but also because of particular socio-cultural and intellectual developments which are imperative before distance education can emerge. If in our society many adults and adolescents decide to study at a distance and not in the traditional way, if they manage to go their own way and do not depend on the traditional educational institutions, they must have qualities which distinguish them from people who lived in earlier eras. It is elucidating to analyse these qualities.

A first precondition is a particular relationship between humans and their environment. Human consciousness of the environment has changed in a long process which started with archaic-mythological ways of thinking which were gradually replaced by empirical-realistic ideas and concepts (Heimann 1966: 10). This process was accentuated by the Renaissance and the Enlightenment as they helped to emancipate human thinking from earlier limitations. At this point it is sufficient to indicate which of these developments were important in the context of the hypothesis presented at the beginning. In the Renaissance, many people became aware for the first time that education can be also used for secular purposes. There was a growing need for the establishment of town schools and of an urban education. In the era of the Enlightenment, teaching and learning were secularized even further. People were inspired by the image of the individual who is able to change unsatisfactory conditions of society by means of reason. For the first time reason was attributed to everyone. And there was an eagerness to educate people in such a way that they learned how to use reason in an efficient way. There was a widely published popular literature in the form of moralizing periodicals and scientific treatises at that time. The enlightened individual was to become emancipated. He was to learn 'to use his reason without the guidance of anybody else' (Kant n.d.: 1). It is evident that teaching and learning received new directions in this era. For the hypothesis mentioned it is important to note that the inner relationship between instruction and practical and useful activities was seen. Instruction assumed a rational-utilitaristic meaning. Furthermore, it is remarkable that in people's conceptions of life, vocational efficiency and success in practical life became significant – an idea which was propagated in Germany above all by the philanthropic movement. Only then did it become possible for long-term systematical work in an occupation to be valued and considered to be a 'sense of life' and 'a standard for success in one's life' (Behrendt 1962: 53). Seemingly, this is one root of the motivation for vocational qualification which was to become so important for distant students in our time.

Further preconditions have been described by David Riesman (1958) in his theory of various constants of social behaviour which can be identified in European and American societal development. According to this theory, people in pre-industrial society were tradition-directed; that is, that their observation of the external rules of behaviour was regulated and forced upon them down to the last details by customs, habits, ceremonies, rites and etiquette. When society became industrialized, however, it developed entirely new mechanisms of maintaining conformity. In childhood or adolescence, people now internalized specific principles of the desired behaviour which took effect on the whole of their lives like a steering gear. In this way, types of persons emerged who succeeded in determining their lives without a strict and obvious direction by tradition. They became inner-directed. Only now did they become able to act on their own discretion. And only in the industrialized society did they have options of doing so, as traditions fragmented, many new goals of life emerged, and conditions of life changed increasingly. Those who intended to realize the career prospects provided by the new society had to learn to take the initiative and to disentangle themselves from tradition-directedness.

Whereas the tradition-directed individual could not choose between work and spare time, as their lives were regulated by tradition with regard to this as well, the inner-directed persons had the possibility of separating leisure time from working time and being able to have it at their disposal. Under the influence of the Protestant success ethic this happened increasingly in favour of useful activities, for the endeavour to be efficient, to control oneself permanently and to fight the 'demon of indolence' was religiously motivated. The then popular motto *per aspera ad astra* was internalized by the inner-directed person. This led to a striving after vocational success never known before, and partly even to a 'passionate drive to earn and gain'. At the same time the individual in the inner-directed society 'was dissociated and sheltered from others' and became, thus, isolated and more vulnerable (Riesman 1958: 135).

The relevance of such developments for the emergence of distance education can easily be seen. It is evident that distance education would have been unthinkable in a tradition-directed society. Only the inner-directed society provided the necessary subjective preconditions for it. Every characteristic trait used by Riesman to describe the inner-directed person can also contribute to the explanation of the situation of distant students. Their decision to enrol in a distant study course is already behaviour according to their own discretion. Their strongest motivation is derived from vocational career prospects. When they study at a distance they dispose of their leisure time, make sacrifices, have many difficulties and are typically 'dissociated and sheltered from others'. Hence, it can be assumed that the phenomenon of the adult distant student is in accordance with an inner law of development of our culture in the era of industrialization. It influenced the student's socio-cultural and intellectual development in such a way that the motivation of millions of distant students became strong enough and their inner-directedness so stable that it caused them to stay outside of the institutions of traditional education and to commit themselves to an unorthodox way of teaching and learning.

Furthermore, it can be postulated that the individual's consciousness is also influenced by life in an industrialized society itself. These influences prepare the individual for being able to study at a distance in special ways, as can be illustrated by reference to the following four experiences:

1 the practice of dealing with people, who – in a given situation – are charged with the performance of single functions only;
2 the adjustment to the permanent reception of coded information;
3 the development of attitudes towards substitute persons;
4 the orientation towards new basic personality types.

In agrarian society people lived in villages and had relatively few interpersonal relations, which, however, were long-lasting, emotional and integral. No matter what the reason for their interpersonal relation was, the persons involved were expected to be dealt with as total personalities. If, for instance, someone did business with someone else, it certainly mattered whether the persons involved had a liking for each other, whether they were of the same religious faith, how they had led their lives so far, whether they enjoyed a good reputation, and so on. In such a village, a teacher, for instance, played a role which exceeded that of just teaching pupils, and which affected the adults also. His impact was a unique one. Hence, he was considered not exchangeable.

Man in the industrialized society is, on the other hand, typically a town-dweller and has as such usually many interpersonal relations, which, however, are relatively short, not emotional, and used for specific purposes. Even with an unusual transaction such as the purchase of an automobile the interaction between the customer and the salesman will, as a rule, no longer be influenced by their personal likings, their religious beliefs, their political leanings, their family situations or their social status. Customer and salesman interact merely as persons who serve in a specialized function, and the two expect from each other that this function be performed well. This means that only a small fraction of one person interacts with a small fraction of another person. Each person is fragmented and consists of many functional parts. This reduction of persons can be demonstrated by referring to the example of a teacher in a city school; that is, to a teacher specializing in one or two subjects. It is true he teaches pupils, but, as a rule, he cuts out his personal background in this process. He separates official and private functions sharply. As he is reduced to someone who serves certain functions only, it is easier to imagine that he could be replaced. In comparing him to the teacher in a village school it can be seen how far this process has gone. At the same time it must be seen that the teacher in a city school is still a partner in a continued process of communicative acting which induces him to perform more functions than a teacher in a system of distance education. Considering the stages of development from the teacher in a village school to a teacher in distance education, the teacher in the city school can be classed somewhere in the middle between the extremes.

As individuals in industrial society are able to make contact with many persons in order to perform special functions, they enjoy a freedom never known before. They have disentangled themselves from old bonds which involved their emotions as well, and even the totality of their persons. Now, they are principally also ready to approach complete strangers and to communicate with them – if it is necessary for objective reasons – without doubt, a new human skill. This freedom must have been a favourable precondition for readiness to teach and to learn at a distance, if a specific educational need could not be satisfied otherwise. If the individual, in doing so, did not meet 'real' teachers and 'real' students, but only persons charged with the performance of often highly specialized functions, this experience was not new to them, as it was in harmony with so many patterns of interaction which are taken for granted in industrialized societies.

Individuals in industrial society distinguish themselves from persons in pre-industrial society by their ability to receive and to work with information which is technically mediated. First of all, they are reading men. The mass media with their modern methods of production and distribution enable them to take part in the doings around them and in the world in a very specific way. As oral forms of information were more or less substituted by printed ones they got used to their presentation by technical means. At the same time, in industrial society people see and listen to many things which remained closed to them in agrarian society. A permanent supply of information from radio and television has certainly an effect on them, whereby the same information can be coded in different ways; for instance, by newspaper, radio or television.

In order to acquire the ability to study at a distance – that is, to work with mediated instruction – it may be very important that people have already gained the experience of receiving many pieces of coded information which are independent from the persons and occurrences in their immediate neighbourhood. This experience is new, for pre-industrial man received typically only relatively few pieces of information, which were accidental, not coded, and connected to persons and events. The difference is obvious. Through his daily experience, industrial man has learnt to use purposeful (that is, constructed) communications which tend to be concentrated and concise. Such communications are intentional to a high degree, they avoid unnecessary repetitions, and try each time to reach the highest level of information (Toffler 1970: 131). Evidently, experiences of this kind are better preconditions for learning at a distance than oral communication as practised nearly exclusively in agrarian societies.

The ideas and the behaviour of persons in industrial society are not formed and shaped by their interaction with their primary and secondary groups only, but also by their relations to human beings whom they know exclusively from the mass media: sports idols, filmstars, politicians, scholars, authors. They learn about their developments and their life style, observe how they react to actual occurrences, and even develop a lasting attitude towards them. Thus, they are already used to dealing with 'substitute persons' and have accumulated a considerable skill in this respect. In distance education the students meet, so to speak, 'vicarious teachers' whom they know only from printed texts or aural and visual presentations. This shows again that people in an industrial society are prepared for distance education to a higher degree than those in a pre-industrial society, in which corresponding relations were established by myths, legends and rumours, and remained, therefore, vague and uncertain.

A corresponding sociological analysis shows that industrial society has also developed new models of human development. With regard to this Richard W. Behrendt (1962: 57) speaks of a 'change of basic types of man' which was caused by the industrialization of society. Referring to pre-industrial time, he speaks, for instance, of the ruler, the subject, the patriarch, the heroic warrior, the missionary, the wise man and the scholar. In industrial society, however, these lose their importance and are substituted by types; as, for instance, the conscious man, the emancipated man, *Homo faber*, the technically competent man and the mobile man. Further types are 'the radically organizing and manipulating man' on the one hand and 'the radically organized and manipulated man' on the other (1962: 59).

This change of basic types of human is a profound one, and so serious in its consequences that one can consider it a major transformation in the development of mankind. This transformation has been already dealt with in regard to its relevance in intellectual history. At this point it can be postulated that only human beings who can be classed with the basic types in industrial society are ready for teaching and learning at a distance. That is to say, if one scrutinizes these basic types, one cannot but agree that all of them have a special affinity to industrial education.

Conscious man, who tries successfully 'to become aware not only of the physical and societal world around him, but also of his inner psychic structure, which is often still unconscious', is more easily ready to assess himself and his abilities and, hence, make decisions with regard to realistic educational or training goals. In addition, he is presumably also more likely to assume responsibility for his learning. Emancipated man, 'who has disentangled himself from transcendental and traditional ties' and 'claims an original and autonomous orientation in new situations of life', is certainly more easily motivated to acquire new qualifications which he needs to adjust to such new situations. Only *Homo faber*, the type of man, 'who considers the world in all its non-transcendental aspects and also man himself as producible or at least malleable', has self-confidence enough to be able to change an unsatisfactory situation of life purposefully by learning. Technically competent man is 'the archetype of an era with a relatively developed technology'. He no longer carries loads and no longer eats his bread in the sweat of his brow. Instead, he operates machines, whereby his work is mostly reduced to the control of mechanical energy. This deliverance from heavy manual work and involvement with machines and technical appliances, which save time and energy, is a good precondition for learning, and especially for dealing with technical teaching–learning systems. Mobile man, who no longer accepts being rooted for his lifetime, geographically speaking, in his native country, in the spiritual sense in his religious belief, and with respect to society in specific social strata, but claims a maximum of mobility according to his abilities and opportunities is emancipated enough to be able to learn without the local, temporal, and personal ties which are usually necessary in face-to-face instruction. Finally, the negative types of Radically organizing and manipulating man and Radically organized and manipulated man can be applied to distance education organizers and to distant students too. Here it becomes evident that industrialized education brings forth dangers of its own. The structural roots of it will be dealt with later, in the discussion of the language as a medium.

On the whole, the special aspects referred to so far facilitate the formulation of the hypothesis at the beginning of this chapter in more concrete terms: the establishment of distance education and the teaching and learning in this type of industrialized education require that a certain intellectual development and the orientation

A cross-disciplinary interpretation 151

to new types of man have already taken place. The ability to detach oneself from the direct guidance of a personal teacher and from the social inspiration and pressure of the learning group, and to determine oneself the time and place of study, the amount of study, and possibly even the ways in which it is controlled, is obviously based on intellectual and socio-cultural experiences which build up enough self-confidence and self-assurance in the individual learner in such a way that he or she can, indeed, 'use reason without the guidance of anyone else'.

If such a stage is reached, a barrier has been overcome. This event can be compared with overcoming the barrier of illiteracy, as it had a similar importance in setting free intellectual potentialities and for the further development of the educational system. It may even be thought that an 'absolute threshold of culture' (Gehlen 1961: 133) has been crossed.

The discussion on the intellectual and socio-cultural preconditions of distance education shows that possible reservations of the critics of culture with regard to this form of industrialized education can be modified in so far as individuals of the European-American industrial civilization are much better prepared for this form of education than people in preceding eras ever could have been. In other words: persons who teach and learn in the industrialized way are basically different human beings. In many ways – it has been possible to name only a few aspects – they are prepared and ready to benefit from abstract, objectified procedures of imparting knowledge. Furthermore, the constructed, abstract relation between teacher and student fits into a net of manifold abstract social relationships, which together form a kind of 'secondary system' (Freyer 1963: 79). Man in industrialized societies is used to assimilating 'secondary experiences' instead of making the respective experiences himself. He does not live any longer in 'primary, organic, natural relationships, but in a produced, planned, organized, and very often manipulated world' (Heitger 1963: 101). Those who accept the changes of man's consciousness caused by industrialization because they think that these intellectual and socio-cultural adaptations are indispensable for coping with the economical, political and cultural tasks of the future will see that the objections of the critics of culture lose some of their significance. Possibly, they will even become critics of culture the other way round, as they might think that the persistent adherence of traditional schools to pre-industrial methods of teaching and learning can be considered as a serious dysfunction of the educational system – in an age which is already developing structural elements of a post-industrial society.

SOCIOLOGICAL CHARACTERIZATION

As industrialization is at the centre of sociological research (Dahrendorf 1959: 135) and as dealing with it has grown from the need for orientation and understanding in view of the rapid changes in our time (Behrendt 1962: 15), which were caused and accelerated exactly by this industrialization, it will be advantageous to analyse and characterize the concept of industrialized education in its sociological aspects as well.

According to Behrendt (1962: 15), sociology strives towards knowledge of 'generally accepted regularities of the interactive and collective behaviour of man'. As there are teachers and students in distance education as well as in face-to-face teaching who interact in special ways, the question arises whether such generally accepted regularities can also be found in this particular form of instruction. In trying to answer this question, emphasis will be laid on the transition from traditional to industrialized instruction. It should be possible to characterize the social changes which have taken place in this process by means of categories of sociology more succinctly and in a more differentiated way than with categories of educational theory.

The hope for a corresponding gain in knowledge can be founded on the fact that sociology – in contrast to theory of education – has fully understood and clearly described the 'overwhelming phenomenon of technology and industrialization and their effects on social change' (Heitger 1963: 106). Many sociologists even think that industrialization has caused such far-reaching processes of cultural change that they interpret it as the beginning of a new cultural era in the history of mankind, quite comparable in importance with former cultural eras – for instance, those of the hunting and gathering society and the agrarian society (Behrendt 1962: 51). And – still more important – the blending of technology and the production process is considered an absolute pre-condition for the continuation of the existence of mankind. In view of such a fundamental philosophy one is not surprised to learn that the industrial production of goods is considered one of the dominant shaping powers of modern society (Lepsius 1958: 122). Helmut Schelsky (1965: 160) emphasizes that 'there is practically no sector of life of modern man in which the industrial production has not caused decisive changes of

A cross-disciplinary interpretation 153

behaviour'. The analysis of distance education has shown that the educational sector has not altogether been left out of this development. Comparing the sociological interpretation of the industrial era with the superficial and dilatory way in which, for instance, technical media are dealt with by didactical experts – to say nothing of the rationalization of instruction by planning and organizing it professionally – the different approach of the two disciplines becomes evident. Advocates of the use of technical media for instruction have only been marginal in the theory and practice of education. Educational technology has not become a central issue in the methodology of teaching and learning, and did not even get beyond the beginnings. The general attitude in this matter is that technical media are merely added to traditional instruction. The insight is lacking that in view of the changes of the consciousness of modern man, the enormous impact of the teaching capacity of industrialized mass media, which so far have only been used to a small extent, and the enormous increase of teaching and training tasks – taken altogether – will make new structural forms of teaching and learning imperative. Only such an approach would correspond with the tendencies of industrialization in our present society. Only in such a way could 'cultural lag' in this sector be reduced.

The methodology of teaching and learning has, so far, not been in position to describe the social change caused by a form of instruction in which the teaching is transported to the student, and to clarify the social conditions in it which are structurally quite different. Typically enough, when trying to explain the teacher–student relation in programmed instruction some authors refer to old, traditional patterns of instruction such as the individual instruction of a prince (Flechsig 1969: 11) and the private instruction by a tutor (Cordt 1963: 111). An attempt will therefore be made to clarify the structural change of social relations when traditional instruction is substituted by industrialized instruction. This change can be identified on several levels.

Max Weber, Ferdinand Tönnies and other representatives of the older sociology have described at an early stage the changes which took place under the dominance of purposeful, rational action and as a consequence of the scientific-technical permeation of traditional social subsystems. Jürgen Habermas (1968: 60) summarized the results of their thinking by remarking that they characterized this change with the help of pairs of concepts, for instance, *gemeinschaft* and *gesellschaft*, organic and mechanical solidarity, primary and secondary relations, and traditional and bureaucratic dominion.

Accordingly, one could understand face-to-face instruction in a classroom as a traditional social subsystem; distance education, however, as a 'modern' one. Thus, distance education would be characterized as a system based on rational planning and development just like the organization of industrialized work processes. On the other hand, face-to-face instruction in the classroom would then be a system handed down by tradition which is not, or is only slightly, affected by the consequences of industrialization.

This would mean that traditional instruction in a classroom could be classed with the category of *gemeinschaft*, as there is a special type of closeness or familiarity between the teacher and the students as well as among the students. The persons involved are also more or less conscious of this familiarity. They approve of it and try to deepen it in order to profit from the solidarity of the *Klassengemeinschaft*. It can be assumed that in such groups of students 'archaic personal relations' (König 1958: 86) are fostered. According to Tönnies, the learning group in the classroom would be founded on 'a *gemeinschaft* of place and spirit'. Subjectively experienced forms of action and their traditions and rites play an important role. In each group a balance of power is developed, a process which might become so dominant that the original objectives for bringing together teacher and students temporarily lose some of their significance. Accordingly, distance education would be classed with the category *gesellschaft*, as there the teacher and the students form groups of persons which are 'not basically close to, but basically separated from each other' (König 1958: 100). Their social relationships are not derived from socio-cultural traditions, but rather from objective necessities.

If the concept of *gemeinschaft* is applied to teaching and learning in a classroom, the following categories could be subsumed: organic solidarity which can develop in direct social interaction, informal grouping, the dominance of primary social relations, and traditional forms of control, which, for instance, are mirrored in the hierarchy of principal–teacher–student.

If, on the other hand, the concept of *gesellschaft* is applied to distance teaching, the following categories help to explain its structure: mechanical solidarity – that is, the artificial solidarity which is brought about by means of technical media; formal groups – that is, the importance of the formal organization of the learning groups in individual distance study courses; secondary relations with little

A cross-disciplinary interpretation 155

intensity and without familiarity of the participants, and bureaucratic control which helps to maintain the contacts between school, teachers and students.

However, it should be mentioned that the characterization of distance education with the help of the category 'secondary relations' does not apply to all cases. Faris has shown that an emotional relationship can be maintained in spite of physical separation, whereby he explicitly mentions the medium of correspondence. Therefore, elements of primary group relationships can also be found in distance education – whereas, the other way round, emotional closeness can be missing even under favourable face-to-face conditions (König 1958: 107).

Jürgen Habermas (1968: 61) has observed that Talcott Parsons' catalogue of possible alternatives of value-orientation can also be used to characterize the change of dominant attitudes as a consequence of the transition from traditional to modern society. Parsons presented the following four pairs of alternative value-orientations:

Traditional society	Modern society
affectivity	affective neutrality
particularism	universalism
ascription	achievement
diffuseness	specificity

With the help of this catalogue it is possible to describe more precisely the characteristic traits of industrialized education proposed so far.

The above-mentioned familiarity between teacher and students in the traditional classroom indicates that affectivity plays an important role in face-to-face teaching. Indeed, there the range of emotional relationships is wide as has been shown by many empirical studies of social interaction in the classroom (Withall and Lewis 1963: 696). On the other hand, distance education is normally characterized by affective neutrality – as here the teaching and learning is not achieved by an interaction of persons, but, strictly speaking, of isolated functions. As Faris also suggested, this does not necessarily mean that technically mediated instruction cannot be affective at all. Now and then one can find initial stages of it. Generally speaking, however, it remains safe to say that in distance education the social relations tend to be neutral.

Traditional instruction in the classroom is oriented to a particular frame of reference: a given teacher teaches a given learning group in a given temporal and locational situation. Industrialized instruction, on the other hand, disregards particular conditions of this kind, as it has a more general, if not principally universal frame of reference. Distance education tends, indeed, towards universal application.

With traditional instruction in the classroom teacher and students orientate themselves to certain ascribed qualities. Students, for instance, are 'diligent', 'good companions', 'well-behaved', 'cheeky', or 'exercise restraint'. Teachers are 'strict, but just' or 'soft'. The orientation in this dimension may become more important than the original objectives of instruction. A proof of this is the student who is the best one with regard to his school work, but plays only a peripheral part in the dynamics of the learning group. With industrialized instruction, however, students and teachers orientate themselves exclusively towards the achievements which are assessed with the help of tests.

Traditional instruction can be characterized by diffuse value-orientations. The reason for this is that the norms of the learning group and the experience of 'group life' are usually not considered and, therefore, made conscious to a slight extent only. They become effective in direct social interaction in a global-holistic sense. Correspondingly, the teachers often think that precise objectives of instruction cannot be described, the methods to be chosen cannot be predicted and the sequencing of instruction cannot be fixed in advance. In contrast to this, in industrialized instruction the indirect interaction is orientated towards the specific qualities of teachers and students in the sense that these are characteristics which are of great importance for the actual achievement of the intended learning process. This tendency for clear determination corresponds with the efforts to lay down detailed definition of learning objectives and to acquire as much relevant empirical data as possible for the learning process in each case.

In an approach of his own Jürgen Habermas (1968: 62) went beyond Max Weber, Ferdinand Tönnies and Talcott Parsons, and developed a categorization with the help of which it is possible to describe in greater detail the relevant structural changes of institutional subsystems which were caused by industrialization. He started out with Hegel's fundamental distinction between 'work' and 'interaction' in his *Phenomenology of Spirit*. Work is defined by him as 'rational acting', interaction as 'communicative acting'. By developing seven pairs of categories for both of them he succeeds

in characterizing more closely those sectors which Tönnies called *gemeinschaft* and *gesellschaft*.
The seven pairs of categories are shown in Table 1 below.

Table 1. Habermas's seven pairs of categories for distinguishing symbolically mediated interaction from rational acting (1968: 64)

	Institutional frame: symbolically mediated interaction	Systems of rational (instrumental, strategic) acting
Rules orientated towards acting	Societal norms	Technical rules
Level of definition	Intersubjectively divided colloquial language	Language free of context
Kind of definition	Reciprocal expectations of behaviour	Conditioned prognoses, conditioned imperatives
Mechanism of acquisition	Internalizing of roles	Learning of skills and qualifications
Function of the type of action	Maintaining of institutions (conforming of norms)	Solution of problem (attainment of the goal by means to an end)
Sanctions because of breach of rules	Punishment by means of conventional sanctions. Failure because of authority	Lack of success. Failure because of reality
Rationalizing	Emancipation. Individuation. Extension of dominance-free communication	Increase of production capacity. Extension of technical power of disposal

If this categorical framework is applied to instruction, the idea suggests itself that traditional face-to-face instruction could be dealt with as an institution of communicative acting, whereas industrialized instruction would be a system of rational acting using means to an end. An analysis of these two forms of instruction reveals their decisive structural differences.

Even a rough comparison shows that the two forms of instruction could, indeed, be compared with each other with the help of these seven pairs of categories. It is evident that instruction in the classroom is regulated by norms. The direct interactions of teachers and students are more or less caused by binding expectations or value concepts developed by the learning group, the school, the families and society. How much this is, indeed, the case can be seen from the fact that there are often conflicts of norms in classrooms which lead to critical intensifications of social interactions. As societal norms determine the actions of the teachers and students, their interactions are influenced by socio-cultural traditions, whereby they themselves become part of the socio-cultural life of society.

Distance education, however, is basically determined by technical rules. Most behaviour possibilities for the teachers and the students are carefully planned, calculated, formalized and standardized. Originally global and complex behaviour patterns are reduced to the setting and control of specific functions. The students are informed about the rules of the teaching–learning system, and these rules must be followed.

Instruction in the classroom is a system of 'communicative acting' and uses intersubjective divided colloquial language. This language is characterized by the traits of special persons, groups of persons, places and times. Thus, in a special sense each communicative situation is experienced as being unique. Distance education, however, uses a language which is taken out of its originally associated surroundings, and is thus free of its context. The technically mediated communication of necessity remains unaffected by particular circumstance, as it addresses students everywhere.

In the classroom the communicative acting is determined by reciprocal expectations of behaviour. This means that the teacher who acts expects the students to react in a special way and vice versa. The expected reactions take place with a higher degree of probability the more the interacting persons have internalized a role consensus and the more the expected behaviour has become ritualized by habit.

In industrialized distance education the segments of interaction are constructed on the basis of conditioned prognoses and conditioned imperatives. Again, particular sequences of a global behaviour become objectified and isolated.

In face-to-face instruction the dominant mechanism of acquisition is the internalization of roles. The students live up to expectations by internalizing the norms of the group. Knowledge and skills are transported by means of this particular role identification, role taking and role performance. In distance education, however, the teaching–learning process is reduced to the learning of skills and qualifications. Every measure in this system has the sole function of achieving this goal. Communicative action and role performance are cut out.

In face-to-face instruction the social interaction helps to maintain the institution. Teachers and students are subject to external and internal control. In distance education, however, the indirect interaction is subject to the attainment of the learning goals by using means to an end.

Correspondingly, the reactions to breaches of the rules are different in the two subsystems. In face-to-face instruction, the students are punished by conventional sanctions; they fail because of the authority of the institution. In distance education, however, they fail because of lack of success; that is, they fail because of reality.

Finally, the two subsystems also differ with regard to their particular ways of 'rationalizing'. Face-to-face instruction leads to the emancipation of the student, to his individuation, and to the extension of 'dominance-free communication'. Distance education leads to an increase of effectiveness by using technical devices.

In Table 2 (overleaf) the results of this comparison are summarized.

On the basis of this sociological analysis the following definition of distance education can be given:

Distance education is a system of rational actions for the imparting of knowledge, skills and attitudes, whereby the originally direct social relationships between teacher and students are substituted to a great extent by indirect relations which are characterized by technical rules and prescriptions, a context-free language, conditioned prognoses and conditioned instructions, goal attainment with the help of target-means relations, and the systematical increase of effectivity.

With regard to the objections of cultural critics it must be stated here that the described change of behaviour is, indeed, a deep one, and therefore, full of consequences for the didactical structure of distance education. The fears of negative consequences, for instance, the mechanization, functionalizing and depersonalization of instruction are real. Obviously, these processes are inevitable in such a specialized system of teaching and learning. And important educational goals such as individualization and the extension of the domination-free communicative action cannot be reached.

A critic who compares distance education with face-to-face instruction will consider these deficits as really serious ones. The considerable structural difference between the two forms of instruction, however, suggests that such a comparison is not really helpful. Thus it must be regarded as inappropriate to want to use the new systems of rational thinking in instruction to achieve exactly what

Table 2. Face-to-face instruction and distance education compared with regard to Habermas's criteria for distinguishing symbolically mediated interaction from rational acting

Face-to-face teaching	Distance teaching
Institution where communicative action takes place	System of educational action determined by rational means-ends thinking
Students' and teachers' actions are predominantly determined by social norms	Teachers' and students' actions are predominantly determined by technical rules
The medium of interaction between students and teachers is 'the intersubjectively shared everyday language'	The medium of interaction between students and teachers is 'context-free language'
Teaching is determined by 'reciprocal behaviour expectations'	Teaching follows 'conditional prognoses' and 'conditional imperatives'
The focus is on the 'internalization of roles'	The focus is on learning 'skills and qualifications'
Teaching aims at preserving the institution	Teaching aims at 'problem-solving, attainment of objectives by applying means-to-an-end principles'
Students are punished on the basis of conventional sanctions. They fail because of decisions made by the authority of teacher, headmaster, director of education	Students fail because of their inability to cope with the reality of learning at a distance. They drop out of their courses, for instance
Dimensions of 'rationality': emancipation, individuation, extension of dominance-free communication	Increase of the effectiveness of the teaching system. Extension of the teaching system

was thought possible with the system of communicative action. It would be more appropriate to ask whether the standards of communicative action must and may still be valid reference points for the evaluation of the social relationships between teacher and taught. We must also test whether the gains in teaching capacity in the reproducible system of rational thinking are not so great that deficits in the case of certain learning objectives of the type referred to can be regarded as acceptable. In this context the basic question has to be put once again whether all mediation of knowledge and skills has to be a priori permanently connected with forms of communicative action, or whether the socialization and cultural effects – the acquisition of norms, values and symbols either consciously or unconsciously – cannot take place in other experiencing and practical contexts as well.

If, in addition, when answering this question we start from requirements made of people living in industrial societies today, there is another aspect which plays a part. People in industrial societies have had to find their way around the secondary system referred to, and make good use of the subsystems contained in this system. This ability can obviously only be imparted by a form of instruction which is not based on communicative action alone. Exaggerating only slightly, it can be said that a form of instruction based exclusively on communicative action, which by nurturing the 'innerliness' of teachers and students enables them to develop complete, individual personalities, cannot achieve a current generally applicable learning objective, because it will not teach students how to manage the 'apparatus of existence' of the 'secondary school system' in an advanced industrial society.

Reflections of this nature can lead to the conception of a dual educational system in which it will be possible for students to relate communicative and rational actions to one another in lessons. On the other hand, it is necessary to relate the differences between the two subsystems brought out so far to a more fundamental problem. With an analysis of its particular structural elements, distance education can be seen as a system for the extension of our disposal of technical means in education. Therefore, it must be related to another analytical level than face-to-face instruction which is based on the way groups of persons see themselves and their traditions. Following Habermas, it could be stated that the increasing application of techniques of distance education results in a variation of the general problem of how usable knowledge can be employed in a social world. Obviously, there is a clash of two different intellectual traditions: the hermeneutical interpretation of the contexts of life, and empirically obtained and technically used knowledge. In a similar context Helmut Schelsky (1963: 188) distinguished between science as reflection and science as technology. The juxtaposition of two respective different forms of teaching and learning has not yet been theoretically incorporated. It conveys a 'life problem of our civilization' (Habermas 1968: 107); namely, how the relations between technical progress and the social world, which are today still natural, can be reflected and controlled by a rational discourse. This will become a central problem of the new didactics.

ANTHROPOLOGICAL INTERPRETATION

If one relates distance education as a form of industrialized education to anthropological terms of reference, the question arises how to interpret the phenomenon that man uses technical media in order to be able to teach and learn at a distance. To answer this question requires consideration of two general features which were very important in human development: people's attitude towards technology and their ability to be challenged by new conditions of their environment and to renew themselves through it.

Of the many anthropological models of interpretation that of Arnold Gehlen (1958) seems to be most suitable for the purpose of this discussion. Following Herder and Scheler, he sees man as a being characterized by biological deficiencies, lacking specialized organs and instincts, and not adapted to a particular species-specific environment. This means that he must necessarily rely on his own actions and must make his environment himself.

In order to achieve this, people need technology, which compensates for their deficiencies in the sense of the substitution, intensification and relief of their organs. Therefore, technology had a determining influence on man's interaction with nature throughout his development. In a general sense, technology belongs to him, and technology mirrors his being. Technology is, as it were, the 'great being'.

The 'continuously increasing substitution of the organic by the inorganic can be considered a relevant result of our cultural development.' This is a process which began as early as the anthropogenesis and which has accelerated increasingly during the last centuries and decades. 'The development of mankind is, hence, not a purely biological one, but essentially a development of substitute organs for missing ones,' concludes Rothacker, taking Gehlen's approach. And he refers to the first important substitute organs – namely tools, language, abstraction, reason and thinking (Rothacker 1966: 38). In a long course of development man had to get used to handling these and other substitute organs and to learn how to use them; that is, how to substitute by tradition what heredity had withheld from him (Rothacker 1966: 39).

In the context of this argument it is important to note that the substitute organs are media which are also used in instruction, and that tools, language and thinking are assigned to the same categorical level. In order to stress the importance of these media, one of the first substitute human organs – language – will be discussed in a preparatory digression as it shows paradigmatically to what degree even anthropogenesis depended on a medium which first had to be created. Furthermore, with the help of this medium, effects can be identified which are comparable to those which are achieved by the mechanization and industrialization of instruction. Finally, language is chosen as an example as it is certainly above suspicion for even the most severe critics of culture, as it is not considered a part of technology, but rather a part of culture which is allegedly in opposition to technology.

Marshall McLuhan (1964: 79) has, however, typically enough, called language a human technology. By referring to a quotation from Bergson's *L'Evolution créatice*, he emphasized that it enabled the human intellect to separate real objects from its environment. Without language, he explains, human intelligence would have remained totally involved in the objects of its attention. A short reflection shows, indeed, that people can distance themselves from an object only if they have found a word for it – the pre-condition of any detached consideration. Kurt Strunz (1970: 1089) characterized this development in this way: 'Man is released from the prison of the here and now of his environment.' And he added that it was only through language that man was able to give an overview and ordered analysis of reality, including past events and distant phenomena. The fundamental importance of language is further clarified by McLuhan's comparison: 'Language does for intelligence what the wheel does for the feet and the body. It enables them to move from thing to thing with greater ease and speed and ever less involvement.'

The reference to a lesser degree of involvement can be judged positively and negatively. On looking more carefully one can see that already this early use of a medium necessarily connects the advantages mentioned with important disadvantages. As language extends and amplifies man's thinking, and as man learns to handle it as a technical extension of consciousness, it also diminishes his originally very important intuitive awareness of collective consciousness (McLuhan 1964: 79). Thus, 'speech acts to separate man from man, and mankind from the cosmic unconscious'. Strunz (1970: 1089) observes that the spoken word changes human inwardness as it objectifies it. And here he sees dangerous implications. The verbal fixation of contents of the world and the inwardness blinds him with regard to the things we do not understand. His detachment alienates him from reality, its contents are 'talked to death'; and, finally, there is also the misuse of the word, in false gossip, in the distortion of the truth, and in lying. A further danger is that language tends to become independent, to develop in its own way, and thereby to assume an inadequate importance which is separated from reality. This may render communication more difficult, or block it or make it open to manipulation.

This example shows the enormous adaptations which became necessary when humans learned how to use the medium of language. Their structures of consciousness changed to a high degree. One might assume that people acquired language only reluctantly and that they refused to use it in some areas of their life altogether, as they were afraid that, for instance, religious and social relations would become stunted. Even today there are situations in which the exchange of feelings is so subtle that the persons involved believe that talking about them would 'destroy everything'. The use of the medium of language was, on the one hand, an important gain for the development of mankind and, on the other, a considerable loss. The same can be said about the use of newer media in instruction; namely, writing, and later print, and still later electronic media. And the same holds true for industrialized education. It must, however, be acknowledged that the losses were by far outweighed by the extraordinary and even epoch-making advantages. In all cases the use of media made it possible to solve educational tasks which so far had been insoluble.

For the interpretation of industrialized education it is important to see that there are similarities in the consequences of the use of the medium of language and of modern technical media. The following insights have been gained: (1) instruction has been removed from its close attachment to given places, times and persons; (2) teachers and students become detached from reality – that is, from the life of the learning group; (3) as the teaching behaviour is objectified the students have it practically at their disposal. They can actualize the teaching with greater ease and speed whenever they wish to learn. Thus, instruction is released from the prison of the here and now and of a given environment. This opens it up for further developments in new dimensions.

Considering the structural similarities conveyed by this analogy, the question suggests itself whether industrialized instruction can release, intensify and differentiate intellectual faculties in the same way as language has done as it is also no longer tied to fixed places, times and persons.

If we follow Gehlen's approach, industrialized instruction can be understood as a complex technical system of teaching and learning which man is forced to develop as he is no longer able to cope with all the instructional and training tasks of the advanced industrial society by means of his natural organs. In the same way as technology was called 'the great being' this technical instructional system can be called 'the great teacher'. In order to be able to fulfil its tasks, the great teacher operates with the help of substitute organs which are to intensify and extend the following human organs or faculties:

- The voice of the teacher, which can scarcely fill a large auditorium, is intensified and extended by media such as audio tapes, records, television, and in a coded form as printed material. In this way it can reach practically every home on this globe – and with the help of radio waves, even out into space. Some of these media transmit the teacher's picture as well and even their gestures and body language, so that the teacher's total teaching behaviour can reach practically everyone.
- The forefinger, an organ which is so unspecified and so deficient that it had already been extended by the pointer in the pre-industrial era, is extended and intensified by graphical representations, careful camera work, and the application of multisensoric stimuli techniques. The camera, for instance, can be directed to the object to be shown in such a way that it appears more precisely than in reality. With the help of cinematographic techniques, for instance, focusing, close-up, microscopic filming, slow motion, quick motion and trick filming, it becomes possible to present the object to the student, didactically speaking, much more effectively than it is possible in reality.
- The eyes and ears of the teacher which inform her or him about the learning behaviour of his students are substituted and intensified by the empirical collection of data and their evaluation with the help of the computer. In this way tens of thousands of students can be observed at once with regard to their particulars, their relevant previous qualifications, their entrance behaviour, their gains in knowledge and skills, the results of specific tests, and possibly also the change in their attitudes.
- The memory of the teacher, which is often not as firm and infallible as he or she might wish and which is in addition often also tied to certain situations, is extended by powerful external data banks and computer programs and thus becomes extraordinarily exact.
- The art of teaching – that is, the didactical decisions which are

necessarily tied to given persons and situations in face-to-face instruction – is substituted by strategies and technologies which address all students wherever they might live.

In general, the following statements can be made. Human organs can be substituted, intensified and relieved in the ways described in an industrial society only, and the extent to which this happens will increase together with the further industrialization of society. The new possibilities for teaching and learning resulting from this development are not yet fully foreseeable. As, according to Gehlen (1961: 95), 'technology and being human have the same origin' and the 'technical activity belongs virtually to the distinguishing marks of man' (1961: 100), the most consistent and differentiated application of technology in industrialized education may be interpreted as a 'human self-heightening', that is, in this case as the heightening of human ability to provide instruction and academic teaching to extremely large groups of students. This process may certainly be considered as epoch-making.

Having interpreted the technically designed distance teaching system as equipping the teacher with artificial organs, thus enabling him or her to tackle instructional and training tasks of unprecedented magnitude (whereby it also has to be said that new dimensions of consciousness, thought and action are also formed which 'break the bounds of natural man' – Heieck 1969: 54), reasons why the decisive changes which industrialized instruction brings about have to be accepted now have to be given from an anthropological aspect.

Present-day man can be characterized by the fact that he is challenged in an unprecedented way by the extreme disproportion between the possibilities of his natural body and of his teaching and learning habits handed down by tradition – and the immense increase in instructional and training needs. With regard to these needs, which are very likely to increase in the future, the individual, indeed, proves to be a biologically deficient being who, because of his morphological helplessness (Gehlen 1961: 48), is bound to fail in his efforts to cope with them. Since the natural teaching capacity is already at a premium in traditional forms of education and since it will be lacking even more drastically when it has to fulfil the needs of the disadvantaged in industrial as well as developing societies, the only way out is to teach and to learn in an industrialized way. This is a pre-condition for enabling as many people as possible to take part in the emerging industrial world civilization.

A cross-disciplinary interpretation 167

Heinrich Roth (1966: 125), in his *Pedagogical Anthropology*, summed up his discussion about the biologically caused release of man from his environment by saying that man is 'world-open', in the sense that he is not tied to his environment, not adjusted to adaptation, but rather to change. This means that he actively organizes his environment. In fact, he is 'the only being who is able to react to changes of his environment and who is best in experimenting with it'.

Industrialized education must be seen as the result of such a basic disposition as well as of an epoch-making thrust in the development of mankind. Now, people face the necessity of coping with 'a new and greatly advanced situation' (Freyer 1963: 233). If they employ industrialized forms of education they will surely have to bear grievous losses of traditional forms of life. But this happened again and again in the history of mankind whenever new media were used. The design and the implementation of further forms of industrialized education will also be risky. However, the difficulties to be expected are part of those critical developments typical for our time of transition from the last phase of the last western civilization to the first phase of the emerging global industrial civilization (Gehlen 1961: 132). This development may raise mankind to a high general level of civilization never reached before.

Seen anthropologically, man is also 'a being open for the future' (Roth 1966: 49). As such he will be able to overcome the critical structural changes which result from such transformations of civilization and in education especially from the juxtaposition of traditional occidental forms of instruction and the industrialized forms of teaching and learning in the coming world civilization. History has shown that 'man has repeatedly been able to overcome extremely advanced alienations which were caused by transformations of humanity' (Freyer 1963: 245).

The arguments of the critics of culture that the humanity of education is threatened by the use of rational planning and organization, and of technical media, no longer hold true in the light of this anthropological discussion. Seen in a larger context the construction of complex technical systems of teaching and learning and their successful implementation must be interpreted as a real proof of man's capacity to react to fundamental changes of society. It is a building block for the 'secondary environment' which people must create in order to survive. In the same way in which technology was not anything strange or even hostile to the inner nature of man in the anthropogenesis, their efforts to industrialize instruction, their ability and skill to instruct extremely large groups of persons with the help of technology can be interpreted as a condition for the possibility of survival in the forthcoming industrial world civilization.

REFERENCES

Adorno, T. W. (1967) *Ohne Leitbild. Parva Aesthetica*, Frankfurt on Main: Suhrkamp.
Behrendt, R. F. (1962) *Der Mensch im Licht der Soziologie*, Stuttgart: Kohlhammer.
Brunner, H. (1957) *Altägyptische Erziehung*, Wiesbaden: Harassowitz.
Cordt, W. (1963) 'Revolution oder "New York" in der Erziehung', in *Auswahl*, 5, Hanover: Schroedel, pp. 108–16.
Dahrendorf, R. (1959) 'Betrachtungen zu einigen Aspekten der deutschen Soziologie', in *Kölner Zeitschrift für Soziologie*, 2: 135.
—— (1965) *Gesellschaft und Demokratie in Deutschland*, Munich: Piper.
Enzensberger, H. M. (1963) *Bewusstseins-Industrie*, Frankfurt on Main: Suhrkamp.
Flechsig, K-H. (1969) *Die technologische Wendung in der Didaktik*, Konstanzer Universitätsreden No. 23, Konstanz: Universitätsverlag.
Flitner, W. (1967) *Europäische Gesittung. Ursprünge und Aufbau abendländischer Lebensformen*, Zurich: Artemis.
Freyer, H. (1963) *Theorie des gegenwärtigen Zeitalters*, Stuttgart: DVA.
Fuchs, W. R. (1969) *Knaurs Buch vom neuen Lernen*, Munich: Knaur.
Gehlen, A. (1958) *Der Mensch. Seine Natur und seine Stellung in der Welt*, Bonn: Athenäum.
—— (1961) *Anthropologische Forschung*, Reinbek: Rowohlt.
Gehlen, A. and Schelsky, H. (eds) *Soziologie. Ein Lehr- und Handbuch zur modernen Gesellschaftskunde*, Düsseldorf/Cologne: Diederichs.
Habermas, J. (1968) *Technik als Wissenschaft und Ideologie*, Frankfurt on Main: Suhrkamp.
Heieck, L. (1969) *Bildung zwischen Technologie und Ideologie*, Heidelberg: Quelle & Meyer.
Heimann, P. (1961) 'Film, Funk und Fernsehen als Bildungsmächte der Gegenwartskultur', in *Film, Bild, Ton, 11* (8): 5–15.
—— (1966) 'Die modernen Massenmedien Film, Funk und Fernsehen als Bildungsmächte der Gegenwartskultur', in *September-Gesellschaft, vol. 7: Technische Helfer in Unterricht und Erziehung*, Frankfurt on Main.
Heitger, M. (1963) *Bildung und moderne Gesellschaft*, Munich: Kösel.
Huber, L. (1970) 'Forschendes Lernen', in *BAK, Schriften der Bundesassistentenkonferenz*, No. 5, Bonn: BAK.
Kaltschmid, J. (1965) *Menschsein in der industriellen Gesellschaft. Eine kritische Bestandsaufnahme*, Munich: Kösel.
Kant, I. (n.d.) 'Beantwortung der Frage: Was ist Aufklärung?' in E. Aster (ed.) *Immanuel Kants populäre Schriften*, Berlin: Deutsche Bibliothek, pp. 1–9.
Keay, F. E. (1950) *Indian Education in Ancient and Later Times*, Oxford: Oxford University Press.

König, R. (1958) 'Gemeinschaft' in R. König (ed.) *Soziologie*, Frankfurt on Main: Fischer, pp. 83–8.
—— (1958) 'Gesellschaft', in R. König (ed.) *Soziologie*, Frankfurt on Main: Fischer, pp. 96–104.
—— (1958) 'Gruppe', in R. König (ed.) *Soziologie*, Frankfurt on Main: Fischer, pp. 104–12.
Leeuw, van de, G. (1956) *Phänomenologie der Religion*, Tübingen: Mohr.
Lepsius, R. M. (1958) 'Industrie und Betrieb', in R. König (ed.) *Soziologie*, Frankfurt on Main: Fischer, p. 122.
Litt, T. (1959) *Das Bildungsideal der deutschen Klassik und die moderne Arbeitswelt*, Bonn: Bundeszentrale für Heimatdienst.
Marcuse, H. (1969) *Ideen zu einer kritischen Theorie der Gesellschaft*, Frankfurt on Main: Suhrkamp.
McLuhan, M. (1964) *Understanding Media: The Extensions of Man*, New York: McGraw-Hill.
Nishimoto, M. (1971) 'Das akademische Fernstudium in Japan', in O. Peters (ed.) *Texte zum Hochschulfernstudium*, Weinheim: Beltz, pp. 95–113.
Peters, O. (1968) *Das Hochschulfernstudium*, Weinheim: Beltz.
—— (1971) 'Vier ausländische Projekte für ein Fernstudium im Medienverbund. Eine vergleichende Betrachtung ihrer didaktischen Struktur und bildungspolitischen Begründung', in G. Dohmen and O. Peters (eds) *Hochschulunterricht im Medienverbund*, Heidelberg: Verlagsgemeinschaft VRMV, I, pp. 109–49.
Rademacker, H. (1969) 'Zum Einsatz von programmiertem Unterricht an Hochschulen', in *Arch + 2*, pp. 37–50.
Reble, A. (1968) 'Geschichte der Pädagogik', in *Pädagogisches Lexikon*, Stuttgart: Kreuz.
Riesman, D. et al. (1958) *Die einsame Masse. Eine Untersuchung der Wandlungen des amerikanischen Charakters*, Reinbek: Rowohlt.
Roth, H. (1966) *Pädagogische Anthropologie*, Hanover: Schrödel.
Rothacker, E. (1966) *Philosophische Anthropologie*, Bonn: Bouvier.
Schelsky, H. (1963) *Einsamkeit und Freiheit*, Reinbek: Rowohlt.
—— (1965) 'Industrie- und Betriebssoziologie', in A. Gehlen and H. Schelsky (eds) *Soziologie. Ein Lehr- und Handbuch zur modernen Gesellschaftskunde*, Düsseldorf/Cologne: Diederichs.
Scheuerl, H. (1970) 'Kulturkritik', in W. Horney, and J. P. Ruppert and W. Schultze (eds) *Pädagogisches Lexikon*, Gütersloh: Bertelsmann, 1970, II, col. 134–5.
Strunz, K. (1970) 'Sprache', in W. Horney, J. P. Ruppert and W. Schultze (eds) *Pädagogisches Lexikon*, Gütersloh: Bertelsmann, 1970, II, col. 1097–8.
Tausch, R. (1960) 'Das Ausmass der Lenkung von Schulkindern im Unterricht. Eine empirische Untersuchung der Fragen. Befehle und Anforderungen von Lehrern', in *Psychologische Beiträge*, 4: 127.
Tausch, A. and R. (1966) *Erziehungspsychologie*, Göttingen: Hogrefe.
Toffler, A. (1970) *Der Zukunftsschock*, Berne: Scherz.
Withall, J. and Lewis, W. W. (1963) 'Social interaction in the classroom', in N. L. Gage (ed.) *Handbook of Educational Research*, Chicago: Rand McNally, p. 669.

Part III
Distance education in practice

7 The concept of the Fernuniversität (1981)

Peters published *Die Fernuniversität im fünften Jahr* (The *Fernuniversität* in its fifth year) in 1981. It has 256 pages. It has the subtitle: 'Report of the Foundation Vice-Chancellor' and deals with educational politics and distance education didactics. It tells the story of the development of the Fernuniversität from its legal foundation in November–December 1974 and its opening in October 1975 and seeks to present a rationale for the directions taken. The Fernuniversität was a highly innovative German university structure which broke with centuries of German university tradition; it was a *Gesamthochschule* – a comprehensive university – that is, a university that combined traditional German university faculties with the new technological disciplines; and it chose didactic strategies, media, standards and approaches that differed markedly from other distance education universities.

At the end of 1972 it was realized in the Federal Republic of Germany that estimates of the increase in the number of university students had been too low. New estimates revealed that even a radical extension of the universities could never meet the rapidly growing demand for university places – a process which was aggravated by the increased output of secondary schools and the high percentage of secondary school graduates who intended to enrol at universities. The numbers of students who actually went on to university rose, and reached its peak in 1972 at 90 per cent.

In this situation the Minister of Higher Education and Research of the *Land* North Rhine-Westphalia considered the possibilities of distance education which had been discussed in the preceding years with more or less commitment on various levels. Since the planned Federal University for Distance Education, which was to involve all *Länder*, all universities and all broadcasting corporations of the

Federal Republic, obviously did not have any chance of being realized, the government of North Rhine-Westphalia decided to establish an autonomous university for distance education. This decision was justified, as it was foreseeable that the different groups planning the federal scheme would never agree – mainly for financial reasons – and the success of the Open University started to convince even sceptics that distance education is feasible in higher education. The cabinet agreed on a plan for the establishment of the Fernuniversität on 9 October 1973. Thus for the history of the concept of the Fernuniversität one has to keep in mind that the original reason and the starting point for founding it was the unexpected and unusually high increase in the number of persons who were entitled and wished to become enrolled at a university. The early plans envisaged distant students who had just graduated from secondary school. Consequently, the new university was to provide study places for nineteen- to twenty-year-old applicants who were to study full time at a distance, that is about forty hours per week. This means that the Fernuniversität was to be, so to speak, a conventional university for conventional students, which, however, taught at a distance. It is true that it was also to become a reform university in the sense that it was to be a comprehensive university, but this applied also to five other newly founded universities.

While the first plan was being discussed, however, it was already being repeatedly suggested that there would also be a demand for university places from adults who worked for a living, and that these applicants might even be in the majority. The Planning Committee, therefore, decided to provide a special quota for them, namely 50 per cent. Furthermore, the Planning Committee ruled that continuing education was to be another important objective. Anyone should be able to enrol for single courses. For these students – as well as for students of other universities taking single courses – the quota was to be 25 per cent. Only 25 per cent, then, remained for persons who had just graduated from secondary schools.

These decisions were fundamental alterations in the original concept. Their consequences for educational policy were of great importance. Some of the critics of the planned Fernuniversität changed their minds and began to accept it, and those experts advocating the establishment of continuing education at all universities now began to support the idea of the Fernuniversität. The suspicion of the other universities grew a little less as the Fernuniversität was no longer expected to become a rival institution to them.

The concept of the Fernuniversität 175

In spite of this dramatic change in the clientele, the Planning Committee confirmed, however, that the courses, the study material and the regulations for examinations should nevertheless be exactly the same as in conventional universities. This was deemed necessary for two reasons: it would be easier for the Fernuniversität to become recognized by the other universities, and it would facilitate the transfer of students from the Fernuniversität to other universities.

At the same time, the special possibilities of the Fernuniversität for the establishment of continuing education were discussed in Parliament as well as in political circles outside Parliament. Everybody saw that the new institution could open its doors to working people to continue their education and that this could be achieved more easily than in conventional universities. On the other hand, it was perfectly clear that continuing education could never be the only mandate of the Fernuniversität and that the Fernuniversität was not to become another institution for adult education.

While discussing the Enabling Law for the Fernuniversität, some experts criticized the establishment of new universities, arguing that the number of jobless graduates was steadily increasing and that this would hold true in the case of the Fernuniversität. The then Minister of Higher Education and Research, Johannes Rau, reacted to them by saying: 'Until the warnings against a saturated labour market are confirmed – and so far all warnings against more students for the professions have been wrong – the Fernuniversität will see to it that as many persons as possible will get chances to study if they wish to do so.'

This decision can be justified by stressing that education and training not only contribute to the achievement of vocational or professional goals, but also to the development of personality. A higher level of general education can, indeed, increase social, political and humanistic competences and facilitate active participation in our social and political life.

The Fernuniversität Act of the *Land* North Rhine-Westphalia was passed by Parliament on 26 November 1974. On 4 October 1974 the Fernuniversität was opened in an official ceremony at the Stadttheater of Hagen.

Right from its beginning the conceptual impulses of the planning period were taken over and integrated in the discussions which now continued in the governing bodies of the new university. Its programme profile was shaped by following three main goals: extension of the capacity of the universities, university reform, and continuing education. These were proclaimed by the Prime Minister,

Heinz Kühn, as well as by the Minister for Higher Education and Research, Johannes Rau, during the opening ceremony, and remained the main orientation for the development of the Fernuniversität in subsequent years.

Whether these three goals are of equal importance, and whether they should and could be realized right from the beginning and at the same time, became the central topic which was discussed by the Fernuniversität Senate, the central committee (*Rektorat*), and in the faculties – often vividly and with deep involvement. This was because the structural orientation of the new university was at issue. Should the Fernuniversität become an institute for continuing education or higher continuing education, or should it rather become a conventional university, that was the question – admittedly in very simplified terms. The discussion was nourished by political convictions, tactical considerations and naturally also by sound interests. Above all, it became obvious that the majority of the university teachers were not only interested in a new future-orientated university, but, legitimately, also in chances for their academic careers. They, therefore, were of the opinion that a Fernuniversität with a traditional structure would be more suitable for their becoming recognized in the scientific community. On the other hand students in the various bodies of the university's self-government had the situation of their fellow students in mind, and had to consider their chances, difficulties and needs – especially of those who were in full employment. They advocated more practice-orientation and free access for applicants without formal entrance qualifications, and emphasized the importance of continuing education. Between these two positions there was also a number of mediating and integrating points of view.

The debate about the right concept for the Fernuniversität reached its peak in April 1977. It was temporarily concluded by a declaration of the Founding Rector in the Senate on 21 April, which mirrors the compromise achieved at that time. It was based on the conviction of all groups that the Fernuniversität must necessarily first seek to obtain academic reputation, as only genuine scientific achievements in teaching and research and their recognition by the public would be a good pre-condition for the development of higher continuing education as well as for experiments in facilitating access. Therefore, the consolidation of the already-developed degree courses had to have priority in the first stage. Thereafter, in the second stage, extension of the degree programme was to be implemented. Then, in a third stage, new and separate courses for continuing education were to be developed. Cooperation with the broadcasting corporations and access for applicants without formal entrance qualifications were to be achieved in parallel with the second and third stages. The final passage of the declaration conveys the balance of claims which had to be considered when developing a strategy for the development of the Fernuniversität:

> The Fernuniversität is a university supplementing the system of higher education in order to comply with the new needs for education and training in modern industrialized society. In the first place it caters for adults who have the required entrance qualifications, but have postponed their university studies so far and for university graduates in employment who wish to obtain further qualifications by continuing their education.
>
> By accomplishing these tasks it helps to solve the capacity problem of the universities and gives a strong impulse to university reform. In laying the foundation for its activities the Fernuniversität will not tend to take over tasks of conventional institutions of adult aducation (*Volkshochschulen*). The Fernuniversität will rather bind itself to the quality standards and the spirit of the traditional university. At the same time it is open for new educational tasks, develops new models for university reform and assumes an experimental attitude when solving these tasks. All members of the Fernuniversität must be expected to combine these two approaches.

This concept became extremely useful in the second and third phase of the development of the Fernuniversität.

On 13 June 1977, the then Minister of Higher Education and Research, Johannes Rau, delivered a speech at the first meeting of the Fernuniversität's Advisory Board in which he examined the political objectives which had led to the founding of the Fernuniversität and which had also been the foundation of its concept. He wanted to find out 'whether they are still important or whether they must be modified'. He surprised many participants when he presented the three main goals of the Fernuniversität in a new sequence. According to this, the Fernuniversität was first to contribute to university reform, secondly to develop higher continuing education, and thirdly to increase the capacity of the universities. The original first goal which, as described, had caused the planning of the Fernuniversität, was now relegated to third place. This can be explained by the fact that the capacity problem of the universities was no longer as pressing as at the beginning of the seventies, which meant that the two other main goals assumed more importance. One can speak of a shift of emphasis for the benefit of university reform and continuing education. All three goals, however, become instrumental in striving after Rau's general political goal for the Fernuniversität, namely 'to improve the chances of all citizens to get a university education'.

8 The Fernuniversität after ten years (1985)

'The Fernuniversität after ten years' was published in 1985 as *Die Gründing der Fernuniversität: Wagnis und Gelingen* (The foundation of the *Fernuniversität*: challenge and success). It is the report of the Foundation Vice-Chancellor after ten years. The report looks back over the period in which this experimental institution established itself as a fully accepted university in the rigorous academic world of German university tradition and gives some guidelines for the future.

Ten years have gone by since the Parliament of North Rhine-Westphalia passed the Act for the Establishment of the Fernuniversität, and today we should like to commemorate this legislative act. It made possible all the planning and development activities of the foundation period which has now been completed. It enabled us to establish a unique university which is in a position to tackle new tasks in present-day higher education and continuing education and even more in the future. This legislative act was, therefore, of great social importance.

At the time of the foundation of the Fernuniversität, the combined efforts of the universities, the governments of the *Länder*, of the Federal Government as well as of the broadcasting corporations to establish a university for distance education had lasted for years and had come to a complete impasse. In this situation the then Minister of Higher Education and Research of North Rhine-Westphalia, Johannes Rau, initiated all the activities necessary for the foundation of the Fernuniversität. He did so with a sense of proportion, a nose for political timing, an instinct for the successful approach, and with extraordinary personal involvement. His activities were, moreover, courageous as he suggested new things, and demanded the unorthodox and reorientation. It is true that his ambitious activities were regretted by those who still hoped that the national plan for distance education would nevertheless be realized. But most people interested in distance education, especially the prospective students, welcomed his activities with relief. The dominant feeling was that with the enactment of the Law for the Establishment of the Fernuniversität the Gordian knot had been cut. In the educational policy of recent decades no similar example of such a resolute act can be found.

Those who were invited to occupy themselves with the new project at that time could not, however, avoid being seized by hesitations and scruples. Every foundation of a university is risky. The foundation of a Fernuniversität is even more risky. It was to be expected that it would meet criticism of a special kind because it catered for adult students – a task which was not yet seen at that time as central, and because of the necessity of transmitting knowledge predominantly with the help of a technical system. No other newly founded university would be attacked on these grounds. Accordingly, the members of the Planning Committee, nearly all of them professors of other, that is traditional, universities, had to deal with particular problems. Would the Fernuniversität be attractive for outstanding and experienced scholars? Would the students envisaged really enrol? Would not the intended high level of instruction and the demanding standards of the examinations rather deter persons who had to work for a living? Would not the plan to combine academic teaching traditions with a technological delivery system invite opposition? Would the administration of the university, which is no less in the grip of tradition than the faculties, be able to master the additional management tasks which correspond with those of a medium-sized publishing house? Would the other universities understand and appreciate the newcomer so different in its goals and groups of students? And if they did, would they not consider the Fernuniversität to be a powerful rival institution on account of its 'mass production' of knowledge and its distribution to masses of students living practically everywhere? Would the new university be accepted by the public in spite of old prejudices and new anxieties caused by technological progress? Would not fond remembrances of their own university experiences cause opinion leaders to object to a new university which was lacking so many features of the traditional university? Question upon question, all of which, indeed, indicated uncertainty and insecurity.

The outlines of the venture become even more pregnant if we consider the foundation of the Fernuniversität under the aspect of the history of academic instruction. The establishment of a university in which the spoken word is predominantly substituted by the written word, or by the word fixed to other technical media, indicates a severe turning point. Teaching traditions which have developed over centuries, even millennia, are interrupted. All organizational arrangements and routines which have facilitated oral teaching for ages have to be done away with and have to be changed for new forms of articulation of academic teaching. This is a serious situation of great consequence, the importance of which is underrated by many. The professors are not only bereft of their traditional teaching routines but also of some of their security of behaviour. They have to break new didactical ground and thereby have to make creative and constructive decisions themselves again and again. Would they be in a position to do this? Would they, moreover, come to terms in pragmatic ways with the technical media such as, for instance, audio and video cassettes, television and the computer? Teaching at traditional universities has, as we all know, been more or less resistent to these media. Would they get into the spirit of new planning and have the constructive imagination, the openness to new experiences, the readiness for experimentation and the ability of cooperation, all qualities which are traditionally called for in research, but not so much in teaching? Under this aspect an epoch-making change of methods and media was pioneered in the teaching of the new university, which was decidedly risky if we bear in mind what is known about the general readiness of professors to innovate their teaching in traditional circumstances, and if we realize that attitude changes cannot be planned and arrived at easily. There were many experts who asked themselves whether the experiment ahead of them would turn out well.

The doubts and objections referred to may have been generally subdued at the beginning by the strong enthusiasm which easily sets in when a great project is started. But they definitely were there and influenced the work of the first years. The Scientific Council, after having examined the plans for the Fernuniversität, was also conscious of the risks. Its members, it is true, judged the Fernuniversität as 'an important experiment with great consequences for university policies', but articulated their sceptical reservations by the following remark: 'For such an experiment nobody can guarantee success. Therefore, it should be continued carefully in order to diminish the danger of failure as much as possible.' Obviously, the experts judging this new project were not quite at ease. And finally, even Johannes Rau confessed that he did not found the university with a feeling of elation but 'with trembling and quailing'.

Now, after ten years and at the end of the founding phase, we can see that some of these doubts and objections were groundless and others seem to be obsolete already. The development of the Fernuniversität has overridden them. Other objections and doubts, however, were valid and show all the more clearly how much has been achieved in developing this university under difficult conditions. Five departments came into being and have developed their impact in research and teaching, in spite of the grievous financial and personnel restrictions of recent years. The recruitment of excellent and even renowned professors turned out to be not a difficult task. About 5,000 professors have so far applied for a chair and seventy have been appointed by the Minister of Higher Education and Research. Together with 200 scientific assistants and other university lecturers they have actively developed their research and teaching activities. At present they cater for more than 25,000 students. Their courses for graduate, postgraduate and continuing education have remained attractive over the years.

The number of enrolled students rises from year to year. The graduates are sought after in the labour market. The self-government of the university has developed and has been remarkably successful. Students are represented on its bodies in the same way as at other universities, a fact which is often overlooked or unexpected by observers of the Fernuniversität. An effective administration routinely solves even unorthodox tasks which are specific to distance education. Excellent relations exist between the Fernuniversität and those communities which have established study centres for us, as well as with a number of universities with which the Fernuniversität has entered into agreements of cooperation and also between the Fernuniversität and other distance teaching universities abroad. For activities in continuing education the advice and cooperation of the Fernuniversität is sought after, most recently by the Scientific Council of the Federal Republic of Germany. The Fernuniversität is supported in its ideals and also financially by a 'Society of the Friends of the Fernuniversität' and has friendly ties to the city of Hagen and the surrounding region. There are good contacts to employers' organizations and those of employees, to political parties, to members of Parliament in Düsseldorf and Bonn. Altogether, the Fernuniversität has become an undisputed and self-evident part of higher education in the Federal Republic. As an autonomous institution the Fernuniversität already enjoys a considerable reputation and has, therefore, developed a cautious, but nevertheless distinct institutional self-consciousness and pride.

Summing up, one can say that the Fernuniversität has become a great new institution of higher learning, which has become the reference point of the hopes, plans, and activities of many people to whom it offers the possibility of learning and of studying as well as doing research and teaching. What a difference between the moment in which the idea of distance education was first formed in North Rhine-Westphalia and today when we can deal with a Fernuniversität which has grown constantly in an organic way, which has become mature by experience and has become conscious of itself, a university which has permanent relations to 25,000 students not only in all *Länder* of the Federal Republic of Germany but also in German-speaking countries, as well as in most countries of the western world. What a difference also between those doubts and objections in the planning phase and today's practice. A good piece of work has been done. Those who participated in the planning, in its political implementation and defence, those who took part in developing, extending and consolidating it, those who helped to overcome serious financial crises, those who have, indeed, ventured and 'trembled and quailed' can look back with great satisfaction.

And yet, there are critics who ask themselves and others whether it is really appropriate to speak of successful accomplishment in the case of the Fernuniversität. They argue that there are still unforeseen problems, some difficulties which have only been mastered half-way and also some failures. In spite of these reproaches the question raised can only be answered positively, and I should like to prove this by describing seven dimensions of this accomplishment.

The newly founded university was accepted very quickly, not only formally by its admission to the Rectors' Conferences of North Rhine-Westphalia, the Federal Republic of Germany, of Europe and the world, but also by practical cooperation with these bodies as well as with a number of universities, for instance, in Bochum, Düsseldorf, Frankfurt on Main, Oldenburg, Berlin and Klagenfurt.

The new university was also accepted by students. To many this has been the most impressive experience. The number of students as estimated by the Planning Committee was soon surpassed. Seemingly, we will have to cater for more than 25,000 students in the future – a phenomenon which deserves special attention from educational politicians. The number would even be considerably higher, perhaps twice as high, if the Fernuniversität had developed its departments of arts and social sciences as had been planned. This acceptance by students is, indeed, a splendid confirmation of its founding concept.

Here a compliment must be paid to the founding fathers of the Fernuniversität. They have opened a university for a new group of persons who up to then had not been seen and had therefore been neglected: students often with considerable vocational experience, clear educational goals and with admirable energy and stamina. With them we do not find any of that cavilling which causes many of the younger generation, in the universities as well, to belittle and reject extraordinary efforts and achievements. They form a new type: the adult student in full employment. Their emergence is a peculiar, new and significant aspect of the foundation of the Fernuniversität.

Students of this new type have developed a new way of studying and learning which will be epoch-making. They combine vocational practice and life experiences and demanding academic study. This may become a model for future continuing professional education. They select the courses themselves on the basis of their special needs. They deal with these courses, in most cases, with great involvement and use the criteria of their vocational practice self-confidently when judging them. Only some of them will graduate after long years under great stress and privation. Those graduates, however, who have stood their ground in their jobs and also succeeded in their academic study are sought after, how much so can be shown by quoting the answer of a personnel manager of one of the biggest companies in the Federal Republic. When asked how he would react when being informed that one of his employees had just graduated from the Fernuniversität, he said: 'I would keep him and try with might and main not to lose him!' Meeting such students in study centres or when they take tests is always pleasing and can make clear the real meaning of the Fernuniversität to sceptics and critics as well.

The Fernuniversität has become a remarkable place of scientific research and teaching. Its professors are well known in their disciplines, as a number of honourable calls to chairs of great universities rich in tradition inside and outside the Federal Republic shows. They have varying contacts with universities in other countries and are familiar with the international trends in their disciplines. They take part in international research projects and also serve as visiting and exchange professors abroad. They attend international conferences and organize such conferences themselves in Hagen. In this way a network of scientific contacts has been constructed which comprises the Academy of Sciences in Moscow and Warsaw, the Sorbonne and Oxford University, the University of California in Los Angeles, and Silicon Valley. Professors of the University for Planning and Statistics in Warsaw and of Princeton and Yale universities can be found among the authors of study units for the Fernuniversität. Scientific research is based on international cooperation. The Fernuniversität has taken this into account.

At the same time the education of the coming generation of scholars is in full swing. So far, more than 100 persons have taken a doctor's degree. The professors of the Fernuniversität have been able to gain 30 million Deutschmarks for their projects from sources outside the university. Their projects are regularly documented and published.

The research activities of the Fernuniversität are to my mind the reason for its acceptance by the scientific community. This distinguishes it from some distance teaching universities in which no research is conducted. The founding fathers of the Fernuniversität are also to be congratulated on their insistence on the basic function of research in a distance teaching university, on their adherence to the normative idea of the unity of research and teaching and on the establishment of departments in which the scholars of one discipline can cooperate. Thus, a university was created which certainly cannot be misunderstood as a mere technological instrument for the delivery of scientific knowledge produced elsewhere. This particular feature of the Fernuniversität is the reason for its attractiveness to many renowned scholars and will also remain the reason for its success in the years to come.

The stress laid on research was beneficial to the teaching. The scholars were able to take responsibility for their teaching material themselves. Thereby, their competence, their erudition, their methodological experience, their instructional skills as well as their renown could be directly invested. Thus, courses for distance teaching came into being which have been widely approved.

People outside the Fernuniversität are scarcely able to imagine the long, highly differentiated and troublesome process which has to be finished before teaching can begin. The courses and the teaching units must be carefully conceived, planned, tried out, repeatedly evaluated and tested. The Fernuniversität is the only university in the Federal Republic which has gained considerable experience in this field. More than this, it has also analysed and evaluated these experiences with the help of a special Institute for the Development of Study Material. In this process the professors have developed special teaching skills which are unknown in traditional universities. The way, for instance, in which they employ new media, including computers and television, is remarkable. Some observers even think that the successful adaptation of their teaching to the special needs of distant students can be considered the 'miracle of Hagen'.

The Fernuniversität has contributed to the consolidation of the Comprehensive University and thus performed a good deal of structural university reform. The admission of graduates of specialized schools (*Fachschulen*) has been a success. The short (three-year) courses have proved possible, and integrated courses combining more theory-orientated and more practice-orientated teaching have been developed. These new elements have helped the Fernuniversität to adapt its teaching to the special needs of an adult clientele.

The Fernuniversität has developed an organizational model for distance education, which corresponds to the special conditions of our country, to our tradition and our present possibilities. The dominant role of printed teaching material, the supplementary use of audio and video cassettes, the informative and motivating functions of the television broadcasts on Saturdays, the activities of the mentors in the study centres, the central and decentralized seminars, the tests under strict supervision and the *Dies Academicus* are some important elements of this model.

One of the most impressive features of this model is its unusual reach, which distinguishes the Fernuniversität from conventional universities as they are, with regard to their teaching, only of local or regional significance. The Fernuniversität, however, teaches students not only in Germany, but also in the whole western world. Because of this incomparable reach, accessibility to higher education is considerably improved. Thus, the differentials between education in the cities and in the country, of the privileged and the unprivileged, and the industrialized and the developing countries can be reduced.

This unique organizational model of a university is now fully developed, tested and consolidated. It has already become of general interest to governments of other countries which intend to organize distance teaching universities themselves.

The Fernuniversität has reached the three important goals which were formulated by the Minister of Higher Education and Research at its opening ceremony: new capacities have been provided to relieve the other universities of the burden of too many students, university reform is under way, and continuing academic education has been established on a large scale.

As to the provision of new capacities, the Fernuniversität can claim that 14.2 per cent of its full-time students and 7.7 per cent of its part-time students belong to the age group eighteen to twenty-four years, and relieve the universities *directly*. It is also of interest that one-fifth of all students in the Federal Republic admitted for computer science this year are enrolled at the Fernuniversität. But more important is the *indirect* relief of the universities in the field of continuing education, which they have not been able to establish at all or at least only on a very small scale. The Fernuniversität caters for probably the largest number of students in the field of continuing education of all universities in Europe. This group now comprises 10,000 students, of whom, by the way, 37 per cent do not have formal university entrance qualifications. So far, more than 30,000 persons in employment have continued their education at the Fernuniversität.

With regard to university reform noteworthy achievements have been accomplished. Looking at the universities of the Federal Republic we can ask: where else have entirely new groups of students been recruited? Where else have new models of teaching and learning been developed and tested? Where else have technical media been utilized for teaching purposes to such a great extent? Where else has the whole teaching–learning system been adapted to the needs of adult students?

It can be reported that continuing academic education has become a focal point of the Fernuniversität's teaching because so many students have applied for it. It is coordinated by a special Pro-rector for Continuing Education. A comprehensive and diversified programme is at hand. In order to illustrate this field of activity by means of an example the course 'Special Education and Rehabilitation' may be mentioned. It was developed for parents, teachers, social workers and persons working in the health service. It aims at supporting the socio-pedagogical integration of the handicapped. This course shows how continuing education can have a direct impact on our daily experience. The whole field of continuing education is now consolidated after ten years and will develop further. Because of these developments there are observers who consider the Fernuniversität as a university for continuing education.

The Fernuniversität has had experiences which might help to solve educational tasks of the future. This can be demonstrated by referring to three patterns of attitude change:

• It cannot be irrelevant for the future that everyone working in

188 *Distance education in practice*

the Fernuniversität is committed to the task of catering mainly for adult students working for a living. This means that they find it appropriate to tear down traditional barriers and to secure access to higher education for this particular clientele. To them this task is already the self-evident pre-condition of their work which needs no debate.

- It cannot be irrelevant for the future if the people working in the Fernuniversität and thousands of distance students consider a new pattern of the distribution of university study over a lifetime not only to be possible, but also acceptable and feasible. No longer do they associate university study with the beginning of adulthood only. Lifelong learning, which has been called for and propagated by experts for more than twenty years now, mainly in vain, has been realized by the Fernuniversität and embodied in the minds of its teachers and students.

- It cannot be irrelevant for the future when tens of thousands of students, hundreds of university teachers and a public interested in educational matters have become familiar with the unique possibilities of such a university, have got used to it and have accepted it, not as an interesting experiment, but as a normal addition to the university system.

The changes of attitudes achieved in these three cases mirror and forecast a structural change in the university which is necessary to meet new educational needs in advanced industrialized societies. In the case of the Fernuniversität this change has not remained a mere plan or a postulated requirement, but has been accomplished after ten years of hard work. One can even maintain that these new attitudes have already been internalized by many of the participants. Everyone who has been committed to university reform and who knows about the barriers, hurdles and obstructions involved will see and admit how significant these changes of attitudes are and will be in the years to come. The Fernuniversität is a pioneer in this new field of higher education.

Is there nothing left to be desired? Nobody seriously thinks so. It is true that the foundation of the Fernuniversität is an outstanding achievement with regard to the social and educational policy which brought it about, to its scientific importance, and its organizational-technological structure and unique attractiveness to students. And it is also true that its long founding phase has now come to an end, but, and this must be stressed, its development has not yet been concluded. If we do not want to endanger and gamble away the

The Fernuniversität after ten years 189

success so far achieved we must envisage new goals. I will refer to seven of them.

Disciplines which still suffer from having developed slowly and from the fluctuation of some key professors must be consolidated – in particular, law, computer science and electrical engineering.

The number of teaching programmes and departments must be increased. There is a demand for additional postgraduate courses, and the university needs departments of arts and social sciences. Only after having established these departments can the Fernuniversität become a real *universitas literarum* in which the departments complement each other in many ways and carry out interdisciplinary discussions of scientific problems. This can be achieved more easily when all departments can work together on one campus. Therefore, new buildings must be provided for on this campus in the years to come.

The network of study centres must be extended. Study centres are still lacking in Schleswig-Holstein, Hamburg, Rhineland-Palatinate, Saar, Baden-Württemberg and Bavaria. The in-depth discussions between mentor and students as well as between students and students remain a very important element of the teaching–learning system of the Fernuniversität, although there are many students who manage to pass their examinations without having been in a study centre at all.

The media system must be developed further and become more diverse and differentiated. The university should continue to claim transmission time for radio and television for broadcasting lectures and demonstrations covering the whole Federal Republic and not only North Rhine-Westphalia. A tutoring system for students and study groups by telephone should be established. The use of interactive videotex should be extended and developed further.

The student support service must be improved by rendering additional assistance to the individual student. It should guide and counsel students without reducing their individual activity in the learning process.

The Fernuniversität must continue to intensify its international relations. It caters for students in nearly all countries of the western world and has good connections to many universities and distance teaching universities abroad. This, however, is not sufficient in the face of the vital problems of international developments. To avoid becoming provincial the Fernuniversität must extend and strengthen these relations. One step in this direction could be the development of special courses for the continuing education of teachers of German at schools and universities in other countries. The academic staff of the Fernuniversität should consider and reconsider the spiritual and intellectual foundations of their work. By doing so they could check the tendency to train only the specialized intellect of the students and to neglect them thereby as human beings. This raises the difficult question of what education by scientific study means in our present industrialized society and in the developing scientific world civilization. This question has not yet been answered. It cannot be answered any longer by referring to Wilhelm von Humboldt's still widely accepted philosophical concept of a university which proclaims the self-educating subject to be the main reference point of university research and teaching – a concept which is certainly appealing, especially to educationists. The impulses from Karl Jaspers and Eduard Spranger for the revival of von Humboldt's idea of the university hardly found any echo at all after the Second World War. If we want to find out what 'education by scientific study' means today we must examine the relation between theory and the corresponding vocational and social practice in order to find out how much it has changed. The function of theory is then to analyse and interpret reality in its abstractness and complexity and to keep the results open. By means of such an approach it should be possible to redefine the position of man in this interpreted reality and to become committed to the *humanum* which is threatened in our modern world civilization by alienation as a result of the division of labour, by technological manipulation, by the disintegration of traditions, by ecological catastrophes, and by famines which are tormenting mankind.

If the Fernuniversität thought that the training of specialists in specialized subjects was the only and ultimate goal of its work, it would act without any guiding principles. The problem laid open must be dealt with by academics of all departments who are expected to cross the boundaries of their own disciplines. Dealing with this problem could create a new integration and identification of the teaching staff. This task should be tackled soon, for a university cannot be merely an agglomeration of specialized disciplines and their training programmes – even if they are of utmost importance and work most efficiently. To many this task seems to be Utopian when we consider the many difficulties of our daily experiences. But the Fernuniversität can emerge as a real university only if this discussion has taken place. Strictly speaking, its founding period will not be finished until then.

The Fernuniversität after ten years 191

Considering the accomplishments already achieved and the tasks still ahead of the Fernuniversität, one can say that new dimensions of further accomplishments have become visible. In its second decade the Fernuniversität will serve more people and thereby become more significant. And nothing will remind us of the 'trembling and quailing' of its beginning any longer. The Fernuniversität is no longer a 'venture', but a great success which gives confidence to all involved with it.

Part IV
Contemporary analyses

9 The iceberg has not yet melted
Further reflections on the concept of industrialization and distance teaching (1989)

After his retirement as Vice-Chancellor, Peters published this article on his views on the industrialization of teaching and learning in 1989 in the journal *Open Learning*. The striking title and vigorous refutation of his critics shows his new skill in writing in English. He gives his reactions to a selection of reviewers and commentators on his work, mainly taken from English sources.

When reviewing my book *Die didaktische Struktur des Fernunterrichts: Untersuchungen zu einer industrialisierten Form des Lehrens und Lernens* (1973) (The educational principles of distance education: research into an industrialized form of teaching and learning), Jeavons (1986: 165) used a striking metaphor when saying that 'theories are like icebergs' in order to point out that quite often only one part of the visible tip becomes known whereas the submergent nine-tenths remain invisible. With the help of this metaphor he wanted to explain that only one chapter of the book on the comparison between the teaching and learning process in distance study and the industrial production process had become visible and was hence being discussed, whereas four more chapters containing the theoretical underpinnings remained in the dark, partly because they have not been translated into English. This could be the reason for the existence of a number of misunderstandings. Being invited to respond to such misunderstandings I would like to adopt this metaphor. I consider it well chosen for three additional reasons.

First: Icebergs break away from their original surroundings and often drift into new areas where they do not normally belong. The use of characteristics relating to the industrial production process in explaining the teaching–learning process in distance study was certainly new and unheard of, and in the minds of some not even appropriate or desirable.

Second: Icebergs are often seen as a danger. Many readers when they come across the term 'industrialized teaching and learning' think of smoking chimneys and dirty manufacturing plants and become afraid that these will soil the pure world of learning. Also at a more abstract level, people have strong reservations as they feel that something entirely unfamiliar and dangerous has entered education.

Third: Icebergs change their appearance and become smaller. Jeavons (1986: 168) referred to this aspect when he wrote that 'even the finest icebergs can melt'.

MISUNDERSTANDING 1

> *I must be a proponent of the process of industrialization in the field of distance education, because I have described the process in detail and at length, and I must be trying to bring about and further this process.*

Nothing could be more wrong. This reminds me of the oriental potentates who put the blame for unpleasant news on the messenger and had him hanged. I have not advocated the industrialization of teaching and learning. It was only that I drew attention to this development which nobody had seen until then, and tried to analyse it. I acted as a witness. Most importantly of all, I am not opposed to other forms of teaching and learning, and especially not to face-to-face elements or other forms of the 'guided didactic conversation' (Holmberg 1981: 30) in distance study. I do not want to dehumanize the instructional process in distance learning.

In fact, the case is quite the contrary. In order to prove this I have to refer to an invisible part of the iceberg. In my book I devoted a chapter to the problematic nature of industrialized forms of teaching and learning. I discussed the structural incompatibility of industrialized teaching and learning with a locally organized educational system. Furthermore, I stressed the process of alienation which takes place when students are confronted with technical artefacts instead of live human beings. Personal relations become indirect and depersonalized, and lose much of their reality. This is symptomatic of the great rationalization of society which is going on irresistibly and which leads to 'disenchantment with the world' (Max Weber 1951: 566). Finally, I suggested that dominant political

The iceberg has not yet melted 197

groups might easily seize power by increasing their influence not only in the administration, industry, military, and the transport and communications systems, but also through a centralized industrialized system of education. Such a system would fit easily within an interrelated and integrated mega-organization, and could be used to manipulate people in a subtle but efficient way. There is the danger that people would become more and more instrumentalized in such a system (Peters 1973: 208).

MISUNDERSTANDING 2

As I have made a study of the similarities of distance study and educational technology I must be an ed tech fan. Jeavons (1986: 166) called me 'a great technological optimist'. Schwittmann (1982: 155) is worried and calls my description 'very problematic'. Ehmann (1981: 231) goes so far as to mistake me for a member of the Society for Programmed Instruction (Gesellschaft für Programmierten Unterricht), which I have never been.

Nothing could be more absurd. Of course, I studied the rise of educational technology in the seventies with great interest. This was part of my job. Certainly, I described the rightly significant role it had in the process of industrialization in education. However, I have never been a protagonist of educational technology. On the contrary, I devoted a chapter to a description of the dangers of a technological model of distance study; the over-emphasis on technical devices, the inevitable reduction of possible learning objectives, the fragmentation and compartmentalization of the learning process, the dominance of technical rationality at the cost of 'critical rationality'. Obviously this part of my book is also part of the hidden iceberg.

Perhaps I should repeat what has been said again and again, perhaps most recently by Shale (1987: 15–21); educational technologies have not worked in distance teaching universities as their more enthusiastic proponents initially thought they would, notwithstanding the theoretical and empirical accomplishments of the last two decades (see, for instance, the massive volumes by Romiszowski 1981, 1984, 1986, 1988). The reasons for this are manifold:

- The skills and techniques of educational technology have been too complex and time-consuming to be acquired by academics in addition to their teaching and research duties.
- The idea that experts in educational technology should assume

a mediating function and impart their expertise to academics individually or in course teams has only been partly realized.
- The patterns and routines of discipline-based traditional teaching proved to be very strong, and these have not been replaced by the artificial procedures of instructional design (for example, the definition of learning objectives in operational terms, the construction of tests, the identification of learning strategies, and the planning of evaluation measures).

Obviously the staying power of traditional ways of teaching had been underrated.

On the other hand it would be wrong to say that academic teaching at distance teaching universities has remained unscathed by educational technology. We can register at least the following changes: academics have learnt to plan and to prepare their teaching material carefully and well in advance of delivery. They have assumed an experimental attitude with regard to their own instruction. They have become used to looking at their courses as 'products', which can be improved with the help of relevant data. They have allowed experts to discuss problems of teaching with them, individually or in course teams. They have used mass media and have transformed their instruction according to the requirements of those media, and have enjoyed the fact that they can reach out to thousands of students at one time. They have learnt to use some of the educational technology jargon. On the whole, there is no doubt about it: this part of the iceberg has melted considerably.

MISUNDERSTANDING 3

> *The interpretation of distance study as an industrialized form of teaching and learning was part of the* zeitgeist *which prevailed in the formative years of the first open universities (Shale 1987: 15). It might have been justified in the seventies but after the disillusionment of the eighties it has lost much of its relevance – (Ehmann (1981: 233), Jeavons (1986: 165)).*

I do not see it this way. The industrialization of teaching and learning is only a small part of a pattern of enormous social change. Industrialization has changed and will go on changing our lives fundamentally whether we like it or not: people now work, spend their leisure time, buy, eat and communicate with their relatives and friends in different ways. They also think in different ways and have

The iceberg has not yet melted 199

developed attitudes not known by their grandparents. It is unlikely that education can resist this process. Further, it might be misleading to assume that the technologization of education peaked in the seventies.

We will probably have to face even greater changes of this kind in education if we are seriously to strive for egalitarian educational systems. In the same way as it will not be possible to feed, clothe and house nearly everyone in the developing countries properly without industrialization, so it will not be possible to provide education. The industrialization of education represents a long-term process of historical and anthropological dimensions and not just the consequences of a decade of enthusiastic reform. I dealt with this in Chapter 5 of my book, yet this is almost forgotten in the debate about the 'industrial model' of distance study, the only exceptions to this oversight being found in the work of Bååth (1979: 7; 1981: 212), Keegan (1986: 85), and Rekkedal (1983: 79).

MISUNDERSTANDING 4

The concept of industrialized teaching and learning is more or less typical for single mode distance teaching universities (namely, those teaching only at a distance), but not for dual mode institutions (that is, those teaching both traditionally by face-to-face methods and also at a distance). The issue now is single-mode (industrialized) versus dual-mode institutions. Furthermore, 'the supremacy' of the single-mode institutions 'is challenged' (Jeavons (1986: 167)).

Dual-mode and single-mode institutions differ in their application of the principles of industrialization only relatively. Dual-mode institutions also have to develop learning materials, in Deakin, for example, using the self-same course team approach (division of labour, collaboration of experts, long-range planning, financial investment). They have to duplicate and despatch them using machines and technical media (mechanization) and often they have to keep track of their students with the help of a computer (automation). They cannot, however, exploit the advantages of mass production and capitalize on the economics of the large-scale operation which enables single-mode distance teaching institutions to employ the best teachers and experts in the market.

To sum up, dual-mode institutions are partly industrialized. They are somewhere on a continuum between conventional face-to-face teaching and learning and the instruction of single-mode institutions.

MISUNDERSTANDING 5

By identifying the characteristics of industrial production processes in distance education I have developed a 'theory of distance education' (Rebel (1983: 175)).

I did not do this! I limited myself to describing the structural differences between traditional teaching and learning and distance study. In spite of this, distance teaching remains teaching and distance education remains education. Both forms remain, of course, the object of the current theories of instruction and education. Distance study, therefore, can be analysed and interpreted according to the teaching models of scholars such as Skinner, Rothkopf, Ausubel, Egan, Bruner and Rogers, as Bååth (1983: 76) has shown so convincingly. It can be developed with the help of didactic concepts like, for instance, 'independent study', 'open learning', 'contract learning' or 'video tutored instruction'. I never maintained that my characterization of the structure of distance study could or should replace them. Its industrial structure is just one aspect of the phenomenon which has to be taken into account.

It is true, that, in 1973, I referred to Paul Heimann who had envisaged the emergence of a 'new didactics' because of the growing importance of technical media in instruction, and it may be that I shared this idea and hoped to contribute to it. But I never called my 'comparative interpretation' a theory.

This being so it is, of course, pointless to refer to the criteria which a theory of instruction must meet as described by other authors and to measure my comparative interpretation against them (Holmberg 1985: 25).

MISUNDERSTANDING 6

In distance teaching universities there are two areas. One is industrialized – namely, the collection, production, storage and distribution of teaching material (here the university functions like a business enterprise); while the other is not, it is 'more in the nature of traditionally conceived academic areas' (Kaye 1985: 1432, 1436; Kaye and Rumble 1981: 179).

This is certainly not the whole truth. In fact, I did not limit my comparison of the teaching and learning process of distance education and industrialized forms of work to the obvious factory or business enterprise areas of distance teaching universities but extended it (and this is more important), to the actual teaching and learning. In order to illustrate this by an example I shall refer here to the most striking feature of this development. Traditionally, a professor performed many teaching functions. He or she prepared, invited the students to meet in a lecture room or at home, created a special learning atmosphere, and motivated the students, implicitly or explicitly. The professor transmitted knowledge to the students, using voice and body as media, and decided when and how to use the blackboard or other media. The professor initiated and took part in the didactic dialogues, acted as tutor and counsellor, examined the students and selected students to help in research.

Due to the application of the principle of division of labour, and the cooperation of specialized experts, the personal unity of all these activities is broken up and the functions mentioned are assigned to specialists, groups of specialists or even specialized sections. By so doing, the role of the traditional professor is reduced mainly to the function of a subject-matter specialist, as members of the course team relieve him or her of many tasks of instructional planning. Media specialists, evaluation experts and instructional designers might be involved. Tutors and counsellors are involved at a distance in study centres. A bureaucratic organization coordinates the many separated teaching functions. Most phases of the teaching–learning process take place without the professor's intervention.

The parallel development in the world of work is obvious. The craftworker planned, organized, worked with tools and sold the products him or herself. In the industrialized working process this unity of action is divided into many specialized functions in departments for research and development, production, marketing, sales and so on.

As this radical change in instructional method corresponds naturally with a change in learning behaviour, it is appropriate to apply the term 'industrialized' to both teaching and learning in distance education.

What about research? Is it not organized in the same way as in traditional universities? Yes, but if we take a closer look at it we see that even in traditional universities, especially in the natural sciences and technological disciplines, the process of research has assumed the characteristics of industrialized work processes and takes place in organizations which are similar to factories. Helmut Schelsky (1963: 192) has described this, quoting Max Weber, who pointed to the division of labour in this field back in 1919: 'Research becomes a continuous acquisition of knowledge, a production process, which must devalue the single contribution' (1951: 575). He referred to Helmut Plessner, who found that 'mechanization, methodization, depersonalization of the production process regulate the production of material as well as of intellectual goods' (1924: 472). The division of labour, the cooperation of specialists, the use of machines including the computer, and the possibility for exchanging and substituting individuals in the research project show that the process of industrialization has changed research fundamentally compared to the time when the personality of the individual professor had been of exclusive significance.

Hence, in distance teaching universities the process of industrialization has permeated not only the administration, and the production and dissemination of teaching materials, but also teaching and learning itself and often also research. It is of comprehensive and central significance.

MISUNDERSTANDING 7

Distance education can be industrialized in so far 'as it employs the technology of the twentieth century' and 'produces an unvaried product in large quantities, and therefore, at low cost'. The analogy, however, should not be carried too far. The mediating functions of the support services of tutors and counsellors cannot be industrialized (Sewart 1982: 27, 28).

This concept of industrialization is, indeed, a narrow one. There is much more to it. Tutors and counsellors do not act autonomously but perform well-defined functions in a teaching–learning system. These functions are derived from the instruction designed by a course team or a professor. This is a clear result of the division of labour. They could not work without the rest of the university, especially not without the course material. In a special sense they are instrumentalized as they are normally not expected to teach in their own right. They are specialists and may accumulate experience in their limited field of activity which is greater than that of ordinary academic teachers. Thus they become experts. High-quality teaching becomes possible because of the contribution of such experts amongst whom the work has been divided. They are connected with the teaching–learning system administratively by some sort of supervision, academically by their loyalty to their faculty, and medially by the computer. As they receive relevant information about their students and their learning achievements via this medium, their tutoring and counselling could be called 'computer-aided' (mechanization, automation). They also use other technical media, such as the telephone, as well as the personal letter and in some cases a student magazine.

There is no doubt that industrialized teaching and learning leads to the building of complicated systems in which tutors and counsellors play an important part, but a part. As such their work is also 'industrialized'.

MISUNDERSTANDING 8

> *The 'industrialization idea' does not do justice to all conceivable forms of distance education. It is perfectly adequate to describe activities of large correspondence schools, of the Open University, of large teaching systems based on radio or TV courses. But what about... very small correspondence schools, entirely run by two or three persons?' (Bååth 1981: 213; Duignan and Teather 1985: 42).*

The industrialization of the production process went through many stages beginning with the simple work of small manufacturers and ending with complex and often fully automated enterprises. Thus, the work originally done by a craftworker became more and more industrialized. This development can be studied by looking at the growing importance of technical devices in this process. Their purpose is to free people from routine and hard physical work and to make the process more cost-effective.

In the pre-industrial period tools were used as extensions and reinforcements of the human body, which at the same time was also the source of the energy needed. The teacher in the classroom acts as a craftworker, using the energy of the body when communicating with students. The pointer and the blackboard are bodily extensions.

The situation becomes entirely different when someone teaches at a distance even in its most simple form. For explanatory reasons I refer to the extreme of one person teaching another by means of personal letters. Here a technical device is used and takes over some of the functions of the teacher. In fact, the letter teaches instead of the teacher. It is possible for the student to learn and relearn from it many times without using the energy of the teacher. The teacher, however, needs a certain amount of organization at home or in the office (at least he or she must procure and store stationery and have a calendar and a list of names). Most important of all, the teacher must be able to rely on the help of communication and transport systems (mail, railways, bicycles and so on), now used as media for carrying instruction. Thus, a considerable organizational infrastructure helps to bring about the teaching–learning process which is only possible with division of labour between the teacher and the communication and transport systems.

This new way of imparting knowledge reduces routine work, is labour-saving and can also be more economical than face-to-face teaching even before the teacher decides to duplicate the written lessons and capitalize on the large scale productivity.

Analysing this first and most simple form of distance study we can already recognize tendencies towards the structural elements of industrialization. It is certainly no coincidence that the first correspondence schools were founded and the first railway and postal systems established at the same time, when industrialization began to change our lives.

MISUNDERSTANDING 9

> It is a misconception if someone argues that distance study is structurally different from conventional forms of study. Distance study 'is no more than a method of teaching' (Hopper, quoted by Keegan 1980: 18). 'It differs primarily in the means, the method itself' (Mackenzie, Christensen and Rigby, quoted by Keegan 1980: 18). Rebel (1983: 171) analysed conventional teaching and distance education and found 'more similarities than differences between them'.

In contrast to this I should like to suggest again that distance study is structurally different from traditional face-to-face instruction. I refer to the following obvious characteristic features which can be discerned at first sight: indirect (symbolic) interaction versus direct interaction; highly individualized learning versus learning in groups; course-material-centred versus teacher-centred instruction; the student being responsible for making decisions as to the time, place, sequence and frequency of self-learning activities versus the teacher being responsible for organizing and delivering instruction.

At a higher level of reflection I stress that distance study is

The iceberg has not yet melted 205

different because it has been developed by the application of the following principles:

- Division of labour: many people have to cooperate before learning can take place.
- Planning and organization: the various specialists have to work on projects which are subject to detailed prior planning. Their work has to be coordinated by bureaucratic procedures which are organized by the project management.
- Mechanization: distance study is not possible without mechanical devices, for example, the letter plus the communication media of the post office, printed matter, radio and television, audio or video cassettes, or the computer for the marking of assignments or computer-based tuition representing the highest level of mechanization, namely automation.
- Objectivity of teaching behaviour: the teaching which is traditionally performed subjectively in the classroom or lecture hall becomes objectified in the sense that it becomes an object which can be manipulated. It can be improved, adapted, changed and duplicated and lends itself to mass production.
- Scientific control: as distance study is the result of the cooperation of specialists, the efficiency of the teaching can no longer be judged in the same way as is done by the teacher in the classroom: experts have to do the evaluation.
- Alienation: in the same way as workers become alienated by strict division of labour, so people involved in the teaching system may become alienated as they often have only limited routine work to do with limited responsibilities. Furthermore, the students have a pre-disposition to become alienated as they may be used to instruction based on personal interaction yet have to take part in a teaching-learning process that is predominantly depersonalized. A feeling of isolation and frustration can be the consequence of this.

Thinking along these lines, one cannot but conclude that distance study is *sui generis* as it is the most industrialized form of teaching and learning.

MISUNDERSTANDING 10

Keegan (1980: 18) finds the radical separation of the educational principles of distance education and conventional education objec-

tionable. *He offers a quotation from R. S. Peters in which the 'culminating stages' of education are characterized in the following way: 'There is little distinction between teacher and taught; they are both participating in the shared experience of exploring a common world. The teacher is simply more familiar with its contours and more skilled in handling the tools for laying bare its mysteries and appraising its nuances. Occasionally in a tutorial this exploration takes the form of a dialogue. But more usually it is a group experience. The great teachers are those who can conduct such a shared experience in accordance with rigorous canons, and convey, at the same time, the contagion of shared experience in which all are united by a common zeal.' Then Keegan goes on to say: 'There is a huge gulf between this statement and the industrial process that Otto Peters described' and he accuses me of having 'misinterpreted what occurs in conventional education, especially at university level'.*

To my mind Keegan's quotation confirms my findings that the educational principles of the two forms of instruction are totally different. Developing industrialized instruction means losing things that might be dear to one's heart: the excitement of direct interaction, the feeling of belonging and, possibly, the warmth of human relations. But at the same time you gain something you can never have in conventional instruction, namely, a very powerful opportunity for teaching students who have so far been denied education. This change has parallels in the development of industry. The craftworker quite often puts his or her personality into the piece of work, so much so that he or she likes it and would rather keep it than sell it. This sentiment is lost when the production process is rationalized and mechanized. The process of alienation begins.

The separation of the two modes of instruction could also be demonstrated by analysing their different advantages and disadvantages, opportunities and dangers. In distance education you simply cannot have the 'sharing of experience in exploring a common world' between a well-liked and esteemed teacher and a learning group as the basis of instruction. Distance students cannot enjoy 'the contagion of a shared enterprise'. The interaction is indirect, emotion-free, and depersonalized. On the other hand, continued experiences in the learning group can never induce a student to develop the strategies and tactics of self-instruction needed in distance study or the unparalleled self-confidence and self-reliance of its successful students, not only in its 'culminating stages'.

However, if the process of industrialization becomes stronger and permeates conventional instruction as well, there might be a time in the future when the didactic structure of distance study and conventional study will become similar, if not identical.

If, for instance, university tuition were reformed according to current models of 'open learning' and 'independent learning', and became strongly individualized under the systematic guidance of a mentor; if each student were asked to develop a curriculum for him or herself: if study activities were no longer organized into 'classes' and a great deal of the instruction were taken care of with the help of learning packages prepared by supra-regional research and development centres; if the student learned to initiate professional activities and experience geared to his or her course of study; if he or she were able to work with a personal computer, using electronic mail and profiting from tele-conferencing, then 'the huge gulf' between the two modes of instruction might disappear.

This is even more likely to happen if distance study improves its present structure. Supra-regional, pre-planned, and pre-prepared teaching material could allow also for greater individualizing of learning in order to meet the real needs of the students. Counselling and tutoring could be developed more strongly. More students could acquire the courage and ability to initiate and to manage self-help groups, and if students also learned to use the emerging techniques of electronic communication successfully, then distance teaching might become more a reformed form of conventional study.

In both modes of instruction it will be the strong relationship between the mentor or counsellor and the student which will become the backbone of the individualized course of study. Their meetings will probably be precious events, direct interaction in its finest and most efficient form. It is here they can 'convey ... the contagion of a shared enterprise'. It is clear that such mentor–student relationships can be made possible only because other teaching functions are taken care of with prepared teaching material which is produced industrially.

FINAL REMARKS

What will happen to the iceberg? Will it become smaller and disappear? Will it continue to exist? Is the comparative interpretation outdated after so many years? The many allusions and more extensive reactions to it in the literature, both affirmative and controversial, indicate that dicussion of my concept of distance education as an industrialized form of teaching is still alive. This is, by the way, slightly to my amazement.

Indeed, the 'comparative interpretation' has often been referred to as one aspect of the definition of distance study (Keegan 1980, 1983, 1986; Holmberg 1981, 1985, 1986, 1987; Fritsch 1984, Kaye 1985, Nilsen 1986). It has been used as a theoretical construct in the field of off-line and on-line computer-assisted distance education (Andrews and Strain 1985: 143), in an interpretation for a research design (Rekkedal 1983: 23), because of its implications for costeffectiveness (Curran 1985: 26; Turnbull 1988: 430), and as a concept for formulating suggestions for reducing early student drop-out (Roberts 1984: 60, 64, 65).

Seemingly, the discussion will continue. There is no evidence that people either want or are able to resist, let alone stop, the changes brought about by the process of industrialization. In due course, it will also affect new conventional teaching and learning projects. Dealing with it is not a figment of mind but an important element of sociological and philosophical research.

REFERENCES

Andrews, J. and Strain, J. (1985) 'Computer-assisted distance education', in *Distance Education*, 2: 143–57.
Bååth, J. A. (1979) *Correspondence education in the light of a number of contemporary teaching models*, Malmö: Liber Hermods.
—— (1981) 'On the nature of distance education', in *Distance Education*, 2: 212–19.
—— (1983) 'Theoretical models for planning correspondence courses', in *Epistolodidaktika*, 1: 15–33.
Curran, C. (1985) 'Cost-effective course provision – a pilot project', in *Epistolodidaktika*, 2: 24–46.
Duignan, P. A. and Teather, D. C. B. (1985) 'Teaching educational administration externally at post-graduate level at the University of New England', in *Distance Education*, 6(1): 34–55.
Ehmann, C. (1981) 'Fernstudium – Fernunterricht: reflections on Otto Peters' research', in *Distance Education*, 2(2): 228–33.
Fritsch, H. (1984) 'Fernstudium', in *Enzyklopädie Erziehungswissenschaft*, 10, Stuttgart: Klett-Cotta, pp. 494–6.
Holmberg, B. (1981) *Status and Trends of Distance Education*, London: Kogan Page.
—— (1985) *Status and Trends of Distance Education*, Lund: Lector Publishing.
—— (1986) 'A discipline of distance education', in *Journal of Distance Education* 1(1): 25–40.
—— (1987) 'The development of distance education research', in *The American Journal of Distance Education*, 1(3): 16–23.

Jeavons, F. (1986) 'In retrospect: Die didaktische Struktur des Fernunterrichts. Untersuchungen zu einer industrialisierten Form des Lehrens und Lernens by Otto Peters', in *Distance Education*, 7(1): 164–8.

Kaye, A. J. (1985) 'Distance education', in T. Husen and T. N. Postlewaithe (eds) *The International Encyclopedia of Education*, Oxford/New York: Pergamon Press, pp. 1432–8.

Kaye, A. J. and Rumble, G. (eds) (1981): *Distance Teaching for Higher and Adult Education*, London: Croom Helm.

Keegan, D. (1980) 'On defining distance education', in *Distance Education*, 1, 1: 13–36.

—— (1983) *Six distance education theorists*, Hagen Fernuniversität-ZIFF.

—— (1986) *The Foundations of Distance Education*, London: Croom Helm.

Nilsen, C. (1986) 'On the definition of correspondence education', in *Epistolodidaktika*, 1: 3–30.

Peters, O. (1973) *Die didaktische Struktur des Fernunterrichts. Untersuchungen zu einer industrialisierten Form des Lehrens und Lernens*, Weinheim: Beltz.

Plessner, H. (1924) 'Zur Soziologie der Forschung und ihrer Organisation in der deutschen Universität', in M. Scheler (ed.) *Versuche zu einer Soziologie des Wissens*, Munich: Duncker & Humboldt, pp. 407–25.

Rebel, K. (1983) 'Distance study in West Germany: The DIFF's conceptional contribution', in *Distance Education*, 4(2): 171–8.

Rekkedal, T. (1983) 'Enhancing student progress in Norway', in *Teaching at a Distance*, 23: 19–24.

Roberts, D. (1984) 'Ways and means of reducing early drop-out rates', in *Distance Education* 5(1): 60–71.

Romiszowski, A. J. (1981) *Designing instructional systems*, London: Kogan Page.

—— (1984) *Producing Instructional Systems: Lesson Planning for Individualized and Group Learning Activities*, London: Kogan Page.

—— (1986) *Developing Autoinstructional Material*, London: Kogan Page.

—— (1988) *The Selection and Use of Instructional Media: For Improved Classroom Teaching and for Improved Interactive Individualized Instruction*, London: Kogan Page.

Sewart, D. (1982) 'Individualizing support services', in J. Daniel, M. A. Stroud and J. R. Thompson (eds) *Learning at a Distance: A World Perspective*, Edmonton: International Council for Correspondence Education, pp. 27–9.

Schelsky, H. (1963) *Einsamkeit und Freiheit. Idee und Gestalt der deutschen Universität und ihre Reformen*, Reinbek: Rowohlt.

Schwittmann, D. (1982) 'Time and learning in distance study', in *Distance Education* 3(1): 141–56.

Shale, D. (1987) 'Innovation in international higher education: the open universities', in *Journal of Distance Education*, 2(1): 7–24.

Turnball, A. J. (1988) 'Distance education – the trend setter', in *Developing Distance Education*, Oslo: International Council on Distance Education, p. 430.

Weber, M. (1951) 'Wissenschaft als Beruf', in *Gesammelte Aufsätze zur Wissenschaftslehre*, Tübingen: Mohr, pp. 566–97.

10 Understanding distance education (1990)

This paper was prepared in both German and English for a conference on the theory of distance education at the Fernuniversität in Hagen in 1990. Peters evaluates and analyses a fascinating listing of slogans about distance education by educational managers and a number of views of distance education by educational theorists of the 1970s and 1980s. Particularly striking is his use of the Russian concept *zaochny*, which implies 'lack of eye-to-eye contact' and of the Russian postulate of an intrinsic relationship between study and work as pointing to essential characteristics of this form of education.

Due to the unusual origin of distance education, the peculiarity of its methods, and its rapid, unprecedented growth during the last twenty years, the question of its basic character and true nature has been dealt with several times. It also may well be that practitioners and scholars like to ponder on this phenomenon. The result is quite a number of theoretical explanations (Moore 1973; Wedemeyer 1977; Sewart 1978; Bååth 1980; Holmberg and Schümer 1980).

I do not want to deal with these explanations of the nature of distance education, nor do I wish to present a new theory of it, although it would certainly be appropriate and necessary to redefine its possible functions in the post-modern society. This, however, must remain a desideratum for the time being. Rather, I should like to conduct an experiment.

'COMMON-SENSE KNOWLEDGE' AND 'LAY THEORIES'

In the 1980s, we have learnt or have been reminded again, that the behaviours of people are, as a rule, not governed by elaborate theories but just by assumptions and notions which grow out of

Understanding distance education   211

experience. They form our view of the world and influence our actions. As such, they are especially important for the analysis of our behaviour. These assumptions and notions are part of our 'common-sense knowledge'. As they implicitly contain special views, ways of thinking and even conceptual elements, social psychologists call them 'subjective' or 'lay' theories (Furnham 1988). Lay theories can become influential when they are adopted by other people and assume the functions of stereotypes or clichés. They can be analysed but, of course, not to the same degree as objective or scientific theories. They are rather implicit than explicit. They are incoherent and inconsistent, and can, consequently, contradict themselves. But in spite of this, some researchers (Groeben et al. 1988) see analogies and parallels between lay and scientific theories. They are important for us as we generally are not influenced by the facts in our world of everyday life but basically by our assumptions of and subjective theories about these facts.

With regard to the theme of this chapter, I should like to analyse subjective theories about distance education. In order to do this, I shall examine a number of designations of distance education which have been used widely. I assume that someone who 'invents' a name for distance education must have a certain concept and understanding of its nature. This holds true also for many people who accept and use this name.

Furthermore, I should like to refer to some stereotypes which have been derived from theories of distance education. As a rule, these theories are often reduced to a few words or phrases or catchwords in everyday practice. They start a career of their own – independently from their original theories. Here I am not interested in the original objective theories, but rather in the lay theories which have been developed by people who are using those stereotypes. My hypothesis is that there might be a lot of sound thinking in those lay theories in spite of their being not explicit and consistent. I hope that if we summarize various outcomes of these lay theories we will learn something more about what really matters when dealing with distance education. We might recognize a way of understanding which is really shared by the people concerned with this particular form of education.

DESIGNATIONS

We are aware of quite a number of different designations of 'distance education' in various languages. There are also different designations for the same phenomenon in one language, especially in American English. Dealing with them we have to accept the premise that different designations mean different ways of looking at distance education and of attaching importance to different elements of this form of education. Let us try to describe them.

Fernunterricht (instruction at a distance)

The German word '*Fernunterricht*' characterizes the phenomenon by pointing at a striking difference from face-to-face education: the apartness of teacher and learner. It stresses the physical distance between them which does not allow direct interaction.

A number of associations are still attached to this word, most of them originating in the nineteenth century or the first half of the twentieth century. These associations include the use and misuse of the term in connection with profit-led organizations, and the opportunity it offers to ambitious and gifted but underprivileged people who are denied the possibility of obtaining an education through the usual channels. Strangely enough, if these people engage themselves in instruction at a distance they are quite often still looked at with a mixture of admiration and condescension.

Fernstudium (learning at a distance in higher education)

The distinctive term '*fern*' (meaning distance) proved to be so successful that it was also applied in higher education when it became possible to study at a university without attending classes. Further, it was also translated into English and is now internationally recognized.

The notions evoked by this term are partly similar to those of '*Fernunterricht*'. Here we think of individuals discontented with their socio-economic status who try to change it in the face of many difficulties. Many people are impressed by these individuals who try to elevate themselves in the social strata or just between the more and less educated. However, again they are looked at with mixed feelings – with admiration, envy, suspicion and disdain. Not all people, especially workers, find it really appropriate to take advantage of this new form of education.

As most institutions of distance study are state institutions, this term is not tainted with associations with profit-making organizations.

Correspondence study

Those who decided to use this term were undoubtedly impressed by a new communication medium in the middle of the last century: the letter (or postcard) in connection with the railway system, which guaranteed quick and reliable delivery. Here the concept of the teacher and the learner who send letters, instead of talking to each other, was in the foreground. The term was so successful that it was adopted in the Romance languages and also in Chinese, in which *han shou* means 'teaching by letters'. It dominated the conception of the new form of tuition for nearly a century.

The most important association attached to this designation is the teacher who instructs by writing and the student who learns by reading. Thus, it popularized a new teaching and learning behaviour.

Open learning

This term when being used to designate distance education emphasizes the 'openness' of the teaching–learning process as compared to the 'closeness' of learning in traditional schools. It stresses that access to this kind of learning is easier ('open access') and that the students are allowed to operate with a degree of autonomy and self-direction. This does not refer only to decisions with regard to the place, time, duration and circumstances of their learning but in some cases also with regard to the curriculum, as the students are free to select from pre-planned curricula or to develop curricula of their own.

Home study

This term suggests that the teaching and learning does not take place in the class or lecture room but at home. It generates pleasant feelings connected to one's home: privacy, familiarity, cosiness – as opposed to the often unpleasant experiences at schools or colleges: publicity, the necessity to deal with many (unknown or not well-known) persons, the uncomfortableness of rooms, impersonality.

Angeleitetes Selbststudium (guided self-study)

Here, 'self-study' is qualified by 'guided'. Clearly, this term is to minimize the difference between distance education and teaching and learning at a university by referring to a highly valued element of advanced higher education. As it is the tacit goal of higher education to produce scholars who work independently and mainly by themselves, self-study has a tradition and is in no way questionable. Much postgraduate work is done in this way with only occasional guidance by a professor. Seen in this way it is not so alien, so frighteningly different from academic tradition.

Zaochny

This is the Russian word for 'distance' in distance education. It is remarkable as it means – etymologically speaking – 'without eye contact'. This implies that the decisive criterion according to which distance education can be distinguished from conventional teaching and learning is the lack of eye contact. Distance education does not take place 'eyeball to eyeball' as Wedemeyer (1971: 135) once called it. As the eye is the organ of man's innermost feelings, this aspect of apartness is surely significant. We become aware that a whole emotional dimension of the interaction of the teacher and learner is lacking in distance education. The new form of teaching and learning is defined and characterized by pointing to a severe deficiency, as in a court when the judgment is announced without the accused being present.

Study without leaving production

This designation is, indeed, telling. Obviously it was invented by bureaucrats of a state planning institution. For them, the most important feature of distance study is the possibility that students can study without discontinuing their work. It shows how much work in production is valued and how much the products of the work force are needed. It is easy to see that this designation was coined in a socialist country: the [former] USSR. From there it was taken over by other socialist countries. There is no other designation for distance study which points to its economic advantage so bluntly. On the other hand one should not overlook the fact that it has strong ideological overtones which are important with regard to the general goal of education. This form of study appeared as an ideal solution to the problem of how practice and theory – the world of work and of theoretical investigation – can be combined and united. Small wonder that 'study without leaving production' was considered to be the main and regular form of higher education in the USSR for some years.

CATCH-PHRASES

Guided didactic conversation

Obviously, this phrase suggests that there is a communication between the teacher and the learner going on in distance education and that it is the most important structural element of it. The choice of the word 'conversation' reminds us that dialogue, as the basic traditional form of all teaching, applies also to distance education. The phrase suggests strongly that distance education is not simple self-study as it is organized according to the traditional pattern of teaching and learning. This phrase emphasizes the similarities between traditional face-to-face teaching and distance education rather than the differences. Implicitly, it means that without 'guided didactic conversation' distance education ceases to be distance education.

Two-way communication in distance education

Two-way communication became the catch-phrase in distance education in the 1980s, as Keegan (1983: 83) once remarked. The people who used it again and again wanted to stress this particular attribute of distance education in order to demonstrate that again distance education is not just self-study, that the separation of student and teacher does not mean that communication between them is cut off altogether, that there are many tricks of the trade to establish and maintain two-way communication. Clearly, this phrase has been coined and is understood as an opposite to the 'one-way communication' of television. Perhaps this is the reason for its tremendous impact.

The first motive of those who invented this phrase and possibly also of those who use it frequently is the desire to defend distance education. They want to criticize the opinion that in distance education the student is left alone with his or her learning material, which, as we all know, is quite often the case. They want to drive home the idea that distance education is much more similar to face-to-face education than, for instance, televised instruction.

The second motive behind the propagation of this phrase is the desire to show and mark the way in which much of the current distance education practice should and could be improved considerably.

'Continuity of concern' in distance education

This is another phrase often used. It stresses a feature of distance education which is considered to be of vital importance and which should by no means be neglected. Those who advocate this phrase are opposed to the idea that learning packages could be really self-instructive and that the students should just work for themselves. Therefore, they consider face-to-face tutorials as constituent elements of distance education – being the bridge between the teaching material and the individual learner or a group of learners. Accordingly, they are strongly in favour of study centres. Again we can say: if this element is missing, distance education is no longer distance education. And again we can note that those who are in favour of this phrase are strongly convinced that it is necessary and possible to improve distance education.

Independent study

Here, the liberation of the student from the fetters of school or college routine is emphasized. According to this notion of distance education, it is the student who determines the when, where and how of his or her learning. This phrase suggests that the student assumes more responsibility for his or her own learning than is possible in face-to-face situations. Studying in this way, the student is no longer in the leading strings of a teacher and is no longer subjected to the conformity pressure of the learning or peer group.

The success of this term can only be explained by referring to strong educational and political reform movements. In this respect, it has an ideological bias.

Industrialized form of instruction

This characterization of distance study is referred to quite often. Implicitly, it underlines the fact that distance study must be carefully pre-planned, prepared and organized, and that there is a division of labour, a growing use of technical equipment to work with, and the necessity of formalized evaluations. People become aware that these and other features of distance study are structurally the same as those that can be found in an industrialized production process. Explicitly, these ideas are expressed by using the image of a teacher in the classroom working like a craftsman, as opposed to a teacher being a part of a complicated teaching–learning system organized like an industrialized process. The catch-phrase 'industrialized form of instruction' helps to recognize structural elements which are typical in distance study.

LAY THEORIES AS THEORIES OF LEGITIMATION

If we add up the designations referred to we get a composite picture of the content of the term 'distance education'. This picture must be necessarily illuminative. For whereas the catch-phrases quoted tried to explain distance education by referring to one – considered to be the most characteristic or important – element, this composite picture will refer to seven of these elements. According to them, distance education is a special form of education in which:

- teachers and students work apart from each other – 'at a distance';
- teachers and students do not communicate 'eyeball to eyeball' with each other;
- letters (and other printed material) are exchanged with the help of the mailing system;
- the learning usually takes place in the homes of the students;
- the teaching–learning process assumes the form of self-study, however guided by the teacher;
- the teaching–learning process allows a degree of openness with regard to access, goals and methods;
- the student does not cease to work for a living as it is a study alongside work.

Evaluating this list of descriptive aspects we can see easily that distance education is not a common, but still an extraordinary way of teaching and learning. One of its characteristic features is that because of the apartness of teacher and learner certain emotional dimensions and overtones of instructional interaction are cut off. Hence it is depersonalized to a certain degree. Clearly, this is a deficiency.

On the other hand, the second characteristic feature is clearly an advantage: the student can study alongside work. This opens up the world of learning also to adults and the underprivileged who otherwise are denied the opportunity to learn and to get or continue their education.

Finally, it should be noted that there still is some ambiguity attached to the term. It generates feelings of appreciation and depreciation at the same time. It is depreciated because it is considered to be merely a substitute of 'real' and that means face-to-face teaching, a surrogate, an emergency measure in situations in which no traditional way of learning is possible.

Let us also summarize the catch-phrases. Each of them was coined to characterize distance education by emphasizing its most important aspect. The first four have something in common: the intention of improving distance education. They do not depict it as it is, but rather as it should be. They are prescriptive. Accordingly, distance education is to be developed after the pattern of a 'guided didactic conversation', must necessarily be based on 'two-way communication', must be 'continuously concerned' about the learner's progress, and emancipate the learner from traditional restrictions of time, place and persons by developing a truly 'independent study' which is open enough to allow for a 'degree of autonomy and self-direction'.

The fifth catchphrase ('industrialized form of instruction') is basically descriptive. It characterizes distance education as a form of study which, because of its typical features, is the product of a particular period in the development of our culture: industrialization. It is useful for discerning and understanding particular features in which it does differ from face-to-face education.

Finally, I should like to mention another aspect of this summary. Normally, we are not aware of our 'common-sense' knowledge and of our subjective theories. It is only in critical situations that they are considered and reflected upon consciously (Matthes and Schütze 1973). The number of different designations for 'distance education', the long debate about changing the designation 'correspondence education' into 'distance education' and the various attempts and efforts to improve distance education by defining it in reformatory terms show clearly that distance education has always been in a critical situation. For a long time it was not recognized and not appreciated at all in other areas of education. Hence, some of the subjective theories referred to in this chapter usually have a strong apologetic trend. They mirror the efforts to gain status. Therefore, most of them can be called theories of legitimation.

Has the experiment been worthwhile? I should like to respond to this question by mentioning the following three points:

1 One can be impressed by the many aspects of distance education inherent in the lay theories referred to. Certainly, they can be useful in qualifying and differentiating the lay theories of our own – which are very likely to be also derived from one aspect only.

2 We can see that the composite picture of distance education is not very progressive in outlook – for example, modern technological communications media including television and computer are missing. Maybe common-sense knowledge is necessarily rather conservative by nature.

3 Nevertheless, the comprehensive overview of common-sense knowledge about distance education shows that it seems to be advisable to take note of it. Before developing objective theories about distance education, one should have examined the respective lay theories.

REFERENCES

Bååth, J. A. (1980) 'Postal two way communication in correspondence education', *Epistolodidaktika* 1–2: 11–41.
Furnham, A. (1988) *Lay Theories: Everyday Understanding of Problems in the Social Sciences*, Oxford: Pergamon.
Groeben, N., Wahl, D., Schlee, J. and Scheele, B. (1988) *Das Forschungsprogramm Subjective Theorien: eine Einführung in die Psychologie des reflexiven Subjekts*, Tübingen: Francke.
Holmberg, B. and Schümer, R. (1980) *Methoden des gelenkten didaktischen Gesprächs*, Hagen: Fernuniversität, ZIFF.
Keegan, D. (1983) *Six Distance Education Theorists*, Hagen: Fernuniversität, ZIFF.
Matthes, J. and Schütze, F. (1973) *Alltagswissen, Interaktion und gesellschaftliche Wirklichkeit*, Reinbek: Rowohlt.
Moore, M. G. (1973) 'Toward a theory of independent learning and teaching', *Journal of Higher Education*, 44: 661–79.
Sewart, D. (1978) *Continuity of Concern for Students in a System of Learning at a Distance*, Hagen: Fernuniversität, ZIFF (ZIFF Papiere, 22).
Wedemeyer, C. (1971) 'With whom will you dance? The new educational technology', in O. Mackenzie and E. L. Christensen (eds) *The Changing World of Correspondence Study*, University Park: Pennsylvania State University Press, pp. 133–40.
—— (1977) 'Independent study', in A. S. Knowles (ed.) *The International Encyclopedia of Higher Education*, Boston, CIHED, pp. 548–57.

11 Distance education in a post-industrial society (1993)

In 1992 Peters was asked to contribute a chapter on distance education in a post-industrial era to the book *Theoretical Principles of Distance Education*, edited by D. Keegan and published in 1993. The aim of the chapter was to respond to comment in the literature that the theory of industrialization of education might not be fully relevant if the phenomenon of industrialization were to disappear or might not be valid in countries in which it might be claimed that an industrialized era had not yet arrived or in which a post-industrial era was in prospect. This article applies American and German writing on the ethos of post-industrialization to the world of distance education, and it is his latest contribution to the literature of distance education prior to his introduction to this book. The chapter argues that if distance education can be defined as the most industrialized form of teaching and learning, and as such also as a typical product of industrial society, what will be its role in post-industrial society? In order to be able to deal with this question, characteristic features of post-industrial societal developments and of post-modern value changes are described. Four affinities between post-industrial developments and distance education are explained. In order to support these assumptions, reference is made to three post-modern theoretical approaches to adult education and to teaching and learning.

Distance education has been analysed as a singular product of the era of industrialization (Peters 1967, 1973, 1983, 1989). It could be demonstrated that its structure is determined to a considerable degree by the principles which govern the industrialization of the working process in the production of goods. This means that distance education is also strongly influenced by such principles as, for instance, rationalization, division of labour, the assignment of frag-

Distance education in a post-industrial society 221

mented tasks to specialists, mechanization and automation. Some striking similarities are:

1 The development of distance study courses is just as important as the preparatory work prior to the production process.
2 The effectiveness of the teaching–learning process is particularly dependent on very careful planning and adequate organization.
3 The function of the teacher is split up into several subfunctions and performed by specialists as, for instance, in the production process at an assembly line.
4 Distance education can only be economical if the number of students is great: mass education corresponds to mass production.
5 As is the case with the production process, distance education needs capital investments, a concentration of the available resources and a qualified centralized administration.

These findings justify the statement that distance teaching is – compared to other forms of instruction – the most industrialized form of teaching. This separates it distinctly from traditional face-to-face teaching in classrooms or in groups which, therefore, to extend the comparison, can be called pre-industrial – that is, structurally similar to the work of a craftsman. Looking at distance education in this way it is easy to maintain that this particular form of teaching and learning is most progressive, as it has adapted to the powerful trends of the era of industrialization – which surely cannot be said of our schools, colleges and universities. Even more, one might also think that this structural peculiarity makes distance education specially conducive to tackling some of the big educational tasks of the future, such as, for instance, continuing education for most adults working for a living.

This assumption, however, invites criticism. Do we still live in the era of industrialization? Do we not speak of *post*-industrial developments now? Are the principles of industrialization not already in the process of fading out? Is it not, after all, already somewhat old-fashioned to analyse the structure of distance education in terms of industrialization? Will there not be a working world structured differently in many ways? Would it not be more appropriate to inquire into the problem as to whether there are affinities of distance education to post-industrial work processes also? And, finally, if distance education were adapted to post-industrial trends and expectations in the future in order to keep abreast with new societal developments, what would it look like? I shall try to deal with these questions.

222 Contemporary analyses

Let me, however, make a preliminary cautionary remark before I begin. If we analyse our society in its present state of development we can already discern definite developments breaking away from industrialism. More and more enterprises of the car industry, for instance, are giving up production at the assembly line and are establishing small work groups in which each group member is no longer engaged in one activity but rather in a variety of activities like a craftsman. Opel alone has already established organized teams for roughly 6,000 employees, each of them consisting of eight to twelve members who elect one of them to be their speaker (Eglau 1992: 31). And if we study social, political and cultural developments we can recognize fundamental shifts in values and value orientation. I only draw attention 'to the emergence and generalization of subcultures sharing a rejection and critique of the established order' (Wood and Zurcher 1988: 2) as well as to the attempts to create a 'counter-culture' with all its post-modern developments and tendencies in the fine arts.

Although these changes are very impressive, are they really early signs of a 'new era' which might be called '*post*-industrial'? Admittedly, there are researchers who have thought so already for quite some time (Boulding 1964; Kahn and Wiener 1967; Bell 1976; Fuchs 1968; Brzezinski 1970; Toffler 1970, 1980; Williams 1982; Wood and Zurcher 1988; and Peters 1981). And, it is true, some of them even think that these changes have already become very significant. There are observers 'who compare the quality and pervasiveness of this change to the transformations wrought by the industrializing of our society' and refer to post-industrialism as to 'another "revolution" of momentous and far-reaching change' (Wood and Zurcher 1988: 1). And yet, in spite of all this the 'new era' will still remain largely a matter of the future. Therefore, many of the changes in distance education I am going to refer to will necessarily be futuristic ones and, hence, might perhaps not be realized at all. Dealing with them means leaving firm ground and entering the sphere of speculation. However, considering the expected structural changes of distance education will shed some light on the direction to which it might have to develop in order to be complementary to the principles and tendencies of a post-industrial society.

NATURE OF POST-INDUSTRIAL SOCIETY

What, then, does post-industrial mean? Wood and Zurcher (1988: 22) have suggested that above all society will undergo the following three economic changes:

1 the proportion of labour employed by the tertiary or service sector will dramatically increase;
2 the 'new' technology will emerge;
3 the decision-making structure of the economy, and eventually that in society at large, will change significantly.

The growing *service sector* has already become the major employer of the work force in highly industrialized countries. This leads to significant changes of work activities and attitudes, and especially of social relations. It may well be that the secondary sector – the industrial production of goods – will cease to be of overriding importance. It could even be that it will be 'forgotten' just as agriculture seems to be forgotten in highly industrialized countries (Kahn and Wiener 1967: 152). The service sector, on the other hand (for instance, banking, accounting, transport, legal, education, health, government, domestic, hotel, gastronomy, repair and entertainment services) will assume even more importance. This means that the quota of highly qualified occupations will definitely become larger, as new post-industrial needs must be met. Because of the knowledge explosion, lifelong training and retraining and continuing education will become imperative for them. Bell, for instance, believes that the professionals of the future will never really leave their alma mater as they will have to combine work and academic study (quoted by Peters 1981: 163).

The *'new' technology* comprises the world of computers (mainframe and personal computers, computer networks), communication systems and further inventions of electronics. 'What counts is no longer raw muscle power, or energy, but information' (Bell 1976: 127). This has already changed many work processes structurally and will continue to do so. As production will use more and more very efficient communication networks, 'the physical location of an enterprise is no longer really important' (Norman 1975: 321). And, in addition, the work place of the employee can be chosen at leisure (Peters 1981: 73) – that is, with the help of computer terminals it can also be at his home. This development has already begun. Perhaps the change from industrial technology to 'new' technology will be as fundamental as the change from the craftsman's technology to industrial technology.

The *decision-making structure* will change considerably. 'In the industrial enterprise, power rests with those who make decisions. In the mature enterprise, this power has passed, inevitably and irrevocably, from the individual to the group' (Galbraith 1971: 109).

Indeed, the hierarchy will be substituted by groups in which the members make decisions as a group. These groups plan and control their work themselves. Hence, a big enterprise consists of many small, decentralized units. There is a high transparency of responsibility. The necessary control of complexity is safeguarded by the sophisticated information system. Democratizing is a dominant trend. Co-determination has a high priority.

What will this mean for the organization of labour processes? The man–machine relation will primarily be substituted by 'a game between persons' (Wood and Zurcher 1988: 12); attention and interest will be focused upon persons everywhere and not upon institutions (Peters 1981: 73).

> The central person is no longer the entrepreneur, manager or industrial executive but the professional, for he is equipped, by his education and training, to provide the kinds of skills which are increasingly demanded in the post-industrial society. If an industrial society is defined by the quality of goods as marking the standard of living, the post-industrial society is defined by the quality of life as measured by the services and amenities – health, education, recreation, the arts – which are now deemed desirable and possible for everyone.
>
> (Bell 1976: 127)

Since the employees will render highly personal services, they will also be able to develop and exercise personal skills. Their work experiences will be more completely human and satisfying as they are more creative. Work alienation, a typical result of the industrialized production of goods, will diminish (cf. Fuchs 1968: 189).

All of this, of course, will have consequences for the *organization and management* of labour in a post-industrial society. Elbing and Gordon (1974: 326) assume that changes will take place (see the Table below).

It is also necessary to outline here significant *changes of values* which have been caused by or are concomitant with post-industrial production processes. They have influenced the *Zeitgeist*, the attitudes and behaviour of people and their cultural life at large. More and more we are becoming aware of the emergence of a new type of person – of the 'post-modern self'. This is not a matter of philosophic observation or speculation but can be proved by empirical research. Wood and Zurcher (1988), for instance, have made a quantitative and qualitative analysis of nineteenth-century and more contemporary diaries. In this they have been able to demonstrate

Table. Management in a post-industrial society

Traditional assumptions about management	Future assumptions about management
Planning: An executive function moving the organization	A function for everyone, essentially moving up the organization
Organizing: The manager determines how and when work is to be done, assigns it to employees	The employee determines how and when his work is done within jointly determined deadlines
Authority and responsibility: Rests with the manager. He delegates authority commensurate with responsibility. Each employee has one boss	Authority and responsibility rest with employees who exercise it over their own work. They seek help from managers when it is needed. In matrix organizations employees will have to report to 2 or 3 people
Staffing: Management determines the staffing needs and selects employees based on industrial-engineered work systems	The working group determines the staffing requirements, hires employees, and designates and evaluates managers
Hierarchy: There was some limit to the number of people whom one could control. Extent of control was discussed in terms of quantity of workers per manager	Hierarchy will be significantly flatter since people will be left to manage themselves
Directing: The manager directs and motivates the work of subordinates	Employees are self-directed and self-motivated and turn to management when they need help
Controlling: Uses external control systems for management	Will rely on employee self-control

Source: Adapted from Elbing and Gordon (1974: 326)

definite shifts of values in the following dimensions: from rationality to irrationality, from unemotional performance to emotional expression, from institutional roles and standards to individual roles and standards, from societal duty to duty to self, and from achievement to gratification (Wood and Zurcher 1988: 125).

The sense of duty of the nineteenth-century man included 'school work and study of the student' and 'professional and work activities'. The researchers found ideas and themes 'which together constitute an approximation to the values and world-view of the Protestant asceticism' which was described by Max Weber as being one of the pre-conditions of the rise of capitalism. This means also that they valued 'temperance and moderation' and distrusted and rejected 'creature comfort and sensual experience' (Wood and Zurcher 1988: 126).

It can be easily seen that the new tendencies and trends in the 'post-modern self' have developed as a reaction to, and criticism of, life in the industrial era. This can be illustrated by the following examples, in which the new trends are apparently just the opposite of certain traits characteristic for people in an industrial society.

1 They reject delayed gratification and restraint, but are more easily motivated to enjoy their work. Therefore, they like spontaneity, choose stimulation, and are open for expressiveness (Wood and Zurcher 1988: 13).
2 They are not ready to endure distress, but develop a capacity for joy (Peters 1981: 67).
3 They refuse to do empty routine work, but desire to do something meaningful (Peters 1981: 179).
4 Their work is not directed towards materialistic objectives, but rather towards the fulfilment of human values. Consequently, their life will not be dominated by the restless pursuit of profit, but by their wish to develop their personal potential.
5 The objective of their work is not achievement, but self-realization.
6 They do not like self-control, but seek self-expression.
7 They reject competition. They do not like to rise in the hierarchy of enterprise, but are, rather, interested in a good work climate.
8 They do not like to become isolated, but are interested in social relations. They seek *inter*-dependence rather than independence (Peters 1981: 67). They are ready to restore 'conviviality' (Illich 1973: 2).
9 They will not participate in exploiting nature, but rather develop ecologically harmonious life and work processes (Peters 1981: 66).

These observations indicate, indeed, that the post-industrial era will bring about broad shifts in culture and values. Our modern culture may turn post-modern.

STRUCTURES OF INDUSTRIALIZED EDUCATION

If we analyse the structure of distance education after having dealt with principles and trends both of the industrial and post-industrial period, we can clearly see that distance teaching is still basically an industrialized form of teaching. This is not surprising at all, as the principles and trends of industrialization are still potent in our society and, of course, also in the production of goods. The powerful influences of a development of more than 150 years will not cease to be effective because of the new post-industrial principles and trends referred to, although these latter might become stronger in the future. On the other hand, a closer look at distance education reveals four elements which, indeed, correspond with post-industrial tendencies, not only contemporarily but also right from its beginning: the learner can be dislocated from the class or lecture room to his home or to a working place in his company, as mediated instruction is primarily being used; more than other forms of teaching it calls for the self-reliant, self-directed learner; distance education has always promoted social interactions among the students; and it has a strong affinity towards new electronic media.

1 What is predicted for the production of goods – namely, that the employee will no longer be tied to a given place of work due to the use of technical communication systems – has been routine in distance education already for more than 150 years. Indeed, the students need not meet their teachers regularly at given places but work independently, the main means of communication being the printed paper and the written letter.
2 In distance education it has always been necessary that learners take over responsibilities for their own learning – a function which in other circumstances rests with the teacher or the teaching institution. The learner, therefore, is given the opportunity to develop *self-determination, self-direction* and *self-control* to a high degree. They determine where, when, and how long they want to engage themselves in the learning process. If distance education also comprises contract learning the student is also able to determine or co-determine *what* he or she wishes to learn and *how* to control and evaluate the results of this learning.
3 Although many proponents of distance education expect the development of teaching material which is truly self-instructional – which means that it can be studied without the help of a teacher – it is also well understood that *social interactions in face-to-face situations* are important. Therefore, most open universities have

provided for study centres in many parts of their countries. And these study centres very often provide for social interactions, which ironically are likely to be more personal than, for instance, at institutes of higher learning, especially in European countries. Also, when it is difficult to provide premises and tutors for such activities, the learners are often encouraged to take the initiative in establishing *self-help groups*. Here again they act as self-determined individuals relatively independent of the teachers and teaching institution.

4 Already, at a very early date, distance education has developed a great affinity with the new electronic communication systems: radio and television as well as the computer are being used. And more and more electronic communication media are integrated into the teaching–learning system. It can be predicted that this tendency will become stronger in the years to come. This separates distance education from traditional forms of teaching and learning which have strong tendencies to resist the use of such media.

We can see that within the structure of the most industrialized form of teaching and learning the seeds of post-industrial developments can already be found.

EFFECTS ON DISTANCE EDUCATION

If the post-industrial tendencies referred to become stronger and change working processes in the way I have indicated – and, above all, if the post-modern value system permeates our culture – will this leave distance education unscathed? Will distance education stick to its structure, to its guiding principles and to its accumulated experience which, after all, have established its extraordinary success? Or will it adapt to the societal changes and develop new forms of distance education? Nobody knows, of course. The chances are, rather, that the big distance teaching institutions in particular will be so bureaucratized and structurally inflexible that this will probably never happen. But it may also well be that definite changes will be suggested and tried out. If so, what would a post-industrial distance education look like?

Before I go into this, however, I should like to suggest that postmodern tendencies have already arrived at the Fernuniversität in Hagen. That is to say if we analyse the attitudes of the students we can see that they no longer correspond to the traditional image of the ambitious social climber who desires to earn more money and to gain more status in his company. On the contrary. When students were asked which criteria of job description they valued most, 'work satisfaction' ranked highest, immediately followed by 'independence of work' and 'personal interest in work' – whereas 'high salary' was in seventh place and 'high status and prestige' only in fifteenth place down at the bottom of the list (Bartels 1986: 179). Accordingly, general and academic goals of study which may help in the process of self-realization are already more important than strictly vocational or professional goals (Bartels 1986: 216). Obviously, the image of the 'typical' student of industrialized distance education must now be shaped anew and adapted to these facts indicating post-industrial influences.

It would seem to be all the more necessary to depict a *post-industrial model of distance education*.

Demand

The definite increase of the *service sector* of society will lead to the establishment of many new jobs, just as the process of industrialization in the nineteenth and twentieth centuries created many new jobs beyond craftsmanship. If the key person of the new era is going to be the professional, the role of scientific knowledge and technology will be at a premium and assume even greater importance. This means that, much more than is the case now, schools and institutes of higher learning and providers of continuing education will be a decisive factor in the development of society. As lifelong learning will have ceased to be merely a slogan by then, and will, indeed, be practised widely, and also as many adults will not be able to attend these learning institutions, there could be an even greater demand for distance education than there was in the industrial era in which it developed.

Students

We must, however, also face the possibility that demand will decrease substantially in spite of this if distance education continues to stick to its traditional industrial patterns. We must ask ourselves whether persons in the post-industrial era will still be ready to undergo the strains of learning at a distance in addition to their vocational, professional and family obligations? Will they have the persistence to do this for many years – up to ten and more years, for example, in open universities? Will they really sacrifice so much of their leisure time which they could use otherwise for their family or recreation? Will not the hedonistic tendencies of the new era distract them from carrying this burden? Knowing that post-industrial man will not be ready to delay gratification for his endeavours; that he will reject competition in the working world and in learning processes; that he will not be interested in material satisfaction and, hence, does not react to financial incentives but will rather seek wholesome social relations and cultural satisfaction (Peters 1981: 66); and knowing also that the powerful influence of Protestant asceticism will lessen and, perhaps, eventually fade away, these questions must be answered in the negative. Apparently, in distance education the image of the 'typical' student who wishes mainly to improve his or her vocational status and income by climbing up in the hierarchy of their company or by changing positions does not hold true any longer. This means that correspondence colleges and open universities will lose the majority of their clients and their traditional *raison d'être*. Possibly, an entirely new type of student will emerge with new value systems, new needs and new priorities. He or she will enrol for distance education for different reasons and seek experiences which so far have not been provided for.

Objectives

The dominating goal will be *self-realization*, which will bring about the emergence of the post-modern self which 'chooses stimulation, openness to experience, and expressiveness' (Slater 1970), and stresses the personal duty, happiness and enjoyment (Yankelovich 1981). Furthermore, there will also be the goal of *improving the qualification for a job*, preferably in the service sector. This goal seems to be a continuation of the most important goal of distance education in the industrial society. However, if we take note of and, possibly, appreciate what has been said about the post-modern self, we cannot but assume that this goal will have to be interrelated with the goal of self-realization. Considerable changes will have to take place here as well.

Structure

I believe that – seen from a post-modern point of view – the double burden of a full-time job and a long, intensive period of learning at a distance will be considered as 'inhuman' for two reasons. First, the students have to strain every nerve for too long a time. Second, the additional demands on them divorce them more or less from their families, their neighbours and friends, and reduce their civic, social and political contacts. Because of this neglect of fundamental personal needs this system will no longer be feasible in its original industrialized form. The only way out is a combination of part-time work and part-time study. Already many young persons like to work part-time only in order to have more time for 'themselves' – that is, for family or social activities – and thus have more time to enjoy life while they are young. Why not also use such additional time for learning at a distance in a post-modern way?

As far as continuing vocational and professional education is concerned, it might be possible to develop more of those models which are already practised by big international electronic companies and which integrate distance education into the daily work processes. Learning is thus an important element of the job to be performed and does not require additional time and fees and relieves the learner of the double burden referred to.

Curricular aspects

When deciding about the contents of courses in distance education it is obvious that we have to realize that people in the post-industrial society will be interested in the present rather than in the future; that they – in a nihilistic manner – will reject the tradition of enlightenment, especially the optimistic belief in the unending progress of society and the confidence in scientific advancement; that they will have given up all ideological schemes and Utopian programmes of societal reform; that they will have to find out for themselves what will be 'meaningful' in a given situation, realizing, of course, that, in a pluralistic society, the values they find to be relevant will be different from those of other persons and in no way better. They will have a preference for social relations and social problems; will be open to aesthetic and ethical issues; will seek cultural satisfaction; and will like to live in harmony with nature. A realm of attractive themes can be derived from this new state of consciousness with its reassessment of so many values. Probably, all courses will have to be rewritten.

In addition, courses for qualifying and updating learners for jobs – not only in the service sector – will be influenced by this new understanding. These courses will probably no longer aim at vocational or professional competence in a narrow and one-dimen-

232 Contemporary analyses

sional sense, but will enable the learner to become aware of the complexity of work situations and of multidimensional approaches to the understanding and mastering of them.

If distance education does not comply with such new requirements it can be predicted that there will be a growing discontent with the curriculum of many courses, as students may think that the contents of teaching and learning are too far away from everyday problems of vital importance, be they, for instance, social, political or ecological. Similar arguments to those voiced by the protesting students of 1968 may be aired, but this time for different reasons.

Methods

So far the backbone of distance education has usually been the sustained and careful study of specially developed and painstakingly prepared standardized *course material*. Tutorials and group work, in which the learners meet face to face with a teacher and fellow students, are usually only complementary. In post-industrial society it may be just the other way round. There might be a growing number of students unwilling to study in isolation from other students and teachers as they are mainly interested in people and social relations. The paradigmatic 'lone wolf' who relies on his own learning strategy and on his extraordinary endurance in order to 'survive', and who considers cooperation with other students merely a loss of time, will cease to be typical of many distance students. Since post-modern students will have a strong desire to develop and experience *social relations*, forms of learning which provide for them will have to be emphasized. As predicted for the working process, the emergence of *autonomous groups* will become the main constituent of the learning process. They could be local or regional and meet face to face, and in addition to this communicate with each other with the help of traditional or new technical media (teleconferencing). They will have a 'critical group size' – that is, the groups are not to have more members than can be managed without a hierarchy. These groups will render opportunities for the development of a wholesome and enjoyable work climate. They will allow feelings of togetherness and belonging. And they will encourage spontaneity and self-expression.

Self-study, on the other hand, will only be complementary to the work in these groups. Ideally, it will not be normalized and standardized by special course material but will be 'open' in the sense that the learners themselves acquire the information they need in given situations. Clearly, it will be an important objective of this method of study to enable the students to store and to retrieve information which will be relevant to their learning process with the help of computers and to develop and refine this particular skill.

As post-modern students want to live their lives now and not, so to speak, postpone them for some time in the future, they will look for attractive and pleasant learning experiences which are not only a means to an end but also ends in themselves. They will have to be already rewarded in the process of learning in many ways.

Since post-industrial persons reject dull routine work and prefer creative work in the production process, they are likely to behave accordingly in the teaching–learning process. This means that traits of behaviour such as, for instance, openness, originality and flexibility will be highly valued and that models of teaching and learning will be preferred that provide especially for this type of acquisition of knowledge and skills.

Technical media

The impact of the 'new' technology will, without doubt, become stronger. Distance education will continue to rely increasingly on differentiated electronic communication systems. The tools of learning of the home-based student will no longer consist mainly of printed material and books but will also involve the use of audio cassettes, video cassettes, diskettes for the computer, and compact discs. Furthermore, the students will use the telephone (conference call), telefax, viewdata, teletex/telex, datex, videoconference, as well as radio and television in order to acquire the additional information they need for their studies (Wurster 1989: 9). Thus, the ubiquity of relevant information enables them to stay at home for some of their learning activities. This will be considered to be quite natural as more and more workers are dislocated from the production process by means of sophisticated technical media. It is possible that the image of the learner in distance education as an extraordinary person who does not really belong to the mainstream of education will disappear.

Organization

Will the expected disintegration of hierarchies in working situations have an impact on the relationship between learners and their distance-teaching institution and its representatives? Analysing post-industrial trends one cannot but assume that this will, indeed, be the case. It may well be that adult learners with experience of life and work will seek to emancipate themselves from being dependent on a hierarchy of persons in the teaching institute and its bureaucracy. Rather, they will insist on determining themselves what and how to learn. They will try to become autonomous in this field as well. This means that the functions of the teaching institutions will change in so far as they will become primarily service agencies whose main role it is to motivate, to inform and to advise the students expertly.

This change could also have consequences for the management of learning. Here, I should like to refer again to Elbing and Gordon (1974: 5), who made assumptions about post-industrial management of work processes. It seems to be more than probable that if the principles and trends in a post-industrial society become so strong that they change the management of work processes, as indicated in this comparison, they might also change the management of learning processes. These changes could take place on the following levels. *Planning* would be a function of the student individually or as member of a group and no longer mainly decided upon beforehand by groups of experts in ministries or in the teaching institution. *Organizing*: the student determines 'how and when his work is done within jointly determined deadlines'. *Authority and responsibility* rests with the students 'who exercise it over their own work. They seek help from' teachers, or counsellors 'when it is needed'. *Hierarchy* 'will be significantly flatter since' the students 'will be left to manage themselves'. *Directing*: students are 'self-directed and self-motivated'. *Controlling* will rely on self-control. The definite shifts described indicate that the organization of the learning process in the post-industrial society might become entirely different in many ways.

Institutional aspects

A great number of distance teaching institutions will probably no longer try to impress students by their sheer institutional greatness and importance. Rather, they will place greater emphasis on the students and students' needs, and focus upon students' learning activities in order to prevent them from feeling dependent, unimportant, weak and exposed to a powerful bureaucracy. This will mean a definite departure from a highly centralized organization of the teaching–learning process and a move to small, decentralized units which can be made transparent by the means of new technology.

THREE PERSPECTIVES

When post-industrial models of distance education are discussed and developed in the years to come it will be helpful to have theoretical guidelines at hand and to know about the theoretical underpinnings of the expected changes of teaching and learning. Although the elaboration of such theories is still a desideratum, it seems possible to refer to some preliminary theoretical approaches. I should like to illustrate them with three examples: the *Lebenswelt* perspective, the ecology perspective, and the concept of instructional design.

The *Lebenswelt* perspective

In order to appreciate the changes suggested by this theoretical perspective one should keep in mind that there was a so-called *realistic or pragmatic perspective* of adult education which was very influential in the Federal Republic of Germany from about 1965 to 1975. It is a good case for illustrating how strongly requirements of a growing industrialized economy also influenced the theory of adult education. According to the theoretical perspective, the main objective of adult education was the increase of vocational and professional qualifications on all levels in order to improve industrial production and to remain successful in international economic competition. Critics of this concept called it 'technocratic', as it instrumentalized the learner and the learning process which thus became mere means to an end.

In the 1970s, however, a radical change took place as the *Lebenswelt* of individual learners and their subjectivity assumed a high priority. The general goal of adult education was no longer primarily better qualification for better jobs, but personality building. Experts became aware of how important it is for the teacher to explore and to understand the *Lebenswelt* of the learner, both in a biographical sense and in the sense of how the learner perceives, interprets and understands his or her social environment. The main objective became the development of the learner's identity. All of this could be achieved by direct social interaction only. Dialogues and group discussions were considered to be the best means of accomplishing this, with no other didactic instruments being substitute for them.

This new perspective was developed mainly by experts who were disappointed with the results of the big educational reform schemes of the 1960s and 1970s which were typical outgrowths of an industrialized society. They discovered, instead, the individual adult learner and his or her situation. Thus, the learner ceased to be just a mere element of a teaching–learning system usually dominated by the teaching institution and instead was located directly in the centre of interest. It was the learner's individuality which counted now. This shift of emphasis must be borne in mind when we conceive, plan and prepare post-modern learning situations for distance education – this can be said although the proponents of this particular theoretical perspective never characterized their approach as post-modern. The new perspective suggests that a teaching–learning system, in which thousands of students study the same carefully prepared, standardized and pre-tested learning material and are tested according to the same pre-determined categories, is clearly an industrialized approach. As such it will not be considered educationally sound at all in a post-industrial society.

The ecology perspective

This theoretical perspective of adult education was suggested by Siebert (1985: 589). According to him it not only aims at making the students 'environment-conscious' but also at a radical and far-reaching change of the way in which nature is perceived and understood. It rejects causal and analytical ways of thinking in the tradition of Galileo and Descartes which, on the one hand, paved the way for outstanding scientific and technological achievements and eventually for the triumphant advance of industrial society and, on the other, for the 'control, exploitation, and manipulation of nature'.

In the context of this chapter it is sufficient to point out that the rejection of causal and analytic ways of thinking and of empirical approaches based on them can also be related to teaching and learning. The proponents of the ecological perspective are certainly not in favour of teaching–learning systems which are carefully planned, controlled and evaluated down to the smallest detail. That is, they are opposed to the technology of education. Rather, they recommend 'self-initiated, global learning'. They no longer expect relevant learning to take place in traditional institutions but rather in new social movements and civic action groups. They expect that here new forms of learning will emerge which will lead to 'global, interrelated, systemic, complementary and dialectic ways of thinking'.

Siebert considers this to be an explicitly post-modern development. This perspective is usually presented with a sense of urgency as the continued expansion of the industrial systems endangers and destroys our natural environment which is a fundamental requirement of our life. Distance education in a post-industrial society will have to include the ecological perspective in order to help to change traditional scientific and empirical ways of thinking. The new thinking will have to rely much more on qualitative than on quantitative standards and will have to develop nothing less than a new ethic. This means that distance education will have to redefine its objectives, extend its curricular scope considerably, and employ new methods of self-initiated and self-directed learning.

The concept of 'instructional design'

Flechsig (1987) maintains that the concept of 'educational technology', which is widely used in a number of countries, will no longer be sufficient in a post-industrial era. And, indeed, if we analyse it, we will see that it is a typical product of industrial society. It pre-supposes that instruction can be planned, evaluated and improved considerably in the same way as the production of goods can be planned, evaluated and improved. Therefore, Flechsig seeks other theoretical explanations and looks for a model of teaching and learning which is open for the new phenomena of the post-industrial society. He calls it 'instructional design'. This model revolves around the concept that teaching is more than handicraft and technique, and more than a system which can be fully determined by scientifically based decisions – namely, that it is an *art* as well. It also indicates that not all elements of the teaching–learning process can be at the disposal of those who plan and develop instruction – especially not the student's self-determination in instructional matters. The term 'design' is partly used because of its origin in the fine arts. It suggests that the persons who design instruction are fully aware of unpredictable factors of the learning situation, factors which are new and cannot be standardized and reproduced *ad libitum*. This refers to the more pragmatic, but also to the aesthetic, ethical and moral dimensions of instruction.

In order to characterize the new concept, some of its more typical features will be specified:

1 Students and their learning take precedence over teachers and their instruction.

2 Teaching does not primarily mean the direct intervention of a teacher but rather the development of favourable learning environments.
3 The educational quality of a learning environment is not only measured with regard to professional norms or pre-determined teaching objectives, but also with regard to its functionality, its meaningfulness and the quality of life it brings.
4 Learning environments may have to be separated and isolated from life, but at the same time they will have to represent part of the *Lebenswelt*.

According to Flechsig, the concept of instructional design is a typical product of our time indicating the transition from the modern to the post-modern society.

If developers of distance education want to orientate themselves with the help of this concept they will be urged to accept and to implement fundamental structural changes. Obviously, the role of learners will have to become a more prominent one. Their being presented with standardized and prefabricated course material of some length with computerized control will simply not do any longer. We will have to find ways in which the learner takes the initiative in most phases of the teaching–learning process, and this must include more say in curricular decisions and methods of control and evaluation. The planners of distance education will also have to concentrate on the task of dealing with the students indirectly – that is, by developing learning environments which are conducive to open learning situations in which the students are encouraged to become active in organizing and managing their learning processes themselves. And, finally, the planners of distance education will have to deal with the problem of how to transform the learning experience in such a way that it is no longer just a preparation for some specific future goal but also a representation of life itself, with a resultant improvement in the quality of living.

CONCLUSIONS

Drawing conclusions from the above, the following statements can be made:

1 Distance education is, indeed, a typical product of industrial society. This not only applies to its inherent industrial principles and trends but also to the fact that distance education has been capable of meeting educational needs typical of an industrialized

economy and that it could attract and keep highly motivated students who wish to improve their vocational or professional status as well as their income, sacrificing their leisure time for gratifications often delayed for many years.
2 In a post-industrial society the traditional industrial model of distance teaching will no longer satisfy the new needs of new types of students with their particular expectations and values which, seemingly, not only differ from those of the students in the industrial society but are in many cases even the exact opposites of them.
3 This situation calls for the design of new models of distance education. They will probably be combinations of intensified and sustained group work – highly sophisticated ways of acquiring the necessary information for self-study and increased telecommunication between the participants. They will have different sets of goals and objectives. And they will have to rely on self-directing and self-controlling – that is, on becoming autonomous students.

This means that the shift from industrial to post-industrial distance education will be a Copernican one. Slight and superficial alterations will certainly not do.

REFERENCES

Bartels, J. (1986) *Die Absolventen des Fachbereichs Wirtschaftswissenschaft. Eine empirische Untersuchung*, Hagen: Fernuniversität, Zentrum für Fernstudienentwicklung.
Bell, D. (1975) *Die nachindustrielle Gesellschaft*, Frankfurt on Main: Campus Verlag.
—— (1976) *The Coming of Post-Industrial Society: A Venture in Social Forecasting*, New York: Basic Books/Harper Colophon.
Boulding, K. E. (1964) *The Meaning of the Twentieth Century: The Great Transition*, New York: Harper & Row.
Brzezinski, Z. (1970) *Between Two Ages: America's Role in the Technetronic Era*, New York: Viking.
Eglau, H. O. (1992) 'Schlank und rank. Deutsche Industrielle übernehmen die Methoden der Japaner', *Frankfurter Allgemeine Zeitung*, 14 February, p. 31.
Elbing, A. and Gordon, J. (1974) 'Self management in flexible organizations', *Futures*, 6, 326.
Flechsig, K-H. (1987) *Didaktisches Design: Neue Mode oder neues Entwicklungsstadium der Didaktik?* Göttingen: Universität Götingen, Institut für Kommunikationswissenschaften und Unterrichtsforschung.
Fuchs, V. R. (1968) *The Service Economy*, New York: National Bureau of Economic Research.

Galbraith, J. K. (1971) *The New Industrial State*, New York: The American Library/Mentor.
Illich, I. (1973) *Tools for Conviviality*. New York: Harper & Row.
Kahn, H. and Wiener, A. J. (1967) *The Year 2000*, New York: Macmillan.
Norman, A. L. (1975) 'Informational society', *Futures*, 7, 321.
Peters, N. A. (1981) *Arbeits- und Organisationsgestaltung in einer postindustriellen Gesellschaft*, Stuttgart: Haupt.
Peters, O. (1967) *Das Fernstudium an Universitäten und Hochschulen*, Weinheim: Beltz.
—— (1973) *Die didaktische Struktur des Fernunterrichts. Untersuchungen zu einer industrialisierten Form des Lehrens und Lernens*, Weinheim: Beltz.
—— (1983) 'Distance teaching and industrial production. A comparative interpretation in outline', in D. Sewart, D. Keegan and B. Holmberg (eds) *Distance Education: International Perspectives*, London: Croom Helm.
—— (1989) 'The iceberg has not melted: further reflections on the concept of industrialisation and distance teaching', *Open Learning* 6: 3–8.
Siebert, H. (1985) 'Paradigmen der Erwachsenenbildung', in *Zeitschrift für Pädagogik*, 31 (5): 577–96.
Slater, P. E. (1970) *The Pursuit of Loneliness. American Culture at the Breaking Point*, Boston: Beacon.
Toffler, A. (1970) *Future Shock*, New York: Random House.
—— (1980) *The Third Wave*, New York: Morrow.
Williams, F. (1982) *The Communications Revolution*, Beverly Hills, Cal.: Sage.
Wood, M. R. and Zurcher, L. A. (1988) *The Development of Postmodern Self*, New York: Greenwood Press.
Wurster, J. (1989) *The Future of Media in the Fernuniversität*, Hagen: Fernuniversität, Zentrum für Fernstudienentwicklung.
Yankelovich, D. (1981) *New Rules: Searching for Self-fulfillment in a World Turned Upside Down*, New York: Random House.

Conclusion

Desmond Keegan

The purpose of this chapter is to provide a context for the study of Professor Peters' concept of the industrialization of education and to evaluate that contribution. The chapter begins with brief indications on Professor Peters' career, the characteristics of his university and some differences between continental European distance university education and the structures that would be more familiar to English-speaking readers. Some comments are then made on his achievements, on his critics and on the consequences of his positions for those who wish to study distance education.

CAREER

Otto Peters worked at the Educational Centre (*Pädagogisches Zentrum*) of the Ministry of Education of Berlin, at the German Institute for Distance Education (*Deutsches Institut für Fernstudien an der Universität Tübingen*), at the Berlin College of Education (*P-H Berlin*) and at the Fernuniversität (*Fernuniversität-Gesamthochschule in Hagen*), where he is now Professor Emeritus of the Methodology of Distance Education in the Faculty of Education, Sociology and Humanities.

In 1964 he was asked by the Berlin Minister of Education to prepare a report on distance education. His subsequent contribution to the literature of distance education, partially listed in the appendix to this book, is substantial. It is also original. The concept of the industrialization of education is a striking one. It has fundamental implications for sociologists, educationists and all who have to do with the field of distance education. In any survey of theoretical contributions to distance education, Peters' work has an important place (Amundsen 1993) and his position will be studied in any university course on distance education (Sauvé 1993).

The purpose of this book is to bring Peters' work on the industrialization of education to a wider audience. Up to 1989 nearly all the published work is in German. Peters writes a relatively complex German and a competent ability in that language is needed to study the original texts. Of the earlier work only the original theoretical formulation has appeared in English before (Sewart *et al.* 1983: 95–113) together with an edited version of a speech on the same topic to the 1969 ICCE conference (MacKenzie and Christensen 1971: 223–8).

The field of education in which Peters worked is distance education and training. In German the words are '*Fernstudium*' and '*Fernunterricht*'. '*Fernstudium*' means 'distance education at higher education level' and '*Fernunterricht*' means 'distance education at further education level'. '*Fernstudium*' is translated into English as 'distance education' provided one realizes that at times one has to use the cumbersome phrase 'university-level distance education' to translate it. *Fernunterricht* is best translated into English as 'distance training' provided that one realizes that it can refer also to children's distance education. As stated in *The Distance Teaching Universities* (1982), it is considered that 'the Fernuniversität' is the correct English translation of *Fernuniversität-Gesamthochschule in Hagen*.

It is clear from the start that Peters knows this field well. He does not make mistakes about what is included in the field or what is excluded from it. The confusion of researchers in the 1970s and the 1980s about what distance education is and what educational technology is and what is some other form of flexible or open or non-traditional provision, is absent from his work. There is from the start a precision and analytical skill in research that is impressive.

The comprehensiveness of the research carried out in 1964 is astonishing. The 1,157 closely packed pages of the two books *Der Fernunterricht* (1965) and *Das Fernstudium* (1968) give an impeccable database for his future work, and no subsequent theorist or contributor to this field has provided such a comprehensive basis for research. One looks in vain in the literature in English of the 1970s, the 1980s and 1990s for comprehensive treatment of countries like the USSR, Bulgaria, Cuba, Mexico, Colombia, Vietnam. The accuracy of the data allows conclusions of far-reaching importance: '*Die Südafrikanische Republik ist neben der Sowjetunion das einzige Land, in dem es eine Fernuniversität gibt*' is on page 115 of the 1965 volume. This may well be the first use in German of the word 'Fernuniversität' but what is more important is that it flows from the text that the USSR and the RSA, strange bedfellows one would have thought, should have been the first countries to develop open universities. Peters goes further and lists all the Soviet distance teaching universities with their foundation dates, faculties and enrolment in 1960 (1968: 549–54). Here is the start of the list:

Northwestern Polytechnical Distance University in Leningrad (1929)
USSR Distance University for Economics in Moscow (1930)
USSR Polytechnical Distance University in Moscow (1932)
USSR Textile and Light Industry Distance Institute in Moscow (1932)

Ilyin of the USSR Distance University for Economics explains in an article commissioned for *Distance Education* in 1983 how these distance universities offer qualifications at technician, polytechnic, Candidatus of Science (four-year degree) and Doctor of Science levels (1983: 142–8).

The accumulation of so much data led a trained analyst like Peters to certain observations and conclusions. To analyse his vast database he, as one might expect, used the dominant School of Educational Theory in Germany of the mid-1960s, the Berlin School of Didactics of Paul Heimann and Wolfgang Schultz. This school had developed a six-level model for didactical analyses leading to a scheme for didactic decisions, comprising:

- the aims of teaching (*Intentionalität*)
- contents (*Thematik*)
- methodology
- media
- human pre-requisites
- socio-cultural pre-requisites.

Peters applied his distance education data to the Heimann-Schultz structural model and was clearly excited by the results. Although his data fell within the Heimann-Schultz framework he had little difficulty in showing that on each of the six structural elements his new field of distance teaching was essentially different. He realized immediately that conventional forms of didactical analysis taken from children's classrooms or university lecture theatres would be inappropriate for furthering our knowledge of this form of education, and cast around for new categories that would explain the genuine nature of the phenomenon.

The conclusion was remarkable, unusual and original: distance education resulted from the industrialization of education and it could best be categorized as a more industrialized form of teaching and learning. Peters quickly (1967) published a 41-page monograph in which he sets out what he calls *Ein Beitrag zur Theorie der Fernlehre* (A contribution to the theory of distance teaching). The full title is *Didactical Structure and Comparative Analysis of Distance Education at Universities and Institutes of Higher Education*. The next years were spent in justifying his position, and resulted in the 1972 thesis published in the 1973 German book, *The Didactical Structure of Distance Education. Research into a more industrialized form of teaching and learning*, from which the major extracts in this book are taken. The two most important conclusions are highlighted here:

1 distance education is a more industrialized form of teaching and learning (1973: 1);
2 anyone professionally involved in education is obliged to assume the existence of *two* forms of instruction which are strictly separable: traditional face-to-face teaching based on interpersonal communication, and industrialized teaching which is based on an objectivized, rationalized, technologically produced interaction (1973: 310).

CHARACTERISTICS OF THE FERNUNIVERSITAT

Complex developments in educational politics in Germany at the time form the background to this research. It is important to realize that the Bundesrepublik has a federal structure with reasonable differences in education policy from state (*Land*) to state as in Canada or Australia; that Tübingen is in the state of Baden-Württemberg in the south and often associated with the CDU; that Hagen is in the state of North Rhine-Westphalia in the north and is sometimes associated with the SDP; and that my interpretation of the events I am about to describe would probably not be shared by Professor Peters.

Planning for a German open university began in the mid-1960s. The planning received a noticeable boost in 1965 when the Volkswagen Foundation funded a distance education research and materials development centre known as the German Institute for Distance Education (*Deutsches Institut für Fernstudien an der Universität Tübingen*). The DIFF became a major promoter of the FIM project, a plan to develop a cooperative German open university combining the DIFF, conventional universitites, state (*Länder*) and federal ministries of education, radio stations, television stations and so on. The talks were interminable, the costs were extensive and the negotiations went on from year to year. Finally, one of the delegates – the Minister of Higher Education of the State of North Rhine-Westphalia – walked out of the discussions and founded his own open university. The Minister, J. Rau, got the legislation through the North Rhine-Westphalia Parliament in November 1974, had it approved by December 1974 and the new open university opened in October 1975 with an extraordinary seventy-five courses designed, written and published. Rau needed a figurehead as *Rektor* of his daring new German university and he chose Otto Peters.

The book *The Distance Teaching Universities* (Keegan 1982) and Chapter 7 of this book (Peters 1981) give an analysis of the Fernuniversität's charter, its goals and objectives. This analysis is summarized here as it is important for those who claim that Peters' theory of industrialization had little or no influence on the university of which he was *Rektor*.

Rau's legislation gave the Fernuniversität these goals:

- to provide extra places for school leavers;
- to develop a system of university continuing education;
- to reform university teaching.

In my view these goals were unrealistic and the focus of the university evolved in its first five years to new and different goals. By 1981 it was clear that the first goal was unimportant: German school leavers chose to enrol in normal universities. They did not choose to study at a distance. There are other structures in Germany for continuing education and a distance teaching university was unlikely successfully to compete with them. The final goal is misconceived – if you want to improve university lecturing you don't found a university at which, by definition, lecturing doesn't take place.

As early as June 1977 the Fernuniversität was setting itself new and much more difficult goals:

- to demonstrate that German citizens would enrol in large numbers in a distance teaching university;
- to attract employed students;
- to produce printed learning materials that would not be criticized by other German academics;
- to award qualifications that would be accepted as on a par with other German universities;
- to achieve a throughput of graduates per professor and group of lecturers at least equal to that achieved by a professor and equal

group of lecturers in a conventional university (Keegan 1982: 92–3).

My evaluation would be that all these goals were satisfactorily achieved by 1981 and represent a considerable accomplishment for all concerned.

The reasons for the evolution of the goals of the Fernuniversität, for its positioning itself in the structures of conventional German university provision and for the relationship of theory to practice in German university distance education are embedded in the history and traditions of the German university ethos. In editing a book about German university distance education for an English-speaking readership one does well to realize that scholars in the English-speaking world may not support certain aspects of the European academic and university ethos. As a consequence they may not see how certain features of these traditions can, on occasion, work in favour of distance education. Italian university examinations, for example, are oral: it seems entirely appropriate that students who study at a distance should be examined face-to-face. French government syllabuses and examinations control certification and awards at most levels in that country: distance students who pass the examinations thus get the same awards as conventional students.

Three aspects of German university education are mentioned here to give a further context for the evaluation of Peters' writing:

1 *The German Abitur*. The German High School Graduation Certificate is a demanding standard and essential for entrance to German universities both conventional and at a distance. Fernuniversität courses take it as their starting point and build upon it. This has the benefit that all Fernuniversität courses are immediately acceptable in all other universities, that students can transfer from the distance university to a conventional one with ease, and that the *Rektor* of the Fernuniversität was immediately accepted into the highly prestigious German University Vice-Chancellors Committee (*Westdeutsche Rektorenkonferenz*). It also shows up precise differences between 'open learning' and 'distance education', terms which some English-speaking commentators use almost as synonyms, and has the consequence that courses which are judged as being below *Abitur* level are regarded as being for children and could not figure in a university degree.

2 *German drop-out*. In Germany a university degree is seen as a standard, often a demanding standard. This can simplify the question of drop-out. If students cannot, for one reason or another,

meet the standard then they drop out. A German distance university, therefore, might not engage in expensive student support services merely to keep students enrolled in the system.
3 *German printed materials.* There is a very long tradition of the importance and primacy of the academic text in German universities. As a result there is little discussion of multimediality amongst the academics at Hagen, and choice of didactic medium is simplified. 'We use print because it is the best' is a frequent attitude. Television broadcasting is usually rejected as inferior. Video cassettes, if used, are clearly produced so that students can take notes from them and they are interspersed with didactic activities.

EVALUATION

A necessary pre-requisite for an evaluation of Peters' work has been suggested with some details on the context of his research, the context of the Fernuniversität and the context of some features of European university systems. Some aspects of his achievement will now be listed and critics of his position will be cited.

Data

Peters built up an impressive database on distance education in the mid-1960s. He relentlessly set out to track down every phenomenon of distance education and training, every distance education institution, and statistics, it would seem, that would include every distance student world-wide. During his long years as *Rektor* of the distance university he kept reasonably well in touch with the field. He avoided the pitfalls of omitting major groups of evidence (children's distance education, proprietary distance education, communist distance education) that have characterized some writing in the 1980s when at least one-third of distance education was in the USSR or China. The accuracy and precision of his knowledge of the phenomena he was dealing with is one of the strengths of his work.

Analytic approach

All of Peters' work in distance education is characterized by the cold, unemotional approach of the analyst. He does not mix up the roles of researcher and manager of a distance institution, or researcher and enthusiast for this form of education or researcher and apologist for this form of education. There is an absence of hype in his work. There is no exaggeration about the didactic possibilities of the latest telecommunications technology, no attacks on conventional schools or universities, no coloured writing about openness or access in distance education. Research is separated from managerial or promotional tactics. Almost alone among distance education researchers, he does not hide the darker side of distance education only too well known to many students who try to study at a distance or to managers who have to administer staff teaching full-time at a distance.

Insights

The concept of the industrialization of education and the view of distance education as a more industrialized form of teaching and learning is a striking and original insight. In the mid-1990s it retains its value especially in the fields of mass education and employment. Many nations today need university systems capable of enrolling 100,000 students a year or more. Peters' insight points the way for them. In the employment crisis of the mid-1990s the institutional structures of the more industrialized form of education will provide lasting employment for many categories of workers in contrast to non-industrialized forms of non-traditional education which tend to provide only short-term consultancies. The use of the Russian concept *zaochny* and its linking to Wedemeyer's 'absence of the eyeball to eyeball and ear-pan to ear-pan' communication, is a decisive insight. Peters correctly points out that the attempt to educate people without the emotional and psychological dimension of eye contact is fraught with limitations, and poses queries for educationists both inside and outside the field of distance education.

Theoretical contribution

Peters called his first presentation of his views in English 'Theoretical aspects of correspondence instruction', and there is no need here to go into the question of whether it is technically a theory or not. To evaluate a theoretical position one needs to evaluate the adequacy of the theory to comprehend all the data, the forecasting value of the theory and its explanatory strength. The implications of Peters' views of the industrialized character of distance education are very far-reaching as it predicts that this form of education will be characterized by the evils and benefits of industrialization. It forecasts that distance education institutions will have monopolistic tendencies and this has certainly proved to be the case. If distance education is a good thing, one would have thought that an open university would welcome a second or a third open university into its territory. Peters' theory forecasts that distance education will be characterized by alienation, and this has proved to be the case: alienation of students, alienation of staff, alienation even of institutions which sometimes seem to want to get out of the industrialized field and back to normal provision.

The explanatory value of the theory also has its uses. It makes it easier to explain the centrality of the warehouse in distance education institutions, whether schools or colleges or universities. It makes it easier to explain the size of the warehouse – at Stoney Stratford, for instance – or the padlocking of the teaching into the university as at the Beijing Television Open University. It helps one to explain to people that in distance education it is often management rather than pedagogy that is the central problem and the constant preoccupations with deadlines, shooting scripts, print runs, transmission times, fonts and mailing lists.

CRITICS

The critics of Peters' position are here divided into two groups: German and English-speaking. Comments by Christoph Ehmann (1981), Manfred Hamann (1978) and Karlheinz Rebel (1983) will be taken as indicative of German attitudes.

Ehmann complains that Peters' position is characterized by categories of the 1960s: the importance of programmed learning, confidence in industrial planning, faith in technical progress, faith in the calculability of social processes. All these faiths of the 1960s had been dissipated by the 1980s, especially in German academic circles, with the realization that technological models of social processes have little validity.

Hamann would represent critics of a Marxist orientation who would claim that no progress towards cost-effectiveness in education has been achieved by systems theory from the weapons industry, or the systems approach of the military establishment or media didactics and taxonomies, or technological models – all of which are the context of Peters' industrialization of distance education. He claims that Peters simply applied the Heimann–Schultz categories of conventional education to the data of distance education and nothing more. Rebel and other distance education theorists are also unhappy with the use of the Berlin (Hamburg) School of didactics and claim that a theory of industrialization is unsustainable and unfalsifiable and that data to justify it could not be collected.

English-speaking critics clearly recoil at the harshness of much of Peters' terminology. They are ill at ease with talk of alienation in education, of the industrialization and mechanization of educational processes and the division of educational labour. Much work has been expended in the literature in English to prove that distance education is 'a good thing'; that it is linked to ideas like student centred learning, educational independence, educational access, educational individualization and so on. Peters' position clearly throws a certain amount of cold water on many of these heartfelt beliefs. Some of the criticism has been misinformed by lack of access to the original documents or by criticizing them from citations. It is one of the purposes of this book to provide texts in English that will lead to balanced evaluation.

CONSEQUENCES

As the study of distance education enters the mid-1990s, a number of issues are becoming central to the literature and research. The acceptance or rejection of the positions taken up by Peters greatly influences the answers by researchers and practitioners to these questions:

- Is distance education a form of education or an educational mode?
- Is distance education theory and research to be located in the mainstream of educational theory or not?
- What is the rationale and focus of bachelors', masters' and doctoral degrees in the study of distance education?

There are a considerable number of references in the literature to the distance education 'mode', and as a corollary to this one speaks of 'dual-mode institutions' and of a continuum of provision fusing one educational strategy into others (Jeavons and Guiton 1993). Peters takes up quite a different position in his major writings and there is little diminution in the 1993 introduction to this book. He had used the Heimann–Schultz categories to show that distance education differed from conventional provision; his analysis of the communication processes used showed radical differences between the two forms of education. The continuum is broken and his conclusion is clear: 'Anyone professionally engaged in education is obliged to presume the existence of *two* forms of education which are strictly separable.' (The italics are in the German.)

There have been varying calls in the 1980s for distance education to enter the mainstream of conventional education (Smith and Kelly 1987). The issue here is whether distance education research is to be combined with research on classroom provision or whether research on conventional classrooms and research on distance education are to be seen as two different and complementary fields both of which combine to elucidate education. Peters has given compelling reasons for seeing the second position as the more valid.

One of the more striking developments in the 1990s has been the development of degree courses in distance education from universities in a number of countries. Peters' work has provided a basis for these degrees in his delineation of the characteristics of the more industrialized form of education, and the study of his contribution will provide a stimulating challenge to students in these degrees and all who are interested in the study of distance education.

REFERENCES

Amundsen, C. (1993) 'The evolution of theory in distance education', in D. Keegan (ed.) *Theoretical Principles of Distance Education*, London: Routledge, pp. 61–79.

Ehmann, C. (1981) 'Fernstudium/Fernunterricht: reflections on Otto Peters' research', *Distance Education*, 2(2): 228–33.

Hamann, M. (1978) *Fernstudienkonzeptionen für den tertiären Bildungsbereich*, Hamburg: Arbeitsgemeinschaft für Hochschuldidaktik.

Ilyin, V. (1983) 'The USSR Financial and Economic Institute for Distance Education', *Distance Education*, 4(2): 142–8.

Jeavons, F. and Guiton, P. (1993) 'Distance education and internal studies: interlocking study modes', in G. Ortner, K. Grass and H. Wilmersdoerfer (eds) *Distance Education as Two-way Communication*, Frankfurt on Main: Lang, pp. 252–62.

Keegan, D. (1982) 'The Fernuniversität', in G. Rumble and K. Harry (eds) *The Distance Teaching Universities*, London: Croom Helm, pp. 88–106.

MacKenzie, O. and Christensen, E. (1971) *The Changing World of Correspondence Study*, University Park: Pennsylvania State University.

Peters, O. (1967) *Das Fernstudium an Universitäten und Hochschulen. Didaktische Struktur und vergleichende Interpretation: ein Beitrag zur Theorie der Fernlehre*, Weinheim: Beltz.

Rebel, K. (1983) 'Distance study in west Germany: the DIFF's conceptual contribution', *Distance Education*, 4(2): 171–8.

Sauvé, L. (1993) 'Media and distance education: course description', in K. Harry, M. John and D. Keegan (eds) *Distance Education: New Perspectives*, London: Routledge, pp. 305–16.

Sewart, D., Keegan, D. and Holmberg, B. (eds) (1983) *Distance Education: International Perspectives*, London: Croom Helm/Routledge.

Smith, P. and Kelly, M. (eds) (1987) *Distance Education and the Mainstream*, London: Croom Helm.

Appendix

Major publications on distance education by Otto Peters

BOOKS

Der Fernunterricht: Materialien zur Diskussion einer neuen Unterrichtsform, Weinheim, Berlin: Beltz, 1965.
Das Fernstudium an den Hochschulen der Sowjetunion, Hamburg-Rahlstedt: Walter Schulz, 1967.
Das Fernstudium an Universitäten und Hochschulen. Didaktische Struktur und vergleichende Interpretation: Ein Beitrag zur Theorie der Fernlehre, Weinheim, Berlin: Beltz, 1968 (Pädagogisches Zentrum: Veroffentlichungen. Reihe B, Bd. 8).
Das Hochschulfernstudium: Materialien zur Diskussion einer neuen Studienform, Weinheim, Berlin: Beltz, 1968 (Pädagogisches Zentrum. Veroffentlichungen. Reihe C. Bd. 5).
Die didaktische Struktur des Fernunterrichts. Untersuchungen zu einer industrialisierten Form des Lehrens und Lernens, Weinheim: Beltz, 1973. Tübinger Beiträge zum Fernstudium, Bd. 7.
With Ehmann, C., Gerhard, V., Köhler, G., Schwittmann, D. and Wurster, J. *Das Fernstudium im Medienverbund. Informationen und Arbeitsmaterialien. Ein Studienpaket*, Tübingen: Beraterkreis Fernstudium im Medienverbund, 1974.
Die Fernuniversität. Das erste Jahr. Aufbau. Aufgaben. Ausblicke. Bericht des Gründungsrektors, Hagen: V. d. Linnepe, 1976.
With Dohmen, G., Müller, K., Petersmann, J., FIM-Glossar, *Informationsbausteine zur Aus- und Fortbildung wissenschaftlicher Mitarbeiter an Fernstudienprojekten. Studien und Berichte zum Fernstudium im Medienverbund*, Schriftenreihe des Deutschen Instituts für Fernstudien an der Universität Tübingen, Bd. 16, 1976.
Die Fernuniversität im fünften Jahr. Bildungspolitische und fernstudiendidaktische Aspekte. Bericht des Gründungsrektors, Köln, Verlagsgesellschaft Schulfernsehen, 1981.

EDITED BOOKS

Texte zum Hochschulfernstudium, Weinheim, Berlin, Basle: Beltz, 1971.
With Dohmen, G., *Hochschulunterricht im Medienverbund*. Teil 1: *Probleme. Projekte. Pläne*; Teil 2, *Didaktische Aspekte*, Heidelberg: VRMV, 1971.
With Gollhard, H., *Jahrbuch 'Wissenschaft Ausbildung Schule'*, WAS, Cologne: Verlagsgesellschaft Fernsehen, 1972–1981.
Die Offene Universität in Japan, Tübingen: Deutsches Institut für Fernstudien an der Universität Tübingen, 1974.
Unterrichtstechnologie und Schulreform. Perspektiven zu Erziehung und Unterricht in den 70er Jahren, Düsseldorf: Pro Schule-Verlag, 1973 (Technology and Innovation in Education).
With Pfundtner, R., *Studium neben dem Beruf. Ergebnisse eines Forschungsprojektes*, Weinheim: Beltz, 1986.
With Güttler, R., *Grundlagen der Weiterbildung: Praxishilfen*, Neuwied: Luchterhand, 1989.
With Keim, H. and Urbach, D. (für den Verein Grundlagen der Weiterbildung), *Grundlagen der Weiterbildung*: Journal (since 1990).

FERNUNIVERSITÄT PUBLICATIONS

Gedrucktes Lernmaterial. Arbeitsunterlagen für Hochschullehrer und Mitarbeiter, Hagen: Fernuniversität, 1975.
Hinweise zu einem allgemeinen didaktischen Konzept für die Entwicklung von Fernstudienmaterialien, Hagen: Fernuniversität (ZIFF-Papier No. 1), 1975.
Unterrichtstechnologische Arbeit an der Fernuniversität, Hagen: Fernuniversität (ZIFF-Papier No. 8), 1977.
Fernsehen und Fernuniversität, Hagen: Fernuniversität-Gesamthochschule, Lehrgebiet für Methodenlehre des Fernstudiums, 1977.
Das Studium neben dem Beruf. Ausländische Entwicklungen und Modelle. Studienbrief, Hagen: Fernuniversität, 1988.
Anmerkungen zum Studienabbruch, ZIFF-Papier No. 73, Hagen: Fernuniversität, 1988.

Author index

Adorno, Th.W. 129
Amundsen, C. 241
Andrews, J. 208
Bååth, J.A. 199, 200, 203, 210
Bandura, L. 5
Bartels J. 18, 229
Basedow, J.B. 90
Bauer, W. 73
Behrendt, R.F. 145, 149, 152
Bell, D. 222, 223
Bischofs, J. 75
Bjerstedt, A. 85
Bollnow, O.F. 90, 140
Boulding, K.E. 222
Brudny, W. 79
Brunner, H. 132, 136, 138, 139
Brzezinski, Z. 222
Buber, M. 90, 140
Buckingham, W. 110, 114
Burk, F. 75, 76

Calvin, J. 61
Canisius, P. 66
Childs, G.B. 5, 82
Christensen, E. 242
Cicero, M.T. 61
Comenius, J.A. 68, 94, 108
Cordt, W. 153
Curran, Ch. 208

Dahrendorf, R. 134, 152
Delling, R.M. 11, 63
Diderot, D. 66
Dietze, G. 50
Dohmen, G. 58

Duigman, P.A. 203
Durkheim, E. 112

Eglau, H.O. 222
Ehmann, Ch. 197, 198, 249
Elbing, A. 224, 234
Enzensberger, H.M. 129
Erasmus, 61
Evers, Carl-Heinz 2

Faris, E. 155
Flechsig, 51, 91, 153, 237–8
Flitner, W. 63, 129
Francke, A.H. 94
Freyer, H. 151, 167
Freyhoff, U. 75
Friedmann, G. 110, 111, 122
Fritsch, H. 208
Fröbel, F. 94
Fuchs, W.R. 136, 222, 224
Furnham, A. 211

Galbraith, J.K. 223
Gaudig, H. 75, 93
Garrison, D.R. 7, 11
Gehlen, A. 151, 162, 164, 166, 167
Glaser, R. 83
Goethe, J.W. 128
Gordon, J. 224, 234
Graff, K. 63
Groeben, N. 211
Guiton, P. 250

Habermas, J. 153, 155, 156, 160
Hamann, M. 249
Hausmann, G. 108, 109

Hawkridge, D. 5
Hegel, G.W.F. 156
Heieck, L. 131, 166
Heimann, P. 9, 79, 81, 109, 131
Heinrichs, H. 81
Heitger, M. 151, 152
Henningsen, J. 64, 66
Herbart, J.F. 90, 94, 140
Herder, J.G. 128, 162
Hölderlin, F. 128
Holmberg, B. 5, 11, 20, 196, 200, 208, 210
Huber, F. 57, 89,
Huber, L. 137
Humboldt, W. von 128, 190
Husén, T. 78

Illich, J. 226
Ilyin, V. 243

Jaspers, K. 190
Jeavons, F. 195, 196, 197, 198, 199, 250

Kahn, H. 222, 223
Kaltschmid, J. 130
Kant, I. 145
Kaye, A.J. 200, 208
Keay, F.E. 132, 135, 138, 141
Keegan, D. 18, 20, 199, 204, 205, 206, 208, 215, 245
Kelly, M. 251
Kempfer, H. 85
Klotz, G.R. 86
König, R. 112, 115, 154, 155
Kosiol, E. 118

Langbehn, J. 128
Langenscheidt, G. 63
Larsson, H. 84, 85
Leeuw, G. van de 136, 140, 141
Lepsius, R.M. 152
Lewis, W.W. 155
Litt, Th. 109, 128
Locke, J. 140
Loyola, I. 61, 66
Lumsdaine, A.A. 51
Luther, M. 65

MacKenzie, O. 45, 242

MacLuhan, M. 163
Marcuse, H. 129
Matthes, J. 218
Mayntz, R. 118
Michael, B. 57, 68, 76
Möhle, H. 5
Montessori, M. 75, 76, 93
Moore, M. 11, 210
Morrison, H.C. 75, 76

Nietzsche, F. 128
Nishimoto, M. 5, 139
Nilsen, C. 208

Otto, B. 90, 94

Parkhurst, H. 75, 76, 93
Parsons, T. 155, 156
Paul (Apostle) 61
Perry, W. (Lord Perry of Walton) 13
Pestalozzi, J.H. 94
Peters, N.A. 222, 223, 224, 226, 230
Peters, R.S. 206
Plato 65
Plessner, H. 109, 202

Rädel, F.E. 5
Rademacher, H. 137
Rau, J. 177, 178, 179, 182, 245
Rebel, Kh. 200, 204, 249
Reble, A. 90
Rekkedal, T. 199, 208
Riesmann, D. 145, 146
Roberts, D. 208
Röhrs, H. 63
Romiszowski, A.J. 197
Roth, H. 167
Rothhacker, E. 162
Rousseau, J.-J. 90, 94, 140
Rumble, G. 200
Ruskin, J. 128

Saettler, P. 76
Sauvé, L. 241
Scheibner, O. 75, 76
Scheler, M. 162
Schelsky, H. 152, 202
Scheuerl, H. 128
Schiller, F. 128
Schleiermacher, F.D.E. 90

Schmidt, H. 122
Schmoller, G. von 112
Schuemer, R. 210
Schulz, W. 79
Schütze, F. 218
Schwittmann, D. 197
Seneca, L.A. 61
Sewart, D. 202, 210, 242
Shale, D. 11, 197, 198
Sheath, H.C. 5
Siebert, H. 236
Singule, F. 5
Sjogren, D.P. 85
Slater, P.E. 230
Smith, A. 112
Smith, P. 251
Spranger, E. 190
Stöcker, K. 57, 89, 92
Stolurow, L.M. 86
Strain, J. 208
Strunz, K. 163

Tausch, A. 138
Tausch, R. 135, 138
Taylor, F.W. 119, 122

Teather, D.C.B. 203
Töffler, A. 149, 222
Tönnies, F. 153, 156
Turnbull, A.J. 208

Washburne, C.W. 75, 76, 93
Weber, M. 72, 109, 153, 156, 196, 202, 226
Wedemeyer, Ch.A. 5, 11, 45, 82, 210, 214
Weisgerber, L. 65
Weniger, E. 140
Weltner, K. 84
Wiener, A.J. 222, 223
Williams, F. 222
Willmann, O. 67, 72, 89, 91
Withall, J. 155
Wood, M.R. 222, 224, 225, 226
Wurster, J. 7, 233

Yankelovich, D. 230
Young, M. 119

Zav'jalov, A.S. 5
Zurcher, L.A. 222, 224, 225, 226

Subject index

accessibility 186
activity 96
adult education 235
advertising 74
agrarian society 147, 148
Algeria 74
alienation 249, 250
AIM-project 85
angeleitetes Selbststudium 213
assembly line 114
attitude change 187–8
audivisual media 79–80
Australia 82
automation 22

basic types of man 149
branching 85

change; dimensions of 133
change of function 121–2
co-determination 224
combined distance education 38
common-sense knowledge 211
communication structures 139
comprehensive university 173, 174, 186
computer aided instruction 85–8
computer conferencing 18
computer data 18
concentration 123
conscious man 150
continuing education 221, 231
continuity of concern 216
cooperation of specialists 202
correspondence schools 3, 4, 27–45; corrector 34; teachers 31–5; travelling teacher 34

correspondence study 213
counselling system 90
critique of culture 128, 129
curriculum 19
curriculum theory 15

Dalton Plan 76
democratization 97, 133, 224
democratization of knowledge 69
depersonalization 10, 12, 131, 202
depersonalized 217
despersonalizing 35
distance education 154;
anthropological interpretation 14; 162–8; designations 21; didactic analysis 57–103; didactic characteristics 98–101; didactic forms 8; historical interpretation 13; industrial production 107–26; intellectual preconditions 144–52; socio-cultural preconditions 144–52; sociological interpretation 14; students 184; teaching functions 33; technological model 50; university level 36–45; university level, types of 37; distant students 38–42; motivations 30–1
division of labour 32, 112–13, 130, 143, 201, 202, 204, 205, 220
domination free learning 137, 138
dramaturgy of teaching 142

ecology 236
educational software 18
educational technology 15, 18, 51
emancipated man 150

Enlightenment 144, 145
equalizing educational
 opportunities 134

face-to-face instruction 154
Federal Republic of Germany 134,
 173
Federal University for Distance
 Education 173
feedback mechanism 81
Fernuniversität 17, 19, 20, 173–8,
 179–91, 228, 242; acceptance 183;
 achievements 182–8; concept 173;
 continuing academic education
 187; establishment 179–82; new
 goals 189–90; research 185; study
 centres 189; teaching 185;
 university reform 187
Fernunterricht 212
Fernstudium 212
formalization 120
France 87
functionalization 130
Funkkolleg 17

gemeinschaft 154, 157
German Institute of Distance
 Education 8, 17
gesellschaft 154, 157
group distance education 38
group instruction 142
Guardian 72
guided didactic conversation 215

Hermods 85
home study 213
Homo faber 150

IML-Project 77
independent learning 207
independent work 77, 92–4
independent study 216
individualization 97
individualizing 85
individual tuition 89–92
industrial education 150
industrialization 108, 129, 140, 142,
 143, 144, 152
industrialized education 130, 131,
 132, 133

industrialized form of instruction
 216
industrialized society 147, 148
instructional design 237
instructional exchange of letters
 60–5
International Correspondence
 Schools 73

language 162–4
lay theories 211
learning by researching 137
learning pace 94
Lebenswelt 235

magazines 73
mass production 115–16, 143, 221
mechanization 114, 130, 131, 143,
 202, 205, 221,
methodization 202
Miami Springs Junior High School
 77
mobile man 150
motivation 39, 41, 47
multi-media teaching packages 77

neohumanistic education 129
Netherlands 87
newspapers 73, 148

objectification 122–3
objectified 142, 143
objectivation 130, 138
objectivity 205
open learning 207, 213
Open University 6, 9, 50, 83, 88, 123,
 133, 174, 244, 249
oral communication 91
oral teaching 140
organization 118–19, 130, 205, 221

periodicals 71–4
personality; development of 175
planning 96, 117–18, 205, 221
post-industrial distance education
 229–35; curricular aspects 231;
 demand 229; methods 332;
 objectives 230; organization 233;
 structure 230; students 229;
 technical media 233

260 Otto Peters on distance education

post-industrial society 152, 226–36
preparation 96
preparatory work 116–17
programmed instruction 21, 77

Quadriga-Funkkolleg 88, 139
Quadriga-Radio-College 9

radio 81–3, 148
rational acting 157–60
rationalization 110–12, 130, 220
rationalizing 142
reach 186
Renaissance 144
repressive teaching behaviour 138
research 184, 185, 201–2
RIAS-Funkuniversität 82

sales representatives 74
School of the Air 82
scientific control 205
scientific control methods 119
Scientific Council (*Wissenschaftsrat*) 181, 182
secondary environment 167
secondary system 161
secularization 136
self-help groups 38
self-instructing material 76
self-instruction 28, 97
self-study 28, 97
South Africa 123
standardization 120–1
study without leaving production 214
supervised correspondence instruction 58
supervised distance education 28
symbolically mediated interaction 157–60

tapes 91

Tatler 72
teaching 185
teaching functions 78
technical media 96
technicalization 130
technically competent man 150
technological turn in the methodology of teaching 51
Telekolleg 17, 82, 103
telephone 81, 87
telephone communication 91
Teletechnikum 82
television 81–3, 148
television broadcasting 18
traditional vs. distance education 155–6
travelling teacher 34
tutorial system 90
TV-College 134
two-way communication 215

United States 77, 82, 87, 93, 95
universal admission 134
university distance education; teachers 42–5
university level distance education 5
university level distance education; models 46–50
University of London 48
University of Lund 48
University of Nebraska 48
University of South Africa 49
University of the Air 124, 134
University of Wisconsin 48
USSR 123

video conferencing 18
value-orientations 155

West Germany 95
written communication 91

zaochny 214

LIBRARY
WEST GEORGIA TECHNICAL COLLEGE
303 FORT DRIVE
LAGRANGE, GA 30240